Free Public Transportation

Free Public Transportation

And Why We Don't Pay To Ride Elevators

Black Rose Books
Montreal

C.P. 35788
Succ. Léo Parriseau
Montréal, QC
H2X 0A4

Black Rose Books No. SS390

This publication was made possible with the financial support of the Rosa Luxemburg Foundation and Concordia University Part-Time Faculty Association (CUPFA).

Library and Archives Canada Cataloguing in Publication

Free public transportation: and why we don't pay to ride elevators / Judith Dellheim, Jason Prince (eds.).

Includes bibliographical references.

Issued in print and electronic formats.

ISBN 978-1-55164-652-7 (hardcover)

ISBN 978-1-55164-650-3 (softcover)

ISBN 978-1-55164-654-1 (PDF)

1. Transportation. I. Dellheim, Judith, editor II. Prince, Jason, 1965-, editor

HE151.F74 2017   388   C2017-906310-3   C2017-906311-1

Ordering Information:

USA/INTERNATIONAL	CANADA	UK/EUROPE
University of Chicago Press	University of Toronto Press	Central Books
Chicago Distribution Center	5201 Dufferin Street	Freshwater Road
11030 South Langley Avenue	Toronto, ON	Dagenham
Chicago IL 60628	M3H 5T8	RM8 1RX
(800) 621-2736 (USA)		
(773) 702-7000 (International)	1-800-565-9523	+44 (0) 20 852 8800
orders@press.uchicago.edu	utpbooks@utpress.utoronto.ca	contactus@centralbooks.com

Contact: info@blackrosebooks.com

Black Rose Books is the publishing project of Cercle Noir et Rouge.

Contents

General Motors's destruction of electric transit systems across the country left millions of urban residents without an attractive alternative to automotive travel. Pollution-free rail networks, with their private rights-of-way, were vastly superior in terms of speed and comfort to smoke-belching, rattle-bang GM buses which bogged down with cars and trucks in traffic. Likewise, electric buses were faster, quieter, cheaper and more durable than gas or diesel units.

No one knew this better than General Motors. To prevent the cities it motorized from rebuilding rail systems or buying electric buses, GM and its highway allies prohibited them by contract from purchasing "any new equipment using any fuel or means of propulsion other than gas." Ultimately, the diesel buses drove away patrons and bankrupt bus operating companies. By the mid-1970's, hundreds of communities throughout the Nation lacked any form of public transportation...

Bradford Snell, statement to the United States Senate Subcommittee on Antitrust and Monopoly, February 26th, 1974.

Acknowledgements

This book would not have been possible without the actions of millions of people around the world who have pushed for free public transportation, and also: the kind, careful and timely contributions of the authors, regular Friday morning burst sessions with the editorial team bridging two continents, careful and intelligent contributions from Patrick Gannon, both on background research and in the editing process, and occasional tech support, and the patient and prompt graphics support of Amy Jin. The cover photo was taken by Marvin Latortue. Thanks also to AJ, Ben, Jolene, Nathan, Phillip and Swan and for help in readying this book for publication. Special thanks to Michael Brie and of course, Black Rose Books. This book was made possible with the research networks and projects of the Rosa Luxemburg Foundation (RLS) and its partners and with financial contributions both from the RLS and the Concordia University Part-Time Faculty Association (CUPFA).

Introduction

The title of this book puts one of our central propositions in the right light. The very notion of paying to use an elevator to get to the upper floors of a tall building is preposterous, as once observed by Michel van Hulten. And in a certain light, so is paying for public transportation, which serves a very similar function in the city, except sideways.

But this book is mainly about how to make cities more attractive for their citizens, more socially, ecologically and globally just, more democratic, and more future-ready. Of course, emerging technologies will help us achieve this, but it does not mean that we must blindly put our faith in technological fixes, thinking they will solve all our problems. And with free public transport, it is just one of the means to achieve a better more just society, not a goal in itself.

We do not always agree with the positions and arguments made by our authors, especially if they sometimes imply that 'transport optimisation' or 'public security' would trump citizen control and the right of citizens to participate fully in decisions that affect them. It is important to state this up front.

First, we must begin by defining what we mean by free public transport, an idea that has taken different forms in different cities, and what has motivated its implementation in these quite different contexts. This is artfully and expertly explored in our first chapter.

We must also examine the rapidly changing landscape of transport in the 21st century city. In the past decade, dramatic changes have taken place, with dozens of major cities taking poetic steps to reduce the place of the private car in the city. New York City abolished automobiles from Times Square. Seoul (South Korea) extracted an elevated highway from the centre of the city, exposing and bringing back to life a buried river, and residents can now hear the birds singing along this linear park and river, in which they can soak their tired toes. San Francisco replaced a collapsed highway with public transport and an urban boulevard. But Montreal (Canada), to cite a regrettable example, is currently rebuilding a highway intersection less than four minutes from downtown, approximately three times larger than the one it will replace, quadrupling its vehicular capacity in a sea of concrete and steel. Not all cities are moving in the right direction.

In many cities, streets are increasingly 'shared spaces' and cars must navigate with much greater care as they heave their weight around the city. Quito (Equador), a long thin city high in the Andes Mountains, already served with an exceptional Bus Rapid Transit system (or surface subway), continues to add space for bicycles and pedestrians. This process of re-commoning public streets and squares is taking in place in cities around the world, both in the city centres and at the edges, at an accelerating pace.

Cars must share the roads, yes, but sharing economy models are also rapidly gaining space in the city economy. The car-sharing company Car2Go recently added luxury Mercedes-Benz sedans to their sharing fleet in North America. A Chinese company with deep pockets is releasing a next-generation bike share option that (technically) can be left anywhere, thanks to geolocation technology. As we are writing this, Uber just lost its license to operate in London, deemed "not fit and proper" by London's transport authority, but the void may quickly be filled by more worker-friendly options such as RideAustin, a non-profit organization that replaced Uber when it was banned from operating in Austin, Texas in 2016. RideAustin announced it had racked up over two million ride shares in its first year of operations, after Uber was pushed out. Cars, public transport, pedestrians, bicycles, car shares, yes Uber and Lyft but also their non-profit competitors, and new and not yet invented hybrid co-operative sharing models using platform co-ops and digital doo-hickeys on smart-phones ...the future is blurring quickly.

Our second chapter attempts to project current technologies and imagines the play of economic and institutional forces in the coming decade, making a vivid case that public transport authorities need to get out front with emerging technology—not shy away from it or ignore it—and use it to maintain and even increase modal share. A striking example of a proactive public authority trying to stay ahead of a rapidly changing technological revolution may be found at the beginning of the 20th century in England, at the birth of wireless. Marc Raboy's recent biography of Marconi details the wrangling between England's Post Office, a publicly-owned crown corporation, and the Irish-Italian inventor whose innovations in wireless technology rapidly transformed the world. This second chapter raises serious unresolved questions for this book's editorial collective, as well as for the broader group of collaborators that has put this book together. It risks doing the same for the critical reader.

Our third chapter presents an analysis of the political economy underpinning the global transport sector, exposing the contemporary power structure acting to protect and extend the dominance of the private automobile in our cities today. This chapter is essential reading if one hopes to understand the forces at play in our regulatory environments, in politics at every level in our countries and cities, and in our economies.

The remainder of the book presents a handful of case studies of efforts to achieve fare-free public transportation as a public right. We have roughly organised the rest of the book in chronological order, starting with an extract from an exceptional little book from the 1970s called *Red Bologna*, detailing the experience of an Italian city that broke bold new ground in wresting space away from the private automobile. Both the New York Times and Newsweek trumpeted in 1973 that Bologna—under the guidance of a Communist-led city administration—was one of the best-managed cities in the world. Given its special status in the history of 'shared space' we include a detailed update on the City of Bologna and how it has evolved since the publication of *Red Bologna*.

Montreal's (then) new grassroots municipal party—the Montreal Citizens' Movement—was inspired by Bologna and adopted free public transport as a central plank in its platform leading up to the municipal election of 1974, where the party won 45% of the popular vote and gained a third of the City Council seats, just six months after its founding congress. The Montreal chapter explores the dynamics at play during an explosive year of civil disobedience—against a backdrop of labour and student unrest—and political upheaval that will lead to the election in 1976 of a separatist government in Quebec, and never-before-seen rates of inflation.

The next two chapters provide more recent examples from two European cities where free public transport has been implemented. In 1993, rejecting a regional government's proposal to foist yet another ring road on the ancient medieval city of Hasselt (Belgium) to facilitate automobile flow, citizens elected a young mayor with a dramatic new vision of their city—with fewer cars—perhaps signalling the end of the car-oriented model of transport in Europe. To achieve this, the new mayor implemented free public transport, along with a battery of other tricks and tools, which saw public transport use explode from 350,000 users per year to over 4,500,000 in just a few years while making the city centre—now with dramatically fewer cars—much more attractive to residents, workers and tourists.

Tallinn, the capital of Estonia, is currently setting the example as the largest city in the world offering free public transport. This chapter presents a sparkling interview with city's acting mayor. The experiment in Tallinn has received lots of media attention and has inspired many cities to aspire to follow its lead. In this case, the price tag for making the transition has been relatively small, because the public transport systems were already heavily subsidised. The Tallinn interview is followed by an eight-point critique, written by an emerging expert on free public transport systems around the world.

Changing speed, we then explore two grassroots movements pushing for social justice in their cities by eliminating user fees for public transport. Planka.nu, forged in the context of massive protests in cities across the globe against the onslaught of the neo-liberal political and economic juggernaut in the early 2000s, was spurred by a proposed increase in public transport fares in the city of Stockholm. This feisty and creative civil disobedience movement, run entirely by volunteers and with no formal leadership, encourages turnstile hopping and manages an emergency legal fund, funded by contributing members of the collective, for any member who gets caught and fined. Planka.nu has gained international notoriety for its creative hacking of the public transport system, but ultimately presents a very serious and reflected critique of society and has become a legitimate voice in public debates in Sweden.

In the city of Toronto, hosting one of North America's most used public transport systems with over 2.75 million passengers daily, a coalition of activist groups has pushed free public transport as a lever to change social and economic relations in the city, arguing that transport—like water and sewage in most of Canada—should be fully paid for out of the public purse, as a social right and a common good.

It may be helpful to recall that most public services at the city level started out as private initiatives or insurance schemes: fire services and policing; public lighting; provision of water and sewage and electricity, these were all started by private companies providing a dramatic and popular social innovation (as we would say, in modern parlance). But common sense, combined with local political pressure and changing sensibilities in the voting population—and in some cases dramatic and popular moves by inspired municipal leadership—gradually transformed them, in many cities, into public services, wholly owned and managed by municipalities or public authorities, albeit sometimes in partnership with the private sector.

At this juncture in the development of the city, in 2017, after over 75 years of city development rooted in the assumption (backed by powerful corporate interests) that the private automobile is the principal mode of transport, are we poised for a new model? What will this model look like? How will it be funded?

The chapter on Greece makes a case against the automobile. Athens developed rapidly and unsustainably after joining the EU, following a pattern of "automobile-oriented development" (as distinct from transport-oriented-development or TOD), causing a household debt crisis and leaving behind a planning disaster that is only partially and poorly fixed with a badly planned program of free public transport. This chapter provides some lessons on what not to do when implementing free public transport.

The next two chapters explore political dynamics in two Latin American countries. In Brazil, a country embroiled in a complex legal and political battle against a backdrop of corruption at all levels and in all parties, we find a raging grassroots movement fighting for free public transport as the most obvious and immediate way to improve the quality of life of poorer residents who must pay a significant percentage of their income just to get around in these vast Brazilian cities. This case study illustrates the importance of a strong grassroots movement, and militant mobilisation in the streets, to hold a progressive municipal government to its electoral promises. Citizens should never rely on simply voting now and again to achieve real changes, they must be prepared to hold a fire to the feet of their local elected leaders, and give them support so they can pursue their promises at other levels of government and jostle a new vision of society with other (richer) stakeholders in the political arena.

In Mexico City, a completely different approach is illustrated, rooted in the Right to the City discourse, but also involving the mobilisation of citizens in the streets in support of transport justice goals. Our contributor sketches out the emergence of a new civic right demanded by political movements that has gained traction and is migrating into international covenants at the United Nations and in other international bodies. The emerging concept of transport justice—rooted in the common sense notion that poorer residents must be able to get to public amenities like parks, markets and schools if they are to properly enjoy them—is now codified in legal documents in Mexico City and is being circulated to other jurisdictions around the world. This "right to public transport" could become an important political tool in efforts to achieve free public transport in other cities.

All this is fine and good, you may say: "free" public transportation. But who will pay, if not the users?

Our final chapter puts forward an argument for a new municipal funding formula that pushes the financial burden of public transportation from the user (a price barrier that reduces the use of public transit) onto the true beneficiary of the system: the owners of the land. An accepted axiom in urban geography is that land value increases with proximity to transport hubs: who doesn't want to go to work in their pyjamas, if they could? In this view, imagining public transport as a kind of horizontal elevator network, each parcel of land in the city would pay its fair share of the transport costs, based on how well connected it is to that network. On the one hand, big data allows calculating the quality of the mass transit connection from a specific geographical location in the city to another specific geographical location, to a very precise level, using multiple factors and a complex algorithm. But we also acknowledge the practice and danger of surveillance and strongly support the demands for protecting individual data. The author argues that armed with this connectivity calculation, and understanding that quality adds value to the land parcel in question, we are now able to charge that connectivity value to the land.

We will come back to the question of how to fund a fare-free public transport system in our concluding chapter. But we must address another urgent problem up front. Studies suggest that if public transport became free tomorrow, the ridership would immediately increase by at least 50%, immediately throwing the system into lockjaw.

Cities serious about reinventing their public transportation system—about making it the centre-piece of city transport—must also be prepared to reinvest massively in this infrastructure. The city of Curitiba, in Brazil, is perhaps the most striking example of a city that has embraced public transport by pioneering the 'surface metro'—Bus Rapid Transit—over the past 35 years, with the result that over 70% of daily commutes are made by public transit.

But most cities don't have the financial means to reinvest in their public transport. In many jurisdictions, cities are the creatures of a higher level of government and have limited taxing powers. In Montreal, one estimate for doubling the provision of public transportation puts the price tag at $19.7 billion.[1] This is over ten times the actual annual capital budget of the city. If we are moving towards a paradigm shift on how to move people in the city, with public transport at the centre, it will require enormous sums of money—and the willingness of the population to change their daily routine—to play the new game. These are heady questions.

Free public transportation implies many changes, a completely new way to look at the city, both in terms of how we move and how we tax, but also how we live, where we live, how we relate to each other as a society, and our broader relationship to the urban regional and global eco-system.

Some of these issues are addressed in the chapters that follow. Others may require reflection by the reader or discussion and exchange with others interested by the questions we raise here. This book raises many more questions than it answers. Perhaps that is the point of a book with such a curious title.

---

1. Jason Prince and Jacqueline Romano-Toramanian, "Le Mouvement Collectif our une Ville Carboneutre" (Brief presented to the Office de Consultation Publique de Montréal, 2016), p. 7, http://ocpm.qc.ca/sites/ocpm.qc.ca/files/pdf/P80/7.1.40_romano-toramanian.pdf.

1

Free Public Transport: Scope and Definitions

Wojciech Kębłowski

Free public transport may seem like a straightforward idea. However, among the many cities and towns that have experimented with abolishing fares in local transport networks, there are significant differences with respect to how this apparently simple idea has been implemented. Crucially, while in some cities free public transport (or more precisely, fare-free public transport) is holistic, in others it applies to only a specific part of urban society, or urban space.

We should therefore distinguish the key difference between "full" and "partial" free public transport. By full fare abolition I mean a situation in which, within a given public transport system, fares do not apply to (a) the great majority of transport services, to (b) the great majority of its users, (c) most of the time. Additionally, to exclude temporary tests and one-time experiments, I argue that to be considered "full," free public transport should (d) be in place for at least twelve months.

According to this definition, fully free public transport systems can be identified in as many as 97 cities and towns worldwide (see figure 1). More than half of them (56) are in Europe (figure 2), where a particularly high number of examples can be observed in France (20) and Poland (21). The largest city in which fares have been fully abolished is Tallinn, the capital of Estonia, with a population of over 400,000.[1] Outside

Europe, a particularly high number of free public transport towns can be found in the US (27), followed by Brazil (11), China (2) and Australia (1).

While fare abolition may seem to be a straightforward and uniform idea, the rationale behind it differs from place to place, and may be identified as following certain regional patterns. For instance, free public transport in the United States often appears to be justified as an economic measure (aimed at increasing the use of under-used public transport networks, stimulating the local economy, reducing operational costs, etc.), which largely reflects the predominant liberal perspective on the role of public institutions. In Europe, on the other hand, free public transport is often framed as a tool for promoting public transport among car users, and hence as an element of sustainable transport planning. Additionally, in many municipalities with established left-wing traditions (socialist, post-socialist or communist), the idea of fare abolition is strongly related to socio-political rationales, according to which collective transport should constitute a common good, to which all users should have unconditional access. Across the landscape of fare-free towns and cities, the reasons behind fare abolition do not seem to entirely depend on whether the local administration is predominantly socialist, green, centrist or liberal. In other words, there seems to be no direct or strong correspondence between the type of rationale behind free public transport and the political "colour" of the municipal government implementing the policy. In other words, free public transport cannot necessarily be labelled as a left-wing or right-wing policy.

Besides fully free public transport systems, there are myriad cities and towns where fares have been partially abolished. Three main forms of partial free public transport can be identified.

First, free public transport can be limited in terms of *who* can benefit from it. Specific social groups that obtain access to free rides on public transport can include children (for example in Tarnów, Poland), students (Świnoujście, Poland), or the elderly (Cape May County, NJ, US)—discounts of this kind are commonly applied in public transport systems across Europe. Interestingly, they can embrace not only urban but also national networks: the railways in Slovakia provide free tickets to children, students, retired persons and seniors. Thus conceptualised, partial free public transport can form part of a social policy that aims at aiding persons with disabilities (Xiamen, China) and their caretakers (Tarnów, Poland), the unemployed (Rzeszów, Poland), or low-income

---

1. See chapters 8 and 9 in this volume for further details on free public transport in Tallinn.

residents (Timişoara, Romania, where free travel is provided to residents whose revenue is lower than 2,000 RON, equivalent to €435 or US$517). Distributing free tickets can also be a way of promoting public transport usage among tourists (Geneva canton, Switzerland) or car drivers (Wałbrzych, Poland).

Second, free public transport can be limited in terms of *where* it applies. This means that in many cities, free access to transport is available only for a specific service or in a specific area, which exists as an exception within a paid public transport network. For instance, in Boston (US), one may take a bus service for free from the airport to the city (but not the other way around), while in Amsterdam (the Netherlands) and Fredrikstad (Norway) free public transport applies to local ferries. In Chengdu (China) passengers do not have to pay to use short-distance "neighbourhood" buses, while they need valid tickets on board of "regular" bus services and in the metro. In many smaller towns and villages, all public transport services are free of charge, yet they consist of merely one or two free routes, and therefore can hardly be considered as full-fledged public transport systems—as for instance in Carhaix-Plouguer (France), Canby (Canada) and Telluride (Colorado, US). Other cities in which free public transport is limited to a single service within a larger public transport system include Columbus (US) and Kuala Lumpur (Malaysia)

Third, free access to public transport may depend on *when* it is used. This is the case in Chengdu (China), where all buses are free to ride before 7:00am, a measure introduced to reduce the number of passengers during the morning peak.[2] Similarly, free access to public transport is available before 7:45am in Singapore. In Gorlice (Poland), free public transport is available on weekends, while in Stockholm (Sweden) it is provided on the first day of the year, presumably to help everyone return home after the party. In Jelenia Góra (Poland), the timing of free public transport is extremely specific: one can ride local buses for free on the first day of every month and on days preceding long weekends.

Additionally, in many cities free public transport has been introduced only temporarily. This may occur because it was conceived of as a test, one that local authorities did not consider to be successful—as was the case in Guangzhou (China), Salt Lake City (United States) and Valašské Meziříčí (Czech Republic). Temporary abolition of fares is also a common ingredient of the so-called "car-free days," which are

---

2. However, this form of partial fare-free public transport didn't work. The ex-CEO of the Chengdu bus group told me that if he were still CEO, he would offer people free breakfast to convince them to ride buses earlier.

celebrated in many world cities on September 22, and are extended for up to a week in some municipalities. Fares can also be abolished in response to specific events, which are often quite dramatic. Tickets are often suspended in the aftermath of terrorist attacks (e.g. in Paris in 2015 and Brussels in 2016) or natural disasters (Prague flooding in 2002), and during days with high air pollution levels. In July 2015, fares were temporarily abolished in Athens in the midst of a major political crisis when the national government did not reach an agreement with the so-called "Troika."

The distinction between full and partial forms of fare abolition is important for at least three reasons. First, it shows that among the many cases of free public transport there exist important variations: while in some cities fares have been completely abolished, in others the provision of unconditional access to transport is in fact socially, spatially or temporally limited. Moreover, while several towns and villages claim to be providing fully free public transport, the services they provide are in fact composed of only one or two routes, and due to their limited scope cannot really be considered as fully free public transport networks.

Second, in those cities where fare abolition is only partial, it can serve as a practical test of its feasibility. It may function as a visible example that a "fare-free city" is not only imaginable as part of some urban utopia, but actually exists—even if it is currently limited in terms of where, how and for whom it is applied. These temporary and small-scale fare-free experiments can act as important ruptures in "classical" paid transport systems, or—to evoke the critical urban theorist Krzysztof Nawratek—small yet potentially expanding "holes in the whole."[3]

---

3. Krzysztof Nawratek, *Holes in the Whole* (London, UK: Zed Books, 2012).

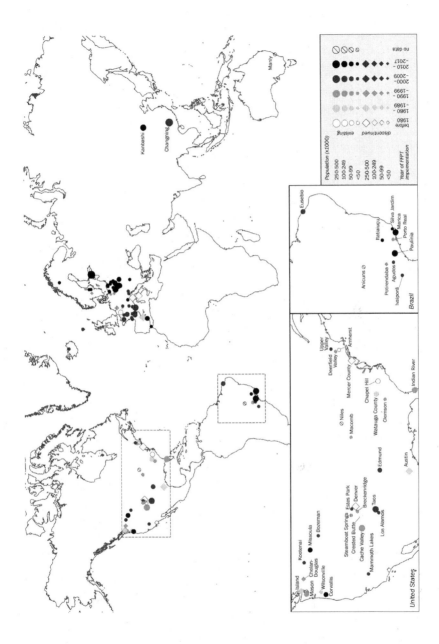

Figure 1. Current and discontinued cases of full free public transport around the world. Maps by Wojciech Kębłowski, 2017.

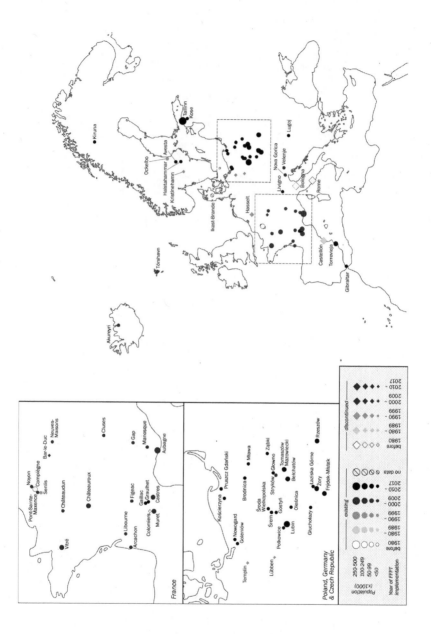

Figure 2. Current and discontinued cases of full free public transport in Europe. Maps by Wojciech Kębłowski, 2017.

2

The Transport Spectrum: Vectors of Change

Jan Scheurer

How do 21st century cities organise their transportation, and what role does public transport have in this mix, now and in the foreseeable future? This chapter explores how the current balance, however precarious, between the roles of walking and cycling, public transport and the automobile, in facilitating urban movement has evolved over time and how this is manifest in the complexity of contemporary urban form. Further, we will discuss the emergence of new and hybrid transport modes such as car sharing and ride sharing services, and the anticipated transition to driverless technology both in the transit and automobile sector. How will this coming technological disruption reshape urban settlements, redefine the roles of public and private transport, and what are the implications on funding transport in the cities of the future?

How cities are shaped by transport

Both public transport and the private car emerged in the late 19th and early 20th century as disruptive transport technologies which, each in their own way, revolutionised urban mobility patterns and the interplay of transport infrastructures and settlement patterns. By enabling greater speed of travel than what was possible during the several millennia of urban history when all land movement was based on walking or animal traction, these mechanised modes of transport provided a greater range of spatial accessibility and thus allowed cities to expand. Since the mid to late 19th century this occurred along linear corridors or in walkable nodes around tram lines and train stations; since the early to mid 20th century, concentric and vast suburban growth was facilitated by the proliferation of the private automobile.[1]

Historically, these shifts in the relationship between transport and urban form have been disruptive in the sense that they overturned the previous regime of city building, and of movement within cities, through forces whose organising principles only gradually became apparent to decision makers. Meanwhile, new transport technologies shaped cities according to their accessibility characteristics. Trams and railways helped rapidly growing and industrialising agglomerations break out of the spatial constraints of the walking city and thus generated a transit-oriented urban fabric where walking became a secondary, supporting mode, and animal traction eventually disappeared.

Half a century later, the automobile began to invade and partially degrade the transit-oriented urban fabric, leading to the decline and in some cases, closure of public transport systems. In the US, the 1974 Snell Report to Congress documented how the automotive industry and political decision makers colluded to dismantle most US cities' streetcar systems in the mid-20th century.[2] Simultaneously, the speed and door-to-door convenience enabled by car-travel helped generate vast swaths of new urban fabric that was outside the convenient reach of both walking and public transport. Yet despite the typical succession in dominant transport mode from walking to transit to automobile during the past 200 years, in the 21st century most developed cities continue to retain functional characteristics from each era and have developed strategies to selectively strengthen elements of the interplay of transport and urban form that the policy process deems desirable.

Thus, pedestrian-friendly environments have been enhanced and expanded in urban centres and around public transport facilities, while the decline of public transport has been halted and reversed through the revitalisation of existing transit infrastructures, the construction of new ones and the intensification of land uses in their vicinity, including in areas that were previously designed for near-exclusive car access.

1. Peter Newman, Leo Kosonen, and Jeff Kenworthy, "Theory of urban fabrics: Planning the walking, transit/public transport and automobile/motor car cities for reduced car dependency," *The Town Planning Review* 87, no. 4 (2016): 429-458.
2. Paul Mees, *Transport for Suburbia. Beyond the Automobile Age* (London, UK: Earthscan, 2010).

Automobiles, public transport and non-motorised modes, and the urban fabric supported by each of these modes, are thus in a relationship of coexistence in the contemporary metropolis.

Across the spectrum of cities in both the developed and developing world, there remains considerable variation: some cities are more walkable, bicycle-friendly, transit-oriented or car-dominated than others, and the policy priorities cities take in developing the interplay of transport and urban form into the future are far from uniform. For example, Beijing (China) underwent a dramatic transformation over the past 30 years, from a modal share dominated by the bicycle and public transport (and the occasional if rare donkey) to become in 2017 one of the most congested metropolises in the world, literally choking on automobile fumes daily. This urban environmental catastrophe has led the Chinese government to announce bold new clean air targets and even the abolition of gasoline fired mobility, in "the near future."[3]

Meanwhile, there is a trend across Western cities to increasingly rely on the knowledge sector to generate and reproduce wealth. Unlike the manufacturing sector which dominated urban economic development in the early transit and automobile ages, the knowledge sector thrives on spatial clustering, on planned and spontaneous human exchange, and thus places pressure on cities to create more spaces where different modes of transport and a variety of land uses can coexist to mutual advantage.[4] Hence, the functional segregation within cities that characterised the 20th century is making way for new forms of integration in the 21st century.

The emergence of new transport modes in the 21st century

In recent years, the traditional modes of urban travel—car, public transport, taxi, walking and cycling—have been complemented by mobility services that increasingly blur the boundaries between public and private transport. Car sharing and bike sharing schemes, now available in many urban areas, allow for the use of individual modes of transport one trip at a time, without the commitment of personal vehicle ownership. Ride sharing platforms such as Uber and Lyft narrow the gap between traditional taxi services and the private car in terms of

3. Agence France-Presse, "China to ban production of petrol and diesel cars 'in the near future,'" *The Guardian*, September 11, 2017, https://www.theguardian.com/world/2017/sep/11/china-to-ban-production-of-petrol-and-diesel-cars-in-the-near-future.
4. T. Van den Boomen, and T. Venhoeven, *De mobiele stad. Over de wisselwerking van stad, spoor en snelweg* [The mobile city. About the interaction of city, rail and highway]. (Rotterdam, Netherlands: NAI010 uitgevers, 2012); and Richard Florida, *The New Urban Crisis. How our cities are increasing inequality, deepening segregation, and failing the middle class – and what we can do about it* (New York (NY), USA: Basic Books, 2017).

user cost as well as scalability. Electric bicycles narrow the performance gap between conventional bicycles, whose usage has grown or consolidated in most Western cities in recent years, and motorised modes.

Meanwhile the car industry, and arguably even more ambitiously the IT industry, are in the process of developing driverless vehicles that, once proliferated around cities, bear the potential to disrupt the interplay of transport technology and urban structure at a magnitude comparable to the introduction of trains and trams in the 19th century, or of conventional cars in the 20th century.

Such disruption can be anticipated on a number of levels. Due to their role as integral components of contemporary communication networks and their resulting ability to identify demand and take themselves there without a human driver, autonomous vehicles lend themselves to shared ownership models or utilisation in journey-by-journey rental arrangements through fleet operators (though it is likely that a considerable number of privately owned vehicles will continue to exist, even with automated driving capabilities).

Fleet operation supports and potentially greatly exacerbates the already apparent trend towards car sharing and ride sharing services while reducing, possibly drastically, individual vehicle ownership. Simultaneously, automated operation of vehicles opens up independent car travel to additional user groups such as children and youth, the elderly and people with disabilities, as the ability to drive oneself is no longer required. This effect, despite the ongoing demographic trend of aging urban societies in Western countries, may reduce the number of residents currently known as 'captive riders' of public transport.

There are several flow-on effects on cities that derive from these disruptions:

Urban space liberated. Declining vehicle numbers and the ability of autonomous vehicles to keep moving and serve customers rather than remain parked for significant periods of the day will reduce the need for car parking spaces. Off-street parking facilities may be redeveloped into more urban land uses and thus support the intensification and clustering trends fostered by the knowledge economy, while on-street parking may make way for enhanced pedestrian and cycling spaces and/or for autonomous vehicle pick-up/drop-off areas.[5]

Changing relations between cars and other users of the road. The deferential behaviour of autonomous vehicles towards other road users

---

5. Wenwen Zhang, Subhrajit Guhathakurta, Jinqi Fang, and Ge Zhang, "Exploring the impact of shared autonomous vehicles on urban parking demand: An agent-based simulation approach," *Sustainable Cities and Society* 19 (2015):34-45.

may tip the balance of space domination in mixed-traffic streets further towards pedestrians and cyclists; though conversely, it may also prompt calls to erect more barriers to effectively segregate pedestrians and vehicles.[6]

Increased speed and safety. On dedicated facilities such as freeways and expressways, a fully autonomous vehicle fleet will increase road capacity and likely the speed of travel, as the electronic synchronisation of movement will enable vehicles to safely travel faster and closer together as platoons. However, it is likely that these benefits will only fully materialise after a transition period during which autonomous and human-operated vehicles (and hybrids between the two) share the roads, and which might last several decades or even lead to a permanent coexistence (and potentially a need for physical segregation) of both vehicle types.[7]

How will public transport adapt to the circumstances emerging in this coming transition?

Competition for public transport? It is conceivable that autonomous vehicles will appear in mass transit markets as a disruptive new form of competition, eroding the passenger base particularly of lower-capacity and lower-performance services such as buses in suburban areas, as their 'captive' ridership base erodes in the presence of a potentially attractive and accessible alternative form of travel.

Autonomous vehicles as public transport? It is also conceivable that public transit agencies will seek to integrate autonomous vehicles into their portfolios in order to greatly enhance and rationalise their service offer and to enable seamless journeys across collective and individual transport modes for their users. For example, autonomous vehicles could provide first- and last-mile feeder journeys to rail stations in low-density or scattered neighbourhoods where fixed-route public transport services tend to struggle. Simultaneously, such feeder services support high-capacity transit such as light or heavy rail in its ability to perform services that are speed-competitive to car-only journeys, and to deliver large crowds of people into space-constrained high-density areas that form the engine rooms of knowledge-intensive urban economies and can only fit a limited number of cars, whether conventional or autonomous.[8]

6. A. Millard-Ball, "Pedestrians, Autonomous Vehicles and Cities," *Journal of Planning Education and Research*, in print (2016), http://journals.sagepub.com/doi/abs/10.1177/0739456X16675674.
7. D.J. Fagnant, and K. Kockelman, "Preparing a Nation for Autonomous Vehicles: Opportunities, Barriers and Policy Recommendations," *Transportation Research Part A* 77 (2015):167-181.
8. Greg Lindsay, *Now Arriving: A Connected Mobility Roadmap for Public Transport* (Montreal (QC), Canada: New Cities Foundation, 2016), http://bit.ly/NCFConnectedMobility.

The integration approach between public transport and autonomous vehicles thus generates synergies that allow each mode to build on its strengths and will likely result in reduced traffic volumes and greater energy efficiency in transport. Conversely, in a competition model, traffic volumes will likely increase, and energy efficiency decrease, as public transport passengers are attracted into (smaller) autonomous vehicles.[9]

Whether integration or competition between public transport and autonomous vehicles can be achieved in practice depends in large parts on the governance of urban transport, the strength and agility of its institutions, and the relationship between public and private sector interests. While acknowledging that the exact pace and trajectory of the impending transition remains highly uncertain,[10] it is critical that transit agencies take a proactive approach in redefining and potentially expanding their position in the changing urban mobility environment by embracing the opportunities offered to public transport through the emergence of automated vehicle technology.[11]

Incidentally, driverless technology has been pioneered in the public transport industry for some time: for example, urban rail systems in Vancouver, Copenhagen, Singapore, London, Barcelona and 32 other cities (in 2016) fully or partially operate without human drivers. Several ongoing on-road tests of automated vehicles concern public minibuses, a mode that under driverless, demand-responsive operation as a shared-taxi service could prove ideal for filling the current gap between the low productivity of conventional buses and the prohibitive user fares of conventional taxis in low-density and rural areas.[12]

Can public transport agencies embrace the autonomous vehicle transition?

What could a proactive approach led by public transit agencies to integrate conventional transit and automated road vehicle technology look like, what are its implications for the ways in which transit is operated and marketed to the public in the future, and critically in the context of this book, how it is funded?

Besides the effects concerning the reduction in private vehicle

9. [UITP] International Association of Public Transport, *Autonomous Vehicles: A Potential Game Changer for Urban Mobility*, 2017, http://www.uitp.org/sites/default/files/cck-focus-papers-files/PolicyBrief_Autonomous_Vehicles_LQ_20160116.pdf.
10. Tom Cohen, Peter Jones, and Clemence Cavoli, *Social and Behavioural Questions Associated with Automated Vehicles. Scoping Study by UCL Transport Institute. Final Report* (London, UK: Department for Transport, 2017).
11. Lindsay, *Now Arriving*, 2016.
12. [UITP], *Autonomous Vehicles*, 2017.

ownership and in urban space used for parking discussed above, the International Association of Public Transport (UITP) identifies a range of further opportunities associated with the roll-out of autonomous vehicles.[18] These include the likelihood that more accessible and affordable fleet-operated driverless vehicles will increase the acceptance of shared forms of mobility among habitual private car users, and the opportunity for transport companies to dispatch staff away from low-interaction driving functions to more customer-oriented positions (though it is legitimate to ask whether driverless operation may also enable transit operators to do away with a sizeable portion of their staff altogether).

Critically, the emergence of automated vehicles offers a plethora of opportunities to integrate conventional public transport, car sharing and ride sharing services into a broader common mobility service if (and only if) transit agencies control access to the associated digital platforms from the vantage point of serving the public interest. New business models emerge here that could include a departure from flat-rate public transport fare regimes towards approaches to pricing that are sensitive to the time of day or week, and differentiate by standard and premium products in terms of user autonomy over the service chosen (eg. an individual, door-to-door robo-taxi journey would attract a higher price than a journey on scheduled public transport). Some types of services might be offered free of cost to the user, financed by general tax revenue or via a major urban tax reform as proposed in chapter 15.

The policy threats summarised by UITP partially revolve around scenarios in which the current private automobile fleet is gradually replaced by automated vehicles, but remains in individual ownership: in these cases, total vehicle travel may increase through empty-running cars (especially in a situation where letting them circulate on the road network attracts a lower user cost than parking them), and through a greater acceptance of long car commutes or even traffic congestion if the vehicle occupant(s) can utilise the associated time for work- or leisure-related online (or offline) activities.

This effect could exacerbate urban sprawl and further promote distance-intensive lifestyles. However, a significant reduction of private vehicle ownership in favour of fleet-operated, shared autonomous vehicles may also translate into a loss of control over public-interest outcomes if such vehicles are predominantly introduced by private companies with the explicit objective to compete against conventional public transport. In such a scenario, not only would public transport see

18. [UITP], *Autonomous Vehicles*, 2017.

an erosion of its traditional business model, as elaborated above; there would also be a growing presence and influence of players in the policy making environment for urban mobility who place profit motives over the public good.

Despite the considerable uncertainty that remains about the pace and trajectory of the autonomous vehicle roll-out in years to come, and the sources and effectiveness of potential resistance to their introduction and proliferation, UITP suggests that public transport agencies need to assume leadership in the autonomous vehicle transition. They need to build the required skills, ensure they have principal input into the regulatory process and take control of the emerging 'mobility as a service' platforms that have already begun to integrate conventional mass transit and more customised products such as car sharing, ride sharing, shared or individual taxis as well as public bicycle schemes.

This is not to preclude private companies from the process (who have a critical role in developing new transport technologies or mobility services, and bringing them to market) but to ensure the sustainability and efficiency benefits of the new products can be maximised. Ultimately, transport users should be able to access the dominant mobility platform in their city as they plan their travel and instantly obtain information on available choices in terms of collective, individual or hybrid modes (or combinations thereof) with associated travel times and prices, including real-time congestion updates, and to pay for their choice using a universal payment system or subscription.

The future of transport funding in a disruptive age

The methods of transport funding in cities are likely to undergo a profound transformation during the transition towards autonomous vehicles, particularly if this process does indeed lead to a steep reduction in private vehicle ownership. Another expected agent of change in this context is the gradual demise of the internal combustion engine in favour of electric vehicles, a transition that may be accelerated in the autonomous vehicle sector.

As a result, many current forms of revenue collection from transport will fall away or be significantly diminished: fuel tax revenue will decline as more easily taxable dedicated transport fuels (such as petrol and diesel) make way for more ubiquitous electricity, far less targetable for transport-specific taxes, as the primary source of transport energy. Vehicle registration fees will decline with the size of the vehicle fleet. Parking revenue will dry up with reductions in the demand for parking. Even revenue from fines for traffic or parking violations is likely to drop considerably, with autonomous vehicles being programmed to diligently obey speed limits and other road rules.

A number of authors have argued that the most sustainable revenue source to replace its declining predecessors in the autonomous vehicle age would be a comprehensive road user pricing scheme.[14] In this model, vehicle users would be charged a per-km access fee to the road system that would be monitored by the GPS and sensor systems with which autonomous vehicles (and some conventional vehicles) are equipped.

As practiced by existing transport providers from airlines to Uber, prices would be governed by demand-responsive algorithms and surge at times or in locations with high usage levels, and drop—potentially to zero—where, or while, usage is low. Similar pricing variation techniques could support the management of the road network: in areas where large numbers of cars are deemed undesirable, such as neighbourhood or city centres with high pedestrian activity or along major surface public transport corridors, permanent access fees could be levied and act as incentives for vehicles to bypass such areas where feasible.

Similarly, toll road operators would charge a specific user fee for a specific (usually higher-speed or higher-capacity) service associated with their infrastructure. Both these mechanisms are already in place as central area congestion charges in cities such as London, Singapore or Stockholm, or as road tolls for particular stretches of motorway, both in public or private operation, in many parts of the world.

But likewise, it is conceivable that shared autonomous vehicle journeys, or parts of such journeys, in particular locations or at particular times may not attract a user charge at all in a dynamic road pricing regime; and/or that the associated cost is picked up by third parties and thus borne only indirectly by transport users. For example, large retailers who now provide free parking to their car-using customers may team up with autonomous vehicle fleet operators to instead provide free rides between their shops and their customers' homes (or workplaces) in the future. In such an environment, it would be exceedingly uncompetitive for public transport agencies to stick to a rigid pricing regime where every journey attracts a marginal user cost.

The transition to autonomous vehicles, likely to occur over the next several decades, thus both exercises pressure on, and presents an opportunity for, transit agencies to fundamentally rethink their funding arrangements. Is it viable for direct user fares, which only recover a portion of total costs in most public transport operations (in the

14. Among others: E. Fishman, and L. Davies, "Road User Pricing: Driverless cars, congestion and policy responses," in *38th Australasian Transport Research Forum (ATRF)*, Melbourne Victoria, Australia (November 2016).

developing world as it stands), to retain their role in the funding mix in a changing urban travel market, or is there a growing case for them to be partially or fully replaced by indirect funding sources, such as employer or property taxes, or congestion and road user charges? This volume explores a range of global examples already undertaken to shift public transport funding away from user fares and explores a number of political alternatives that some cities and movements have used to pursue such options.

Summary

The emergence of new transport technologies has fundamentally reshaped cities and their mobility patterns repeatedly over the past two centuries. In the 21st century, the emergence of driverless vehicles at a large scale is expected to lead to another wave of potentially disruptive change that will influence the future roles of existing transport modes such as conventional (privately owned) cars, public transport, walking and cycling.

The most likely scenario for public transport to retain and expand its role in the urban transport market in the autonomous vehicle era is for transit agencies to engage forcefully and constructively with the new technologies and their promoters, and to closely integrate new forms of shared autonomous mobility such as robo-taxis and demand-responsive minibuses with existing forms of high-capacity transit for a seamless user experience. In the age of ubiquitous communication technology, this is particularly related to transit agencies assuming a central role in emerging digital user platforms that offer 'Mobility as a Service', and to exploring new pricing regimes that cover various forms of public and private mobility and call into question current public transport funding models with a strong focus on individual user fares.

3

Political Economy of Transport

Judith Dellheim

Introduction

Let us consider our typical resident. In our cities, she or he or they live in a flat and must go to work. He must bring his children to school or his sick mother to a care institution. They must buy food and other goods. He may need to see the doctor. She may want to spend free-time with relatives, friends and colleagues. They want to participate in public life. They want to have the real possibilities to plan their own lives and to take part in decisions about the development of their society.

How they do this—and, consequently, how they move in the city—depends on where they live; on their gender; physical and mental constitution; on their social, ethnic, cultural, confessional, national origin and affiliation. Beyond the specific societal and family contexts—but also connected with these contexts—individuals have specific economic possibilities and constraints, as defined by their social, political, cultural, ecological and ideological orientation.

For example, he is unemployed and wants to get a job. But he cannot accept the job offer because he lacks money to buy the car needed to get to this location. Or she has strong ecological values and wants to use public transport, but the service is so poorly organised and underfunded that it takes ages to get around in this manner. Or local communities are angry about air pollution and yet there are more and more parked cars in their neighbourhood. They want to see more public transport in their city but are concerned about budget constraints and banks demanding high interest.

These simple and very concrete examples illustrate what researchers like Castells,[1] Urry,[2] Ascher[3] and Baumann[4] have already explained: mobility in our societies has become increasingly central, and its significance is still rising.

Mobility is more than just transport, but it is significantly connected with transport.

Recent trends in the global transport sector

A recent report by the International Transport Forum (ITF) gives an overview of recent trends and near-term prospects for the transport sector globally.[5] It presents long-term projections for demand for freight transport (maritime, air and surface) and passenger transport (car, rail and air), with related CO_2 emissions for different policy scenarios.

According to this report, carbon dioxide emissions from transport could increase 60% by 2050, despite significant technological progress (if no special measures are taken, global freight emissions could increase by 160%, exacerbated by freight expansion in regions that lack rail links, like South-East Asia). Air travel will continue to grow significantly, increasing every year for the next 15 years, causing CO_2 emissions to grow by 56% between 2015 and 2030, even if fuel efficiency improves.

Motorised mobility in cities is set to double between 2015 and 2050, with the share of private cars continuing to rise sharply in developing regions. Even in alternative policy scenarios, where public transport is incentivised, motorised passenger kilometres reach similar levels, but with buses and mass transport serving more than half of the total demand.[6]

But the ITF report doesn't ask **why** transport is on the rise. It does not ask **how** to enable developing countries to introduce sustainable mobility and transportation. The report authors seem to throw their hands up in the air fatalistically and say: "we haven't got much choice here!" But we do have a choice.

1. Manuel Castells, *The Rise of the Network Society- the Information Age: Economy, Society and Culture Vol. I* (Oxford, UK: Blackwell, 1996).
2. John Urry, *Sociology beyond societies—Mobilities for the twenty-first century* (London, UK: Routledge, 2000).
3. François Ascher, *Postface: Les mobilités et* les *temporalités*, condensateurs *des mutations* urbaines (Presses Universitaires de France, 2000).
4. Zygmunt Bauman, *Liquid Modernity* (Cambridge, UK: Polity, 2000).
5. OECD/ITF, "Mobilities in Cities," in *ITF Transport Outlook 2017* (Paris: OECD Publishing, 2017), http://dx.doi.org/10.1787/9789282108000-en.
6. OECD/ITF, "Mobilities in Cities," 2017.

The transport issue depends on the system of the societal division of labour and the way of life we choose to lead. Depending on how we choose, we could see decreasing freight and passenger transport while overcoming and avoiding societal isolation and hindering economic progress.

The public sees the connection between transport and ecological destruction. Yet, in 2016, globally, consumers purchased 88 million cars—a new annual record.

But if cities want to meet their obligations under the Paris climate agreement, they must reduce greenhouse gas emissions. In many jurisdictions, this means taking radical action to address car-dependency. So municipal officials need to drastically limit the cars on their streets to reduce emissions. Even if city authorities and most of the population do adjust and align to targets established in the Paris climate agreement, they cannot significantly increase their available finances for the reconstruction and retrofits needed to realise the human-scaled city. They cannot change global production chains. Often, they must make the irrational choice between more childcare and more investment in public transport.

This does not mean that a local policy changed in favour of public transport would be unimportant. On the contrary, cities should be empowered and able to expand ecologically responsible transport, but also to avoid such antisocial and irrational choices like having to choose between childcare or public transport. So, clearly, we need to deal with those who are responsible for production patterns and destructive ways of life—and their political supporters.

The transportation web

Obviously, transportation is connected to the production of transport fuel, but beyond this, it is also deeply embedded in the production of the goods shipped, and to the infrastructure on which they travel. As such, the real share of transportation in the emission of greenhouse gases is much higher than standard estimates, which tend to be narrowly defined and miss the emissions of associated activities. And this is not even counting our transport systems' contribution to the pollution of water and soils and the fragmentation, destruction and degradation of ecosystems.

All this destroys human health and threatens the viability of life on Earth. Most texts that purport to explain the 'social costs of transport' are grossly inadequate to the job. The true costs are much higher than the sum of infrastructure costs, traffic accidents, emissions, noise nuisance, direct and indirect land take, and congestion.[7] What about the impacts on our already over-stressed human health and on our ecosystems, and what about all this wasted human labour? And the huge natural, economic, and financial resources wasted? What about resources that could otherwise be directed towards increased quality of life? What about the future?

For the past century, the car industry has shaped the global economy and billions of human lives. In Europe, the automotive industry accounts for approximately twelve million jobs (including related jobs); in the US, more than eight million; and in Japan, more than five million. By 2020, global profits could increase by €25 billion (US$29.8 billion), reaching €79 billion (US$94.18 billion).

Clearly, the economy of the internal combustion engine will not disappear overnight.

In 2007, the BRICs and the rest of the world accounted for 30% of global profits (€12 billion/US$14.15 billion), rising to nearly 60% (€31 billion/US$ 36.55 billion) in 2012. Further, more than half of this growth came from China (€18 billion/US$ 21.23 billion). In 2020, internal combustion engines will still account for more than 90% of all cars. Automotive original equipment manufacturers will continue developing more advanced conventional internal combustion engines even if they need to invest in alternative power technologies to meet future emissions targets.[8]

So the question becomes: what is the reason for the enormous role of the socially and ecologically destructive car industry, aerospace industries and the merchant navy? Of course, there are structural, economic, technical or behavioural barriers to change the global economic structure. The revolving doors between industry and many powerful governments also help to explain this.[9]

But we must look deeper into the power structure of the globalised economy and examine the history of transport and its political economy.

Transport and the capitalist oligarchy

In 1881, Karl Marx exposed the fundamental dynamics of the then emerging transport system, dynamics still very much at play today: co-

7. J.P.L. Vermeulen, B.H. Boon, H.P. van Essen, L.C. den Boer, J.M.W. Dings, F.R. Bruinsma, and M.J. Koetse, *The price of transport - Overview of the social costs of transport*, (Delft: CE, 2004).
8. Detlev Mohr, Nicolai Müller, Alexander Krieg, Paul Gao, Hans-Werner Kaas, Axel Krieger, and Russell Hensley, *The road to 2020 and beyond. What's driving the global automotive industry?* (McKinsey & Company, Inc., 2013).
9. Stefan Gössling, and Scott Cohen, "Why sustainable transport policies will fail: EU climate policy in the light of transport taboos," *Journal of Transport Geography* 39 (2014): 197-207.

operation between the most powerful finance and industrial capitalists and with agents of the state. The starting point of the capitalist mode of production was cooperation between the state and high finance to build large transport projects using brutal slavery, enabling the extraction and transport of materials and goods: Canada's national railroad, for example, or Costa Rica's ill-fated banana railway, are but two examples.

This cooperation was forced through a very specific legal innovation: the joint stock company. Wearing this legal hat, company managers are responsible only to their main stockholders and shareholders and are the drivers of societal and economic development. These co-operations have reproduced—and still reproduce—themselves via the appropriation of the fruits of labour of third parties, as well as through the redistribution and dispossession of value produced.

The main stockholders 'organise' and 'liaise' with their managers, with their partners 'within the state', with their supporters 'in politics' and within civil society, the judiciary, the military and 'security sector', as well as in the spheres of consulting and accounting, science and culture, media, and among all groups of lobbyists. They are capable of mobilising payment bonds, incomes, assets, property, etc. to finance new projects, by continuously being the most powerful actors in the financial markets.

Thereby, they are simultaneously capable of increasing the numbers of the exploited and of further intensifying the practices of exploitation. Indeed, productive structures and structures of social reproduction are developing within this very process, and these are in turn interacting with their corresponding structures of consumption (diet, housing, mobility, recreation, etc.).

In such a comprehensive perspective, it is possible to distinguish six sectors which serve as bases of control by capitalist oligarchies: energy, transport, agriculture (or rather agribusiness), security (the military-industrial complex), finance and high-tech.

These sectors penetrate each other and, taken together, account for the largest consumption of both land surface and natural resources, for the heaviest levels of pollution and, simultaneously, for the highest profits.

Globally, energy related activities produce around 63% of climate-damaging emissions, including 77% of CO_2 emitted. Around 28% of climate-damaging emissions and 36% of CO_2 emissions stem from electricity generation and heating, while transport accounts for one quarter. The transport sector depends on oil for 96% of its energy, and oil is responsible for over 95% of transport emissions. Agriculture produces 14% of CO_2 emissions, while including CO_2 released through deforestation and forest degradation increases this figure to 32%.

The US war in Iraq, alone, cost more than the total cost of investments into renewables that would be needed until 2030 to stop global warming. During the war, more climate-damaging emissions were released each year between 2003 and 2007, than the annual joint production of 139 states.

The ruling oligarchy in these six economic sectors engender violence against living beings and largely determine everyday life, as well as the ecological footprint of the populations in the centres of the capitalist mode of production.

Simultaneously, they work constantly towards organising a consensus of 'more of the same' among the individual members of our societies who are socially, politically, culturally, ideologically, ethnically and sexually differentiated.[10] This consensus is based on a special blend of nutrition, housing, mobility, goods and services. To enjoy this carefully crafted special blend, you need a car: and you also need air transport, either directly or indirectly. Fourteen car companies manage fifty-four distinct car brands, each one corresponding to a niche market lifestyle package to which a cluster of other brands adhere.

Meanwhile, food, clothing, basic goods, even many services are intimately connected to transport. Many people in our societies are unhappy about all this, but they don't see any alternative.

The limits to business-as-usual

Germany loses about 90 hectares of natural land surface daily. Surface coverage by roads increases by 22 hectares daily. Yet the trend towards owning a 'house in the countryside' continues. Owner-occupied real estate, comprising roughly 18.2 million residential units, consists primarily of single-family and two-family homes.[11] While in 1960, an average individual in Germany had 14 square metres of living space, this figure rose to 42 square metres by 2010.

Municipalities compete for the resettlement of commercial districts and residential areas. For land-owners, selling their land for home construction is usually more economically rational than its agricultural or natural use. Both urban and rural land-use planning commonly proceeds from a notion of the 'car-owning citizen'.[12] This 'car

10. Judith Dellheim, "In search of possibilities for action", *International Journal of Sustainable Development* 19, no. 2 (2016): 201–215.
11. ifs–Institut für Städtebau, Wohnungswirtschaft und Bausparwesen "Wohneigentumsquoten in Deutschland und Europa" [Rates of home ownership in Germany and Europe], 2014, http://typo3.p165294.webspaceconfig.de/fileadmin/Daten_Fakten/Wohneigentum-squoten_in_Deutschland_und_Eurpoa.pdf.
12. Bündnis 90/Die Grünen Kreisverband München-Land, "Positionspapier Flächenverbrauch," 2013, www.gruene-ml.de.

community' harms quality of life through pollution and environmental degradation, noise, stress, exclusion of people without cars, lost opportunities for living in decent conditions in an attractive environment, for spaces of communication and solidarity throughout the community, and myriad other social and ecological impacts.

The members of the capitalist oligarchies are equally confronted with contradictions: to stay competitive on a global scale, wages must be depressed. This contradicts the interests of producers of consumer goods, of the providers of human social services as well as those of financial market actors. To stay competitive and dominant on a global scale, corresponding economic structures which exude 'security' and attractiveness are crucial. This 'security' and attractiveness are simultaneously connected to resources of power, ideologies, ethics and surveillance.

The common interests of capitalist oligarchies in Germany and the EU can be summarised as follows: consolidation of public funds, patent and investment protection, active regulation of the economy, unification of capital, banking and energy markets, infrastructural policy, delegation of responsibilities concerning 'employability' and social security to individual citizens, free trade and market deregulation, extensive privatisation, deployment of public funds on behalf of capital valorisation in combination with corporation and wealth-friendly tax policies.

The automotive industry is the largest industrial sector in Germany. In 2016, it listed a turnover of €404 billion (US$476 billion), around 20% of total German industry revenue. Germany is Europe's number one automotive market, accounting for over 30% of all passenger cars manufactured (5.75 million) and about 20% of all new car registrations (3.35 million). One in five cars worldwide carry a German brand and 21 of the world's top 100 automotive suppliers are German. Around 77% of cars produced in Germany in 2015 were ultimately destined for international markets—a new record. In 2016, domestic automotive R&D expenditure is expected to reach €21.7 billion (US$25.58 billion), equivalent to 35% of Germany's total R&D expenditure. Research and development personnel within the German automobile industry reached 110,000 in 2016—with 808,500 employed in the industry altogether.

Between 2007 and 2017, the German automotive industry received €969 million (US$1.14 billion) for research and development from various federal ministries. Additionally, €181 million (US$213.4 million) were paid during this period for investments. But this is nothing compared with €1.529 billion (US$1.8 billion) tax concessions on gas fuels for 2007–2015, plus €794.3 million (US$936.5 million) from vehicle purchases since 2007. State investments account for 2.2% of GDP, significantly into roads.

Manipulated dates, efficiency labels that make no real sense, weak limits for CO_2 emissions, deceptive fuel consumption, generous diesel fuel—the list of ecological failures of transport policy is nearly endless. The impacts affect everyone—in the form of excessive particulate matter, ozone and nitrogen oxides. Germany's ruling party policy has allowed the car industry to pull away from climate protection: in the transport sector, the output of greenhouse gases has risen steadily since 1990. One overriding and patently obvious reason for this: the German car industries and German politics are closely interwoven. Regulatory capture is commonplace, and often the border between lobbyist and politician is blurred.

The industry itself has influenced the political framework successfully. Access is purchased in the form of politicians who are exceptionally talented at networking. The so-called 'side changers'—people who come from industry and go into politics and policy development and vice-versa—are extremely important in this process. But what's even worse still, the German government protects criminals in the German car industries.[18]

This interpenetration of industry and politics also works at the EU-level. Bavaria secured a luxurious, historical building complex for the bargain price of €30 million (US$35.37 million) close to the EU parliament and the EU commission. European institutions are being lobbied to promote Bavaria's interests, such as supporting car manufacturing, notably for BMW. In the 1990s, the car industry committed to substantially reduce CO_2 emissions from cars by 2010, under a voluntary agreement with the Commission. But by 2006, it was already obvious that the target would not be met, and the Commission decided to set a mandatory target. Daimler and other carmakers waged a full-scale lobbying offensive and succeeded in reducing and delaying the implementation of mandatory targets.[14]

Economists call ecological damage "externalities". If global subsidies for fossil fuels (according to the IMF totalling US$19 trillion/€16.1 trillion in 2013) were eliminated and companies were made to pay for these externalities—a decline of up to 13% of global CO_2 emissions would ensue.[15]

13. Greenpeace, *Schwarzbuch* Autolobby [Black book car lobby] (Hamburg: Greenpeace, 2016).
14. Corporate Europe Observatory, *Lobby planet. Brussels: The EU quarter*, 4th edition, fully revised and updated, (Brussels: Corporate Europe Observatory, 2011).
15. Susan George, *Committing geocide: climate change and corporate capture*, November 2016, http://climateandcapitalism.com/2016/11/23/corporate-power-climate-change-geocide/.

And how about digitalisation? Should we be reassured that car companies are dabbling with new technologies that could change the automobile and transportation sectors dramatically? A fully digitised vehicle is foreseen, while advanced info-tainment systems, vehicle-to-vehicle communications, real-time location services and routing based on traffic conditions are imminent. The intelligent car is moving from the drawing-board to the streets. It should give drivers an experience of relinquishing control, with self-braking, self-parking, automatic cruise-control based on real-time road conditions, automatic accident-avoidance features, and more:

> In the future, all aspects of the mobility value chain will be digitalised: From the shortening of product life cycles due to higher software dependency, over the transformation of car dealerships to the actual sales process and maintaining the relationship with the user—everything will be coined by the opportunities and challenges digitalisation offers.[16]

Connected with this digitalisation, the demand for raw materials will change. Copper, bauxite or iron must be secured by companies on the world market, along with an increased need for high-tech metals. Demand could soon dramatically exceed supply on world markets. "The policy must put the issue of raw material security back on the political agenda," demanded the president of the BDI, a powerful business association in Germany). He warned: "for some of these raw materials the safe supply of the industry is in danger." By 2035, demand for raw materials like lithium, rhenium, terbium and dysprosium will double present global production. Also, present production of germanium, cobalt, scandium, tantalum, neodymium or praseodymium won't cover the future demand. German expenses for the military are expected to rise sharply.

GALILEO is the EU's Global Satellite Navigation System (GNSS). This system, sometimes called the 'European GPS', consists of a constellation of 18 satellites and could help optimise transportation and resource exploration. Officially a programme under civilian control, it and its data can be used for a broad range of applications—and also, unfortunately, for the military.

The GHOST project aims to design, develop and validate a GALILEO-based intelligent system for vehicles. It should take advantage of public transport fleet routes. The development of new cross-functional applications for infrastructure maintenance, parking and garbage management should help to more intelligently shape our cities.

---

16. Evan Hirsh, John Jullens, Reid Wilk, and Akshay Singh, *2016 auto industry trends: Automakers and suppliers can no longer sit out the industry's transformation* (PwC, 2016).

Conclusion

We see that transport is rising sharply. Of course, it must rise in many parts of the global South, but this must be offset by reductions in industrialised regions. Public transport, even free public transport, would not solve all of these problems. Rather, at best, it would represent a first step. Nevertheless, it could help go a long way towards solving, or at least mitigating, many immediate problems. Some people cannot afford to use public transport, while some motorists would prefer to travel by bus or train. Moreover, this suggests that the issue of (free) public transport cannot be separated from the broader issues of social inequality, structures of production and consumption, the public sphere and public finances, as well as from the degree of political will existing at various levels.

From what has been argued above, three main political areas of action may be identified. These areas are, in turn, interconnected and interdependent in strategically significant ways:

1. the area of political struggles for defining and implementing binding standards for economic processes with regard to democratic, social and ecological concerns;
2. the area of defending the public sphere and of struggling for its radical democratisation, with a particular emphasis upon stabilising public finance;
3. the area of active struggles against destructive development projects and in favour of a socio-ecologically constructive development, which have already begun to unfold in a local and in a regional dimension.

Global justice demands, as a start, a sharp limit on the use of resources by Western cities, especially those needed to produce cars—including autonomous vehicles. Social justice demands the realisation of equal rights to mobility, a permeable use and combination of transport modes, and a just distribution of the social, economic and ecological impacts of transportation. Finally, ecological justice demands a sustainable treatment of natural resources and ecosystems and a pattern of life in our cities and countries that respects our natural limits.

4

Traffic Policy: 'Free Fares Were Just the Beginning'

Max Jäggi

(reprinted from *Red Bologna*, Writers and Readers Publishing Cooperative, 1977)

'Once we regarded traffic as a purely technical problem,' recalls Mauro Formaglini, Bologna's Traffic Councillor until 1975. Bologna, like every Western city of its size, used to have its daily traffic breakdown. Beautiful streets and squares were congested. A motorized iron avalanche poured daily into the city. Residents, especially in the narrow streets of the

Old Town, where exhaust fumes are worse and noise reverberates more than in the open, were forced to realise that Bologna had more cars in proportion to population than any city in Italy except Turin — with a car for every 2.6 residents (1972).

This was in the car-mad sixties when the historic Piazza Maggiore was being used as a car park. During this epoch of motorised chaos, Bologna's pedestrians were relegated to second-class road-users; and public buses, caught in traffic jams, used up most of their petrol in standing still. As late as 1972, no fewer than 200,000 cars a day poured into the Centro Storico and created an almost permanent haze over the area, causing the leaves in parks to turn grey.

Now Bologna's street scene has changed. Children play basketball and old people rest on benches in the Piazza del Unita — in the workers' district of Bologna — where before endless queues of cars idled at traffic lights. Similarly on the Via Libia in San Donato the schoolchildren can run onto the street without danger; this street, like ten others, which endangered schoolchildren, has been closed to traffic.

Again, the elegant Via d 'Azeglio in the middle of the Old Town where the drivers once hurtled impatiently towards the shops, has now been made into a pedestrian zone where the Bolognese can stroll leisurely when doing their shopping.

The Piazza Maggiore, Piazza Nettuno and Piazza Re Enzo still reverberate to the sound of engines. However, these are no longer the countless private cars which once crawled nose-to-tail over the antique cobbles, but the red, yellow or dark green public buses which run at regular intervals to the outskirts of the city.

Bologna has, of course, not solved all its traffic problems at a stroke. Nor has it suddenly become a pedestrian paradise.

But decisive changes have taken place. City Council and traffic planners are developing a traffic concept directly aimed at the wellbeing and quality of life of the people. This decision is not a mere technical one. Mauro Formaglini says: 'We have now realised that every traffic question has a political side too.'

The best reform plan is not one which promises to increase private profit for a privileged minority, but one which benefits the majority of people. Multi-storey city-centre car-parks which would bring more customers to a few businessmen and bankers, but which would make all the citizens suffer from increased levels of carbon monoxide are rejected. Instead emphasis is on an efficient public transport system which can get workers to work quickly.

The Bolognese do not only travel more quickly. Since April 1973, they also travel during rush-hour free of charge. Workers do not need loose change or expensive season tickets. Bus transport every working day till 9am and from 4.30pm to 8pm, costs nothing. The rest of the time, including Sundays and holidays, it costs only three pence (5c).

Bologna's traffic-planners envisage abolishing even this low, almost nominal, charge. While elsewhere in Europe escalating fares hit directly at the low wage-earner, Bologna is in the process of abolishing fares altogether. As a step in this direction, schoolchildren and students (at specific times) and pensioners (all the time) can travel free outside rush hours. In Bologna, public transport is not seen as a profit-making undertaking.

'We must gradually achieve completely free transport,' declares Formaglini. 'Only then can public transport be what it ought to be, a genuine social service.' Politicians have the support of the majority in this matter. Since the introduction of the rush-hour free-fare, the buses have been experiencing a real passenger boom. At the beginning of the 70s there were 320,000 passenger journeys a day; there are now 480,000 — a respectable 50 per cent increase.

Workers who previously struggled through rush-hour traffic by car, motor-bike or moped; children who went to school on foot or bicycle now use the free-fare buses. Bologna has successfully initiated a radical change in travelling habits, something that traffic technocrats have been vainly striving for in most European cities for years. In some of these cities, there have been experiments with free fares or cheap tickets as attempts to make public transport more attractive to the people. However, these have been complete failures, apparently proving how unsuitable and unrealistic a free or almost free public transport system is. In Rome, for instance, there was a temporary free scheme in 1972, but the streets were still crammed with private traffic. In Hanover, demonstrations forced a 9 per cent reduction in fares, but the increase in the use of public transport was not even 1 per cent.

The Bolognese success in achieving what only a few, ridiculed traffic-experts believed possible, is not due simply to the fact that bus travel is free. 'Of course I would think twice about using a bus if I had to pay for it,' says an electro-mechanic from Mazzini, who works in Bologna and travels six kilometres each way every day. 'But if the bus were always caught up in heavy traffic, even the free-fare wouldn't help.' In other words, free-fare alone would not be enough to change the travelling habits of a car-happy town. For that, one needs an efficient public service.

In Bologna, the free-fare policy is part of a socially-conceived financing policy which protects lower income groups and ensures that a badly paid labourer does not pay as much for a public service as his managing director. The drop in transport takings is compensated for by the deduction from the employers of a sum equivalent to .8 per cent of the total wage bill which goes to the city treasury. This, together with astute planning which sees free-fares as only part of a comprehensive traffic policy, has made bus service in Bologna quick, frequent and therefore a viable alternative to private transport.

In November 1971, in an interview with the communist daily newspaper, 'L'Unità', Mayor Zangheri announced 'co-ordinated measures' to improve traffic conditions within Bologna. 'Apart from the introduction of the free-fare,' he explained, 'we must assure the efficiency of public transport — and that means greater speed and frequency.' When asked when the co-ordinated measures would become reality, the Mayor answered, 'Not before we have discussed the subject thoroughly with the workers and citizens of the city. To achieve positive results we must avoid purely administrative or directive decision-making.'

This answer is indicative of the political understanding of the Bolognese administration. It fits in perfectly with their radical decentralisation efforts which move decision-making away from the town-hall to the eighteen neighbourhoods — to the citizens directly affected by every political decision. Preparing the traffic plan which was to bring 'mobility and ambience' (the motto) to the city, meant holding hundreds of meetings between autumn 1971 and summer 1972 in which politicians, planners and technicians sat down with the traffic committees of the individual neighbourhoods to work out goals and advise on possible measures. When the theme of city traffic was on the agenda, visitors thronged to the regular assemblies. In spring 1972, hardly an evening passed without debates in some assembly hall somewhere between workers and students, shop-owners and housewives, on Bologna's traffic future.

Everything in any way connected with city traffic was discussed — from the future effect of the car on noise levels in an Old Town alley to the creation of an additional one-way street. The consequences of banning parking in the city centre and of special bus-lanes were considered and ordinary citizens criticised the suggestions of traffic experts. They formulated demands, argued about priorities, and above all drew up without compromise a list of their needs.

Bologna's administrators are convinced that this is the only way to democratic, political decision-making. Only if information flows from 'below to above' — from the working people to the authorities — can elected politicians be certain about the concrete political consequences of any change in policy direction.

In contrast with cities ruled by bourgeois parties, a well-developed system of participation and self-determination is open to the Bolognese with their neighbourhood assemblies, committees, and councils. As a member of the Mazzini Council points out, this 'is still not socialism, but at least it involves more democracy.'

Bologna did not arrive at a traffic solution merely by encouraging a direct formulation of the will of the people. Scientific surveys of the volume of traffic in the city and of the behaviour of the people involved in traffic, measuring of noise levels and air-pollution played an equal part in the process. Analyses of the medieval street and alley structure were considered together with latest accident statistics. Representative opinion polls on the habits and desires of pedestrians; computer-directed investigations of shuttle services all played their part.

Figures specifically applying to Bologna, extracted from the Italian census of 1971, show that about one third of the Bolognese make their journey to school or work on foot. This means that a great number of city homes and places of work are close together (the poll also showed that people on average only choose to walk if the journey does not take longer than eleven minutes).

However, the study also brings out some less pleasant aspects of the Bolognese traffic situation. Only about 29 per cent of the people made their journey by public transport; but from four to ten thousand Bolognese sat at the wheel of their Fiat or Alfa Romeo every day to travel to work apparently 'autonomously', but in fact gripped by traffic stress.

Moreover, 75 per cent of Bolognese residents whose work was based outside the city (in 1971 — 18,000) preferred the private car for their daily journey, whether there were traffic jams or not.

One further survey provided information significant to the new traffic-planners. This survey left no doubt that the Bolognese preferred their cars to the uncertain charm of the public bus system. It took the form of a large-scale census of traffic in the historical centre during several weeks in the winter of 1972.

One of the most impressive figures in the census showed that in 24 hours along 36 streets, 200,000 vehicles of all categories made their tortuous way into the city centre. Compared with a 1964 figure, this implies an increase in traffic volume in the Old Town of about 35 per cent.

The results of such investigations and the detailed debates among the residents created a broad spectrum of ideas and suggestions, for an effective traffic reform plan. These encouraged the administration to lay before the City Council a comprehensive catalogue of radical measures to save Bologna from being choked to death by traffic. 9 June 1972 was an historic date. It was then that Mayor Zangheri and Traffic Councillor Formaglini presented the democratically-formulated plan to the City Council, the neighbourhood councils and representatives of political, union, economic and cultural organisations.

- The most important goals of the plan were as follows:
- Limitation of uneconomic use of the private car, especially for the daily journey to work.
- Preference for public transport and introduction of the partial free-fare.
- Investment policy in the public transport sector.
- Merger of the public transport companies of city and province in one consortium.
- Creation of decentralised car parks near the bus termini on the outskirts of the town.
- Creation of new pedestrian zones in the centre and in the outlying neighbourhoods.

Many meetings of the City Council were necessary before the go-ahead was given. The bourgeois opposition was highly critical and antagonistic. Christian Democrats, Republicans and neo-fascists attacked the proposed free-fare, in particular, for five whole sessions.

Finally at the City Council session of 7 July 1972, the programme crossed the last hurdle, as the left-wing parties (Communists, Socialists, and Party of Proletarian Unity) pooled their votes.

It is understandable that the bourgeois opposition should not be enamoured of the new traffic plan. It was not only that the social service, free-fare bus idea fitted in badly with their political credo. Nor was it only that they wanted nothing to do with the proposed policy of massive investment in public transport — since they were committed to savings in public expenditure to improve the critical position of the city's finances. What the bourgeois opposition had to be convinced of, step by step, was the extent to which capitalist urban development was destroying the citizen.

'The roots of modern city misery,' Formaglini told the bourgeois minority 'are to be found in the rape of our society — which has been going on now for almost a hundred years; and in the urban disorder which the post-war development process has created through property and capital speculation, undisturbed by any serious urban planning at all. The deepening crisis and imbalance which can be observed, on the urban as well as national plane have obvious roots in an economic development mechanism which rests firmly on motor-car consumption.'

City-dwellers everywhere are learning where this mass consumption must lead. It is a long proven fact that a single car travelling 40 kilometres uses up as much oxygen as four trees can produce in a day. Many newspapers recently carried reports showing that motorised street warfare causes 50,000 traffic deaths each year in Europe alone. Day after day city-dwellers in Milan, Naples, Turin, Paris, Frankfurt and London learn that car-crammed streets do not bring much-prized mobility to the city but rather cause polluted immobility.

However, not even the Arab oil crisis has succeeded in forcing a really effective change in traffic policy. After all, even if a car cannot move any more because of traffic, it still guarantees the private economy more profits than all other alternatives.

Traffic ideology usually expresses itself in demands for motorways and expressways. These — as economy-conscious planners know — will provide profitable control of a continually increasing flow of traffic. Experience has, of course, shown an increase in thruways and motorways simply means more traffic which then piles up in congested wide streets instead of narrow ones. The fact that whole cities, or at least areas, of cities thus lose their original human dimensions — without their inhabitants profiting in any way from the car boom — seems to be at best a second-rate problem for planners and politicians in most urban centres.

Things are different in Bologna. Instead of extending the inner-city network of streets — which would not have been possible except by destruction of the delicate city structure — the Bolognese decided to deprive the car of its primary place. Instead of degrading the status of townspeople to that of slaves of the internal combustion engine and its financial profiteers, they took note of the fact that cities had once been considered as homes for people. Formaglini explained this alternative aim: 'Our goal above-all is the restoration of the human dimension of our city.'

What is this human scale? In Bologna, it is a narrow branching network of streets, alleys and squares which Bologna of the twentieth century inherited from the Bononia of Roman times and the Etruscan Felsina (as the city was then called). It includes the countless narrow connecting alleys and short-cuts between the Palazzi. These allow the pedestrian to move about the Old Town comfortably and relatively quickly. It means the traditional Bolognese arcades, called 'portici', along which people walk and stand, meet friends, talk, drink coffee. And it means the kinds of manageable distances, widths of streets, and distances between buildings which do not resign people into apathy.

The fact that such a street system was conceived not for cars, but for human needs, some thousand years ago does not constitute a reason for nostalgia for the Bolognese planners. Looking back to a time when all traffic — from horse-drawn carriages to pedestrians — moved under the arcades, only makes the people more aware that a city does not necessarily have to end up as a soul-less, concrete jungle. However, in a community where people are extremely aware of economic and social problems, such a degree of awareness about the quality of life must necessarily be transferred into a still more radical, political consciousness.

'The crisis of the cities is a political crisis, a crisis of the system', explained Formaglini. 'By starting a large-scale discussion about the catastrophic traffic situation, we wanted to provoke a psychological and emotional reaction on the part of the people of the city. And I believe we have succeeded in this. Reaction is followed by reflection. The people consider the causes of the traffic chaos and soon discover that there are clear political reasons for it.' For example, the more quickly a city develops a shopping and administrative centre, the more quickly it sinks into a flood of traffic.   Conclusion: as time goes by such private business as produces traffic, should not be permitted to spread into the already saturated areas of the city, and in particular the Centro Storico and adjacent neighbourhoods. The possibilities of intervention are, however, fairly slim for the present because Bologna is still only one town in a capitalist state. Yet something can be achieved by the careful screening of building projects. For example in Saffi, a neighbourhood immediately adjacent to the Old Town, a responsible committee categorically rejected an application for building permission from the Italian Automobile Club. The reason: the proposed office block would attract too many cars to the district. At its previous location, the club could easily be reached by bus.

The City Council also makes its own contribution towards unravelling the traffic knot. Population control offices, building offices and other much-frequented administrative offices which were previously concentrated in the Town Hall in the City Centre and attracted countless motorized visitors have now largely been decentralised. The basic commitment to 'decentramento' — the delegation of extensive democratic decision-making powers to the neighbourhoods — does not only affect the political participation of the citizens. It also affects city transport and the entire process of creating a more humane city. Mauro Formaglini: 'We must proceed with urban decentralisation at the same time as political decentralisation.'

The achievements of the 1972 traffic plan as well as the plan itself, are a direct result of a policy of decentralisation which allows the people themselves to share and implement their opinions: Bologna's street network signals one such achievement of the plan.

Until 1972 Bologna's city streets (with the exception of a few already designated pedestrian zones) were open to private motorists for unlimited use. Admittedly, the council had already created some one-way systems and prohibited turns in certain areas. These few restrictions did not help much. They were, in most cases, a direct outcome of the city's basic structure, and seldom the expression of a conscious traffic policy. And so, drivers continued to go where they wished in their pollution machines.

All this has now changed. Of a total of 580 kilometres of streets in the city, not quite one-quarter (i.e. 140 kilometres) remain open to motorists for unrestricted use. The use of the rest of the streets has been subjected to various restrictions by the traffic department. Categories include streets which only residents of that district may drive in; access streets which are open only to firms located there and their delivery services; streets or parts of streets reserved for taxis and buses; connecting streets which can only be used at certain times of day; pedestrian-zones which are closed to all forms of transport.

The point of departure for this ambitious project was a conclusion reached in extensive local debates: only a radical reduction of the number of streets available to cars can bring about a radical reduction in traffic volume. This temptingly simple conclusion took months of debate to formulate. Its implementation, however, was not at all simple. While clear majorities in favour of radical traffic reform crystallised in the various neighbourhoods, the proposed car control also aroused violent opposition.

Shop-owners and hotel-keepers, entrepreneurs, garage-owners and the majority of the businessmen who feared dwindling turn-over because of reduced traffic levels, raised an outcry against restricted and partially-restricted zones. 'Most of them,' recalls a bus-driver who regularly followed his neighbourhood's debates, 'were not against limitations of private traffic in principle. But when it came to the street that ran past their door, they found a thousand reasons against restrictions.' Despite this, the will of the majority prevailed. This underlines the major difference between Bologna's planning democracy and the planning demagogy of other cities.

'Of course we don't want to crucify the car,' emphasizes Formaglini, 'but we do want to create a situation where it is only used when its use is rational. It seems to us irrational, for example, if someone goes to work by car. Then it stands around most of the time only to block the streets.'

The nucleus of the street reform is the creation of different classes of streets. Since the completion of the first phase of the plan, every street belongs to one of two main categories: The 'Rete Primaria' (primary networks) in which private traffic is permitted; or to the much longer 'Rete Secondaria' (secondary or subsidiary network) in which private traffic is restricted or completely forbidden.

- The primary network (1974: 140 kilometres) controls the traffic which is going through, to, or away from Bologna. Within this network there are three main street categories:

1. The 'tangenziale': a dual-carriageway by-pass which forms a northern semi-circle with a radius of three to five and one-half kilometres from the city centre and joins the Autostrada del Sole (Milan-Florence) with the motorways to Ferrara, Padua and Rimini.
2. The City Ring: a tree-lined boulevard which circles the Centro Storico along the lines of the Old City walls.
3. The star-shaped streets which act as spokes moving into the centre and join the Northern By-pass and the City-Ring. These streets allow access to certain entrances and exits of the Old Town.

- The secondary network (1974: 440 kilometres) serves internal traffic within the city. It is composed basically of access streets and so-called no-through roads, which formerly connected the present main-traffic areas. The signposting of these streets plays a decisive role in keeping them exclusive to internal traffic. No-entry signs and compulsory direction signs, one-way streets and diversions are arranged in such a way that the streets of the secondary network no longer connect the main traffic arteries. A driver who tries to take a short-cut to the main road on the other side of the town will fail in his aim. Signs will lead him back to the beginning and force him again on to the primary network. In addition, some of the internal traffic streets in the Centro Storico are closed, even for access, at certain times of day.

Clearly, with such a policy, car-parks in the centre become undesirable intrusions. Therefore part of the local reform plan envisages the building of efficient car parks on the outskirts. At five locations near the by-pass, big park-and-ride zones are being set up to absorb motorized visitors to Bologna and allow them to change to public transport. Car-parks, petrol stations, services and a snack bar are planned inside these zones. A unanimously agreed-on regulation states that every new car-park is to have between 30 and 50 square metres of oxygen-generating greenery, for every 100 square metres of parking-space.

Every year the City Traffic department declares a few streets and parts of streets as pedestrian zones. In 1974, 47,000 square metres of public ground in the centre were given over to pedestrian use alone. (In 1970 it had been only a little over 20,000 square metres). Moreover, approximately 25,000 square metres of old city streets — which the Council partially closed to traffic in 1973 and 1974 — are now no longer available as car parks.

Such restrictions to private transport have already produced noticeable improvements in the city centre. Traffic censuses have shown that the motorized invasion of the city has lessened in intensity. In 1972 the number of cars which undertook the doubtful pleasure of a daily journey into the city was 200,000. Two years later it was under 160,000. That means a reduction of 25 per cent, in spite of the fact that the number of cars in Bologna continued to rise over the same period.

The Bolognese planners see the coeval fifty per cent increase in public transport use as being a logical consequence of their policy.

It was clear to them from the beginning that a change in traffic trends away from private to public transport would come about only if measures were introduced in both areas. The free-fare alone achieves nothing, if buses are caught in traffic jams and cannot keep to the time-table. Restrictions on car use do not help either, if citizens who are prevented from using their cars cannot find a place on a bus.

The first World Conference on City Transport took place in Bologna in June 1974. It was attended by 450 traffic specialists from eighty cities in twenty countries. Its aim was to work out concepts for the future of traffic. (See Declaration of Bologna). Traffic Councillor Formaglini formulated the city's concept of reform as follows: 'Without expecting miracles, we have tried to intervene effectively and to provide alternative solutions to traffic and public transport problems ... It is not enough just to talk about priority for public transport. It is necessary to do something to ensure that the leading role does actually fall to public transport.'

What the Bolognese did includes raising the buses to a position of genuine preference on city roads. Streets, such as the Via Archigannasio or the Via de Carbonesi in the Centro Storico, were completely closed to private traffic and are now the exclusive domain of buses and taxis. Even where public vehicles have to share the streets with private ones, there are many bus-lanes on critical stretches. In 1974 on the 140 kilometre long primary network there were more than 30 kilometres of yellow marked lanes reserved for buses and taxis, most of them going the opposite way in one-way streets.

The Bologna Declaration

450 traffic specialists from 80 cities in 20 countries produced this document on the occasion of the First World Conference on City Traffic in 1974.

'The concentration in cities has attained monstrous proportions in our time and produced symptoms of collapse which threaten to destroy the achievements of economic progress and to do irreparable damage to the quality of life.

In certain countries, the lack of suitable restrictions and prohibitions concerning building in the cities has had the effect of letting an over-concentration of buildings, infra-structures and services develop in the centres. This has led to increased density of buildings and increased property rents.

This process has spread in accordance with the 'oil-stain principle' — the cities have spread and the suburbs degenerated. The social effects of an expansion of this kind are obvious to everybody. The imbalance in the distribution of public services and the lack of co-ordination between production plans and housing estates have the effect of an unhealthy increase in demand for means of transport.

The less this demand is met, the greater are the inroads into the free time of the people and the decrease in the rational use of this free time (rest, relaxation, cultural, social and political activities).

The boom in private motoring contributes to an unbearable deterioration of the situation. This is, in many cases, precipitated by the increased road-building with the aim of furthering the ancillary industries (car, tyre, petrol, concrete), at the cost of indispensable investment in public transport. The illusions of those who believe that problems of mobility can be solved in the cities by means of private motorization are exploded when individual motorization becomes a mass phenomenon and causes traffic congestion.

This is already the case in the cities and will apply soon even outside them.

It is clear that congestion, which hinders the transport of people, also quite obviously represents a severe hindrance to the transport of goods and, therefore, to the economy as a whole. The economic crisis in certain countries has shown, on the other hand, that unlimited use of cars causes damage to the environment which is not compatible with a balanced development perspective.

A clear perspective is, therefore, indispensable for planning and traffic policy if the survival of our cities and the maintenance of the quality of life for their residents is to be assured.

For all these reasons the participants in the conference of Bologna regard as essential the formulation of some principles which should be decisive for the organisation of urban life and the search for a harmonious development of the cities.

1. The city must not throttle the people but be built and organised according to their needs.
2. Mobility is one of the basic needs of a person. It must be fulfilled in a way which provides safety, comfort and speed, because it is also an expression of the right of every person to freedom and the free exchange of thoughts and experiences.
3. The interests of the community as a whole must be held superior to those of the individual if these are contradictory. In consequence, collective transport and such forms of transport as are in the public interest, must be given real preference over individual means of transport.
4. The public streets belong to the community and must not be monopolised by individuals.
5. Transport is a public service: it must not be managed and organised with profits as its aim, but for social benefit and must therefore, also serve the special needs of the handicapped, the elderly and children.
6. The citizen is primarily a pedestrian and as such has the right to freedom of movement and to full use of the city. In this sense the rights of the pedestrian are a part of human rights.
7. Traffic policy and urban planning policy are indivisibly united and must aid common goals. Traffic policy must, therefore, be formulated in the framework of comprehensive planning.
8. All planning concerning the utilisation of space and the

organisation of traffic must have the conscious, voiced approval of the people and presupposes a preceding phase of information and discussion among the general public.

For the bus companies it was a new era both in the offices and on the streets. To rationalise the administration of the public transport firms in view of the need for additional buses, higher frequency, and freedom from bureaucratic suffocation, the provincial and municipal bus companies were merged into one consortium.

The politicians of city and province felt that this merger was the only way to make possible the planned development of efficiency and the co-ordination of the bus networks. They were correct in their view. As commuters had already discovered, connections between the two bus companies depended too much on chance. The politicians also believed that considerable duplication between the two was overburdening the already half-empty coffers of city and province. 'The merger of the companies,' wrote Augusto Boschetti, the president of the consortium, 'will prevent waste of public money in the future.'

Local politicians are convinced that this forecast will become reality. If it does not, the people in charge will have to slow their impressive pace in developing the public transport sector. Costs are high and Bologna moves further and further into debt.

To adapt bus capacity to increased demand, the community ordered more than 200 new buses in one two-year period — an order that the local coachwork factory was hardly equal to. The price was four million pounds ($6,800,000). Moreover, to run the buses in 1974, the year of the foundation of the consortium, the city treasury had to put in more than £12 million ($20,000,000) — the second highest item in the city budget. It is hardly surprising then that the deficit for the traffic sector reached over £10 million pounds ($18,000,000) in 1974, covered for the most part by high-interest loans.

As a result, the bourgeois City Councillors do not hold back in their violent attacks on left-wing administrators, when the debates to sanction the deficit take place. During the 1974 budget debate, the Christian Democrat Giuseppe Coccoloni complained eloquently about the lack of 'the will to save' and rejected the budget on behalf of his party, 'because the accumulated deficits of the transport companies have become insupportable.' Amatore Battaglia, Liberal party spokesman stated that public transport was the real villain in city traffic. 'Our streets are invaded by a great number of buses which hinder private transport.'

The opposition politicians did not, however, mention the fact that the precarious financial situation of Bologna and all the Italian cities has little to do with lack of the will to save, and a great deal to do with the catastrophic tax system of the Italian state.

The fact is that the Rome government did away with local taxes from 1 January 1974 and is now trying to reduce the compensatory state-to-city payments which replaced them. Quite apart from that the national government is already years behind in the payment of the once customary city allocation from national taxes.

However, despite this, politicians and civil servants do not believe that the expensive Bolognese traffic reform is in serious danger on financial grounds. They emphasize instead that the demands formulated in an eight-point programme 'The Union of the Cities of Italy', will finally be met by community participation in tax affairs.

Floriano Degli Esposti, a clerk in the Traffic Department commented on the annual bus company deficit:

'We have always had deficits with the bus companies. If a solution to this deficit is unobtainable then let us at least have a deficit that serves the people.' And Mayor Zangheri declared to a mass meeting in February 1975: 'We can tell our critics that the budget deficit in Florence is twice as big as Bologna's, though Florence does not have free fare on public transport.'

5

Learning from Bologna

Maurizio Tira and Michelle DeRobertis

Introduction

An early adopter and innovator of progressive and sustainable transportation practices, Bologna presents an excellent opportunity for considering the effects of a free public transportation experiment on city form over time. But it was never only about free public transportation, as we will see.

Bologna is a medium-sized city with a population of almost 400,000, located in the central Italian region of Emilia-Romagna and home to the oldest university in Europe, founded in 1088. From free public transport to pedestrian streets, Bologna has experimented with several strategies to reduce the presence and adverse impacts of motorised private automobiles on its historic city centre. Many strategies were controversial but they survived a public referendum in 1984. The measures developed in Bologna and other progressive Italian cities were eventually codified into Italian law in 1989 and 1992.

This chapter presents a brief description of the pioneering transportation policies that were implemented during the 1960s and 1970s, and traces their evolution and additional innovations to the present time. These include traffic access restrictions known as *Zone a Traffico Limitato* (ZTL), pedestrian streets, bus-only lanes and bus-only streets, and reduced public transport fares.

What aspects or approaches from the time period remain or were expanded, and what impact did the developments during this time period have on other cities, particularly with respect to decentralized approaches to planning, and the implementation of restricted traffic and pedestrian zones? The chapter concludes with the lessons learned and potential applications for other major and medium-sized cities.

The political context of Bologna after the Second World War

The Emilia Romagna region has always been the most communist part of Italy and the City of Bologna, at its centre, has a long history of communist governments, dating back to the Second World War. While other parts of Southern and Central Italy had been liberated by the Allies (Southern Italy in October 1943 and Rome in June 1944), Emilia Romagna remained under a particularly cruel German occupation, north of the Gothic Line. The region was deeply scarred by atrocities committed against civilians and maybe that is one of the reasons why the population reacted by leaning left. For over fifty years since World War II, the mayors of Bologna belonged to the Communist Party, until 1999 when the first right-wing party mayor was elected.

The first mayor after the war was Giuseppe Dozza, elected on April 21 1945, before Italy was fully liberated, with a promise of greater public participation and transparency to give hope to a war-torn society. He delivered balanced budgets for more than ten years and then built important public works, like the bypass road and the exhibition centre, while reinforcing the role of the University. He was re-elected mayor for 21 years without interruption.

Guido Fanti, was elected as mayor from 1966 to 1970, during which time a new master plan was approved, adopting a strategic view under the banner "Bologna 2000". Kenzo Tange, the famous Japanese architect, was commissioned to head up the city's largest project in years, the new "Fiera District". Under Fanti, demonstrating amazing foresight, Bologna saw the development of a pedestrian area flowing along the historical street (Via D'Azeglio) into the main square (Piazza Maggiore). Fanti resigned in 1970 after being elected the first president of the newly created Region Emilia-Romagna, introduced by the new Constitution of the Republic. Notably, the Communist Party was in power at all administrative levels at the time in that Region. Renato Zangheri, full professor at the University of Bologna, was elected mayor of Bologna between 1970 and 1983. He faced hard times due to several terrorist attacks, namely the big one at the railway station (August 2, 1980).

Over the following decades, until today, the City of Bologna was governed by Community Party mayors and their allies, with one brief exception, between 1999 and 2004, when the city elected a right-wing mayor for a single term. Most of the mayors of Bologna also played important roles in the national and European Parliament, and at the regional level.

The government of the City of Bologna has always been a reference for the country and its mobility policies were prototypes for many others that followed. The post-war reconstruction of the town was led by wise mayors, councillors (Giuseppe Campos Venuti and Pier Luigi Cervellati), civil servants and other advisors that made history in Italian city planning. Housing and public services were constantly planned together, and important infrastructure projects changed the face of the town. Bologna's best-known policies are nevertheless linked to managing and restricting automobile traffic. The city's transportation policies were particularly advanced, although it should be acknowledged that the car revolt was happening in many cities in Italy beginning in the 1960s.

The following paragraphs present a brief overview of the key transportation policies that were implemented in the decades after the 1970s. These include policies affecting public transportation, traffic access restrictions known in Italy as *Zone a Traffico Limitato* (ZTL), pedestrian streets and parking management.

The first pedestrian street

Some mobility management initiatives are worth mentioning as they were particularly advanced at the time they were applied. One of the first streets closed to traffic was via D'Azeglio (1968), including a narrow way that leads to the main square (Piazza Maggiore). After initial fights with shopkeepers, they soon accepted the change and realised the great advantages of closing the street to cars. It was quite an achievement, as this is still an issue in many towns.

Public transport

In the early 1970s, Mayor Zangheri implemented another innovative measure: dedicated bus lanes. In the midst of the ever-increasing motorisation rate in Italy, part of the public street was reserved for public transport. It was a cultural revolution, not just a mere traffic solution, as car parking and movement had co-opted public squares and streets for private use for decades. Suddenly, exclusive bus lanes are

introduced, a major step towards reclaiming public space for public use.
Today, we advance that experience in the "shared space" concept.

One rather unique experience was the implementation of free public
transport.[1] The first free public transport policy was introduced in April
1973, and provided for zero fares for the peak periods of 6:00am to
9:00am and from 4:30pm to 8:00pm. In addition, a special card was
issued to school children to cover one free return trip between noon
and 3:00pm. Another aspect of the free fares policy was implemented
in June 1974, providing for free public transport throughout the day for
low-income senior citizens.[2] Free transport in one form or another only
lasted a few years. Importantly, a fare-free policy would be much more
difficult to implement today than in the 70s due to the adoption of a
national law requiring that local public transport services maintain a
fare-box recovery ratio of at least 35%, to obtain public funding. While
fare-free public transport is not prohibited, it is simply much more
impractical for local public authorities than before.[3]

Bologna has continued to prioritise public transport over the last 40
years. Despite the fares no longer being free, Bologna has continued
to improve public transportation and has implemented several positive
strategies to prioritise public transport and improve the quality of the
service. As stated in *Red Bologna*, it was recognised that free fares alone
would not be enough to cause a significant modal shift to public
transport: transit service would also need to be improved.[4]

The most recent General Traffic Plan (*Piano Generale del Traffic Urbano*,
PGTU, 2006) recommitted Bologna to three strategies to promote
public transport: 1) restrict private motor vehicle traffic (as described in
the next section); 2) gradually replace the fleet of diesel buses with those
using sustainable fuels; and 3) provide many bus-only lanes and bus-
only streets. The plan also extended the innovative bus-only contra-flow
lanes—allowing buses to drive the wrong way on one-way streets—to
improve the network of public transport and called for an increase in the
number of bus lanes by 30%, from 40km to 52km.[5] As of 2017, Bologna
has added new reserve bus lanes but eliminated others, so the total
length has not changed.[6]

1. See the previous chapter of this book for a full discussion of free public transport in Bologna
at this time.
2. Mauro Formaglini, "Bologna (Italy)," in *Better Towns with Less Traffic*, Organisation for Economic Co-operation and Development (OECD) Conference Proceedings, April 14-16, 1975,
(Paris: OECD, 1975), 53-96.
3. Alberto Croce, personal communication with the author, July and August 2017.
4. Max Jäggi, "Traffic Policy: Free Fares were Only the Beginning," in *Red Bologna* (London, UK:
Writers and Readers Publishing Cooperative (Society Limited), 1977), 64.
5. City of Bologna, Urban Mobility Department, "Piano Generale del Traffico Urbano (PGTU),"
2006.
6. Michelacci Carlo, Comune di Bologna, communication with the authors, July 2017.

Today in Bologna, public transport fares are similar to those in other Italian cities: a single public transport fare is €1.30 (US$1.56) while a monthly pass is €36 (US$43.08). An interesting social policy is that, on weekends and holidays, up to two adults and five children can ride together on one person's monthly pass.

ZTL: traffic limited zones

Bologna's 1974 strategy of designating some streets as pedestrian-only zones while preventing through-traffic with the strategic placement of one-way streets[7] was a precursor to what is now known as a *Zona a Traffico Limitato* (ZTL), which translates as *traffic-limited zone*. For the purposes of simplicity and consistency, we will use the Italian acronym ZTL.

Examples of traffic-limited zones (ZTLs). Source: Maurizio Tira.

Bologna and other pioneering cities in the 1970s, which began to restrict private cars from parking and circulating within the historic city centres,

---

7. Piano Urbano Traffico (PUT), 1974; also described in Jäggi, "Traffic Policy," 69-71.

turned the tide in the effort to reclaim city centres and piazzas from the pervasive presence of the automobile.

A ZTL is an area where motor vehicle access is restricted; in other words, only certain motor vehicles are allowed to enter, such as residents, taxis, and/or motorcycles. Each city determines who is authorized to enter during the restricted hours and whether the access restrictions are for a certain time period or are in effect 24 hours a day.

(Indeed, their efforts to restrict traffic in the 1970s and 80s led to the ZTL being codified in national law in 1989 as an official strategy. Today, ZTL are the norm rather than the exception in Italy. They are present in at least 300 Italian cities and towns including all cities with a population above 100,000 and even in towns as small as 3000.)

The city subsequently implemented the ZTL in the late 1980s, which included the following elements:

- motor vehicle access to historic city centre between 7:00am and 8:00pm was restricted to permit holders, emergency vehicles and public transport, and only residents, persons with disabilities and taxis were allowed to obtain permits;
- deliveries were only permitted within a narrow window of time;
- a 30km/h speed limit was imposed within the zone;
- and residents, although allowed within the ZTL, were only permitted to park on the public street within their own neighborhood.

This traffic restricted zone produced immediate, measurable and remarkable results: traffic volumes entering and leaving the historical centre (*centro storico*) were reduced by more than 50% between 1981 and 1989; public transport travel time was reduced; and starting in 1989, bus patronage began to increase again noticeably.[8] The ZTL has since 2002 been expanded and now measures 320 hectares.

Public participation: engaging the residents in the process of change

These remarkable achievements in re-commoning (to borrow a term more common today) were only possible thanks to the strong political support from progressive mayors backed by solid majorities in city council. The link to university knowledge was important: Professor Cervellati, deputy mayor at that time and full professor of the faculty of architecture in Venice, was the innovator behind the first pedestrian

---

8. Hartmut Topp, and Tim Pharoah, "Car-Free City Centres," *Transportation Journal* 21, no. 3 (1994): 231-247.

area in 1968. But it is also crucial to underscore the role of some clever technical civil servants in bringing forward realistic and innovative solutions: Alberto Croce, the engineer heading up the mobility office in the period 1994–2000 was a key player in developing several innovative traffic solutions.

But perhaps most important is that the citizens of Bologna were deliberately and deeply involved in many of the decisions that were being taken, as noted in the book *Red Bologna*.[9] In the early 1980s, Bologna prepared a new urban transport plan (PUT) with various measures for controlling traffic. Prior to implementing them, the council decided to allow the public to vote on the proposed new traffic scheme via a public referendum, even though it was not legally required nor legally binding.[10] The referendum passed overwhelmingly with 71% voting in favour.

The main innovations in Bologna in public participation date back to the first political mandate after the war ended. The mayor organised the neighbourhoods' councils, thus strengthening the force of people's views in public life. Interested readers are strongly invited to read Sil Schmit, "The Preconditions: A Hundred Year Fight for Alternatives," in *Red Bologna*.[11]

Two significant events occurred in the 1990s. First, the centre-right returned to power for the first time since World War II (in 1999). Under pressure from merchants and businesses, the ZTL was suspended on Saturdays, the biggest shopping day of the week. This remained the case until 2012 when the ZTL was restored to seven days a week. At that time, the city also diverted the buses from two major roads in the city centre on Saturdays and Sundays to create pedestrian streets. However, while beneficial for pedestrians and shoppers, this move created a number of logistical problems for bus drivers and their riders.

Secondly, in 1994, to provide better control over non-authorized entries into the ZTL, Bologna implemented a trial program of electronic control for vehicles accessing the ZTL. For this innovative program, which for the first time in the world involved an electronic license plate recognition system, Bologna received the very prestigious Bangemann Award, in Stockholm in June 1999. This was followed by a national law, adopted and modified between 1997–99, that

9. Max Jäggi, Roger Müller and Sil Schmid, *Red Bologna* (London, UK: Writers and Readers Publishing Cooperative (Society Limited), 1977).
10. L. Mazza, and Y. Rydin, "Urban Sustainability: Discourses, Networks and Policy Tools," *Progress in Planning* 47, no. 1 (1997): 1-74.
11. Sil Schmit, "The Preconditions: A Hundred Year Fight for Alternatives," in *Red Bologna* (London, UK: Writers and Readers Publishing Cooperative (Society Limited), 1977), 29-42; see also: Sil Schmit, "Urban Planning: An Old Town for a New Society," in *Red Bologna* (London, UK: Writers and Readers Publishing Cooperative (Society Limited), 1977), 43-60.

permitted electronic methods for access control and administering of fines.

In 2005, Bologna reinstituted the system enforcing the ZTL (called SIRIO) and today (2017), there are seventeen SIRIO telecameras operating in the city and more than thirty dedicated telecameras enforcing the bus-only lanes (RITA). Since the expansion of electronic enforcement, traffic reductions have been even more pronounced.

In 2006, the City of Bologna adopted a new transport plan (PGTU), which is still guiding development. An update of this plan has recently begun and is expected to be completed by the end of 2018.[12] The PGTU calls for the "completion and extension" of the limited traffic zone (ZTL), which includes expanding the ZTL to include an additional 14 hectares (from the present 320 to 334, an increase of 4.4%) and improving the electronic enforcement, with additional control points to prevent evasion.

The plan stated that the city would engage and consult with the public before implementation of these new measures. As of 2017, only the improved electronic enforcement has been implemented.[13]

Pedestrian areas and bicycle lanes

The city has continued to expand its pedestrian areas, as have most Italian and European cities.

The PGTU called for creating two more pedestrian areas in the city centre: Via del Pratello and University Zone, affecting an area of 16 and 50 hectares, respectively. These have both been implemented.[14] In addition, the Sunday pedestrian streets, which initially applied only to the heart of the city centre, were expanded in 2006 to apply to the entire ZTL area (between 9:30am-12:30pm and 3:30pm-6:30pm).

In May 2012, this was again modified to include the six main streets and two main piazzas of the city centre and it now applies over the entire weekend from 8:00am Saturday to 10:00pm Sunday.[15]

Bicycling facilities have also increased in the last 20 years. Between 2004 and 2010, Bologna increased its cycling network from 61km to 80km, a 33% increase.

Bologna has also experimented with allowing cycling counter-flow. Similar to bus lanes, cycling has little space in the middle-aged structures of the town, where cars are allowed. Therefore, allowing cycling   in   the   contra-flow   direction—provided   space

12. Michelacci Carlo, 2017.
13. Michelacci Carlo, 2017.
14. Michelacci Carlo, 2017.
15. Comune di Bologna Ordinance PG. n. :81824/2012.

permits—constitutes a valid alternative and improves bicycling circulation and access.

Also worth mentioning is the new by-pass for bicycles, constructed in the middle of the large ring-road boulevards surrounding the city centre.

Parking management, car share, bike share

Driving and parking are inextricably linked, and therefore Bologna has modified its parking fee policies and park-and-ride facilities. But they have provided park-and-ride lots near bus lines outside the city centre. Car-share and bike-share programs also contribute to reducing the amount of driving.[16] They also have measures to reduce car driving in the city centre, by encouraging two-wheeled motorised vehicles, due to their lower impact both while moving and while parked. For example, in 1998, the city replaced 700 car parking spaces with 3535 scooter parking spaces.[17] As electric scooters become more common, noise in the city centre will also abate. In addition, there are different parking policies and fares for residents versus non-residents in neighborhoods in and near the city centre.

Key national laws behind these strategies

Over the past years, a number of important national laws have been modified or adopted that support and extend the local policies applied in Bologna:
- 1989 – the ZTL and Pedestrian Areas were first defined in the Italian Highway code,[18] which granted the mayor the authority to establish them;
- 1992 – the *Codice della Strada* was modified to require the city council, not just the mayor, to establish ZTL and Pedestrian Areas;
- 1992 – a directive (known as "D.L. 285/92" in Italy) was passed that allows municipalities to charge a fee to motor vehicles when entering or circulating inside the ZTL;
- 1999 – a presidential decree (250/99) approved the installation and operation of automatic access control systems in historic centres and ZTLs.

Of course, there is also the law that requires a fare-box recovery ratio

16. City of Bologna, PGTU, 2006.
17. Alberto Croce (unpublished paper), "Zones de Trafic Limité," 2013.
18. Codice della Strada [Italian Highway Code], Titolo 1, Articolo 3 and 7, 1989.

of 35% for public transport to maintain public operating subsidies, as mentioned above.

Safety impacts and benefits

Traffic incidents in Bologna were analyzed using data provided by the City of Bologna. The annual number of traffic collisions between 2003 and 2013 was compared to the base year of 2002. As can be seen in Figure 3, traffic collisions in general decreased compared to 2002 for each year from 2003 to 2013, except for a slight blip in 2004. Beginning in 2006, the annual number of traffic collisions in both the historical centre (*centro storico*), where the ZTL is located, and the rest of the city (*periferiche*) began a sustained decline. Notably, the number of collisions in the downtown decreased by a much greater extent than the rest of the city during the same period, decreasing up to 45% within the ZTL compared to a citywide reduction of 30%. This indicates that the traffic restriction measures are effective in improving traffic safety.

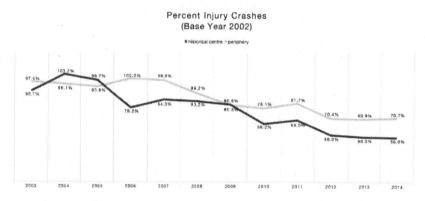

Figure 3. Redcution in annual number of traffic collisions between 2003 and 2013 compared to base year of 2002. Values indicate the percent of collisions compared to the base year (i.e. 100% = the number of collisions in 2002). Source: Maurizio Tira.

Lessons learned

Many strategies working together are needed to successfully control the adverse impacts of traffic in city centres. Bologna was the first in Italy to implement many of the progressive strategies to minimize these impacts, and was also the first compared to many other EU and non-EU countries.

The main lesson we can learn from Bologna is that strong political will, combined with a capable and competent administrative staff, were of great importance in achieving the results in the City of Bologna during the 1960s and 70s. The first four mayors after the Second World War were all important political personalities within their party and were often also members of the Parliament, and they leveraged these connections. They did not shrink from facing and overcoming challenges faced in the implementation of car reduction policies.

The new transport plan expected to be ready in 2018 sets high aspirational goals for improving the modal share for the public transport system. The political will persists to keep many of the measures discussed in this chapter in place, as part of an important reimagining of the European city, going into the 21stC.

The last twenty years have been marked by a breakdown in the political and administrative consensus that previously existed. Debates concerning transport policies have shown stops and starts. Decisions made by one administration may change when a new administration enters office. For example, a metro line has been under discussion for over a decade, and design was even started, but no but no final decision to begin construction has been taken. This highlights the fact that a mix of political will and technical competence is and always has been the only way to develop efficient and lasting solutions.

Three factors are worth highlighting, in the way of concluding recommendations, based on the Bologna experience, (both positive and negative, if looking at the most recent developments):

A strong political consensus behind the mayor: The Communist Party received 38% of the votes in 1946, and reached 49% in 1975. In a proportional electoral system, alliances meant the Communist Party could always lead.

A good administration: budgets were always balanced and therefore the citizens could appreciate and trust in the wise management of public resources, and the civil servants were knowledgeable and competent.

Innovations in public participation. The public was always present in decision-making, with innovations introduced just after the war and deepened and strengthened in Bologna in the 1960s, by dividing the town into fifteen neighbourhoods with real powers delegated, involving all social classes and promoting discussion and decision-making in the neighbourhoods of the town.

These three basic elements must be in place to implement progressive policies that touch residents' close personal habits, like their love affair with the private automobile. What we can learn from Bologna is not a technical—but rather a **political**—lesson, of the highest degree!

[6]

Free Public Transport and the Montreal Citizens' Movement

Jason Prince

...c'est le temps de faire une tentative...
Il me reste une demi-minute, trente secondes. C'est une suggestion, M. le Président. Dans la ville de Rome, actuellement, on fait la tentative, pour valoriser le transport en commun, de rendre gratuit le système de transport en commun aux heures des travailleurs, c'est-à-dire le matin entre six heures et demie et huit heures et demie et, le soir, entre quatre heures et demie et six heures. C'est une suggestion, M. le Président, à laquelle le gouvernement devrait penser de façon que les travailleurs bénéficient d'un tarif soit réduit ou soit gratuit, comme c'est le cas à Rome. Cela permettrait aux gens de laisser leur automobile chez eux, décongestionner le centre-ville, diminuer la pollution et ainsi aller vers une politique de transport en commun qui va vers la gratuité et non pas vers une politique qui est là pour des autoroutes contrairement aux intérêts des travailleurs.

Marcel Leger, Parti Québécois
–Extract from Quebec National Assembly debate November 17, 1975

On Friday August 10, 1973, a front-page article of a major daily newspaper denounced the Mayor of Montreal, Jean Drapeau, and Quebec Premier Robert Bourassa for continuing to ignore cries by senior citizens for reduced transit fares.[1]

---

1. George Radawanski, "Bus fares for elderly now", *Montreal Gazette,* August 10, 1973, https://news.google.com/newspapers?id=BZE-jAAAAIBAJ&sjid=6qEFAAAAIBAJ&pg=6524,2139726.

The article highlights the contents of a 52-page report written by a feisty young Bourassa government backbencher and former football player, George Springate,[2] who had taken up the cause for senior citizens seeking some relief from high transit prices. In 1973, 44 Canadian cities, both big and small, offered fare reductions or free transit for seniors.[3] As 95% of Quebec's 413,015 seniors lived on fixed incomes and in the community and not in senior's homes, and depended on mass transit to get around, and because seniors use mass transit outside of rush hour when buses have many empty seats, a reduced fare would yield greater use off-hours when buses are half-empty, and hence possibly yield even more revenue for the transit authority, Springate argued.[4]

Yet politicians were facing a problem of "insurmountable complexity" observed the journalist. Which level of government is responsible for providing relief?

> Mayor Drapeau is powerless, you see, because this is really a welfare problem, and welfare is a provincial responsibility. And the Quebec Government can't act, because it's not a welfare problem at all, but a transportation matter which comes under municipal jurisdiction.[5]

Seniors had been fighting for years without results and "have been reduced to talking desperately of things like blocking principal city streets, staging sit-ins at City Hall, or picketing Man and His World—at the age of 70 or 80."

In the mid 70s, civic unrest is palpable, it is in the air. Even senior citizens are ready to take direct action to get justice. And Mayor Drapeau's authoritarian leadership over Montreal is the immediate target.

Montreal in the mid-1970s: Setting the stage

The war in Vietnam rages on. In Montreal's coffee houses, hippies make candles in raised tabletop sandboxes. Pants flare, men wear their hair down to their buttocks, and women wear necklaces of large wooden beads. Incense is sold in packets on street-corners.

Quebec's independence movement is growing in strength and the separatist Parti Québécois will win the next provincial election in 1976. A thousand protesters rally in Montreal streets against the execution of Basque separatists in fascist Spain. David Suzuki attracts hundreds

2. Kristian Gravenor,"George Springate: what a slacker!", *Coolopolis*, February 20, 2011, http://coolopolis.blogspot.ca/2011/02/george-springate-what-slacker.html.
3. Radawanski, "Bus fares," 1973.
4. Radawanski, "Bus fares," 1973.
5. Radawanski, "Bus fares," 1973.

of students to a McGill University auditorium giving a speech on the destruction of the environment. Gasoline peaked at 63 cents a gallon in 1973, but has dropped recently to a reasonable 44 cents. Students at the *Université de Montréal* push for greater control over what is taught in the classrooms—and how it is taught. Marijuana smokers perfume the public parks. Cars spew lead-laden fumes into the air, choking pedestrians. Activists occupy housing to protest the demolition of the Milton Park neighbourhood to build high-rise housing, and dozens are arrested. The cost of a movie at the cinema is 2$ and the minimum wage is 2,60$.[6]

Source: Vittorio Fiorucci, "Un jour on Crescent Street," 1973, *Coolopolis blog.*

The Quebec government is in the middle of constructing the largest infrastructure project in its history, harnessing hydroelectricity in the North at a massive public cost. The reservoir for these new dams, known as the "eye of Quebec", can be seen from outer space.

After *Man and his World* (Expo 67), Montreal mayor Jean Drapeau is heading up the team that will bring the Summer Olympics to Montreal in 1976, having said in 1973, to great fanfare: "The Olympics can no more lose money than a man can have a baby."[7]

6. "Minimum wage jobs pay roughly the same as they did in 1975", CBC News, last modified July 16, 2014, http://www.cbc.ca/news/business/minimum-wage-jobs-pay-roughly-the-same-as-they-did-in-1975-1.2708717
7. "Montreal '76: A 'self-financing' Olympics?", CBC Radio News, http://www.cbc.ca/archives/entry/montreal-olympics-1976-self-financing.

(The Montreal Olympics, estimated by Drapeau in 1973 to cost 310M$, will end up costing over 1.47B$, by far the most expensive Olympics ever held up to that time. A special tax on cigarettes is introduced to pay for it. As intended from the very early planning stages, this publicly-funded infrastructure is home to two private and very profitable sports franchises for decades after the Olympics, the Montreal Expos and the Montreal Allouettes.)

Inflation is running into the double digits for the first time in Canada's history, provoking a muscled response from the Canadian government, under Pierre Trudeau. Municipal costs and taxes are skyrocketing after the merging of municipal services in 1970, under an expanded regional government, provoked by a "devastating" strike by Montreal police and an effort to cost-share the demands of the police force.[8]

Quebec's Common Front strike

A common front of Quebec public sector unions crested in 1972, after a 15,000-strong march and ferocious police repression during a strike at the Montreal daily newspaper *La Presse* resulted in the accidental death of student and union activist Michele Gauthier.[9] The Common Front, uniting 210,000 workers or 84% of all public sector workers, called for wage increases of 8%, more control over working conditions and a minimum wage of 100$ a week for public service employees. The government refuses, and public workers go on strike on April 11, 1972.

The government goes on the offensive, seeking injunctions to force workers back to work. When these don't work, despite 103 arrests, 24 years in accumulated jail time, and over half a million dollars in fines, the government passes Bill 19, suspending the right to strike for two years.[10]

Unions ignore the law and the government responds by jailing the leaders of the three largest unions for one year. According to the Canadian Workers' History Project, the following years in Quebec are marked by the largest worker disruption in Canadian history since the Winnipeg General Strike of 1919, including worker takeovers of factories and media outlets, the shutting down of anti-union newspapers and even worker takeovers of several towns on the North Shore of Montreal.

8. Raphaël Fischler and Jeanne M. Wolfe "Regional Restructuring in Montreal: An Historical Analysis", *Canadian Journal of Regional Science* 23, no. 1 (Spring 2000), 89-114, http://www.cjrs-rcsr.org/archives/23-1/FISCHLER.pdf.

9. Robert Chodos and Nick Auf der Maur, ed., *Quebec: A Chronicle: 1967-1972* (Lorimer, 1972), 107.

10. "Canadian Workers' History Project", November 24, 2014, https://www.facebook.com/cana-dianworkershistory/posts/819301868091277:0.

"The downtown area is an immense garage"

In 1961, one in seven Montreal households owns an automobile, but by 1970, this number has shot up to one in four, nearly doubling in one decade. Public transit has also expanded enormously, with the construction of the first phases of the Montreal Metro system, but the vision and financial priority for the region is centred squarely on the automobile.

The automobile is taking up a larger and larger physical footprint in the city. In 1960, surface parking represented 10% of the downtown surface area, but by 1969, parking lots comprise 16%. Developers are demolishing buildings to make parking lots, but even this is insufficient to the meet the need and multi-story parking lots must be built.

"(T)he downtown area is an immense garage," urban geographer Louis Beauregard observes, at an important international meeting of geographers held at Place des Arts in Montreal in 1972. Origin-destination data shows that public transit accounted for 28.6% of all journeys to work, while automobile use is at 59.2%.

The City is pursuing a policy of wholesale demolition of Montreal's historic greystone downtown, including its housing stock. Heritage and housing activists, composed of some of Montreal's anglophone elites, form *Sauvons Montréal* (Save Montreal), which will spearhead efforts to protect Montreal's built environment from the bulldozers.[11]

The Drapeau era

Jean Drapeau has been ruling the City of Montreal for nearly 20 years, by 1975.

A bread and circuses mayor, without much in the way of bread, Drapeau's administrations have seen a string of expensive mega-projects completed during the 1960s, like the mega-tourist event at Expo 1967 which cost twice as much as the revenues it generated, the Decarie Expressway and the Turcot Interchange, demolishing thousands of units of housing in low income neighbourhoods, and the construction of the Montreal Metro, providing heavily subsidized mass transport links to building owners in Montreal's downtown shopping district, funneling workers and shoppers downtown.

And things are accelerating in the 1970s. Another huge swathe of East Montreal has been demolished and the Olympic Stadium is under construction, in anticipation of the 1976 Olympics. The Ville Marie

11. This movement will eventually give birth to Heritage Montreal, still active today. For an account of this moment, see Donna Gabeline, Dane Laken, and Gordon Pape, *Montreal at the Crossroads* (Montreal: Harvest House, 1975).

expressway and tunnel is finally completed, ruining a dramatic geological feature of Montreal, the *Falaise Saint Jacques*. Hundreds of typical Montreal greystone buildings and mansions are being demolished every year, provoking an organised response from Montreal's anglophone elites. Plans are afoot for even more inner-city highways and neighbourhood demolitions.

By 1975, 27,000 homes have been demolished, several neighbourhoods have been razed and traffic in the city has exploded.

Drapeau rules the city with a strong arm. During the 1970 election, Drapeau handpicked each candidate[12] for the Civic Party of Montréal, nicknamed "Draparty rubber-stampers" by one municipal observer.[13]

The Montreal Charter concentrates legislative and executive power in the office of the Mayor, and Drapeau exercised this power with authority, appointing yes men to the City's executive committee. For some voters, this style had a certain appeal. Few municipal observers would deny that it was his style.

Drapeau came to politics with ideals and situated his urban political project squarely within the bigger project of *maître chez nous*, the principle behind Quebec's Quiet Revolution, which called for anti-colonialist state-ownership strategies to wrest economic control from foreign and anglo capital.[14]

But after nearly two decades in power, Montreal is even more deeply and completely in the grip of foreign and anglo capital than ever before, as carefully detailed in Henry Aubin's ground-breaking 1976 book: *City for Sale*.[15] As one observer puts it:

> The net result of the development policies followed in the last 15 years by the state has been the colonisation of Montreal. ... Because of its debt level, its fiscal policy is now tightly controlled by Canadian, American and European bankers.[16]

12. See, for example: "Jean Drapeau a consolidé sa mainmise sur la Parti," *Le Devoir*, October 21, 1970, 3.
13. L. Ian McDonald, "Montreal This Morning," *Montreal Gazette* October 19, 1974, as cited in Kristian Gravenor, "How Auf der Maur got elected", *Coolopolis*, June 11, 2007, http://coolopo-lis.blogspot.ca/2007/06/how-auf-der-maur-got-elected.html?view=flipcard.
14. Abe Limonchik, "The Montreal Economy, the Drapeau Years", 1977, as reprinted in Dimitrios Roussopoulos, ed., *The City and Radical Social Change* (Montreal: Black Rose Books 1982).
15. From the cover of *City For Sale*: "Who really is in charge of our rapidly changing cities? Who are the individuals, dynasties and cartels that finance and provide so much of the impetus for our bleak, alienating urban landscape? Investigative reporter Henry Aubin spent almost two years trying to find out. He sifted through musty files for hundreds of hours and interviewed more than 400 people in six countries to mold this prize-winning account. *City For Sale* examines how Montreal's citizens became disenfranchised residents of their own city. As with many other cities on the North American continent, Montreal's elected officials acted to a large extent as pawns in the game of international finance. *City for Sale* is one of the most penetrating, myth-shattering analyses ever made of land ownership and related forces behind urban development in the 1970s." Henry Aubin, *City For Sale* (Lorimer, 1977).
16. Limonchik, "The Montreal Economy," 1977.

Drapeau grants reprieve to seniors

In 1974, the Drapeau administration announces some relief for senior transit users, adopting a special rate for those already receiving a low-income pension from the provincial government, making Montreal the 45th city in Canada to provide relief to seniors. Only 65% of seniors are eligible, and they must complete the paperwork and carry a special low-income seniors card to benefit from the rebate.

For seniors' groups, this gesture is not enough. With this measure, low-income seniors are stigmatised: they must face down the bureaucracy; travel, wait in lines, complete paperwork. As Springate's document pointed out, 95% of seniors are on fixed income and a 12% inflation rate is rapidly diminishing this fragile population's spending power. This useless layer of complexity is not appreciated.

Montrealers are looking for a change, and the engine of that change is bubbling up from neighbourhood struggles and getting ready to challenge City Hall.

The birth of the Montreal Citizens' Movement

The mid 1970s sees the birth of a new left-wing municipal party in Montreal that will rise out of Montreal's neighbourhood struggles and spearhead a campaign for a more democratic and fair city: the Montreal Citizens Movement (MCM).

The MCM was launched by the political arms of two of Quebec's largest unions as part of a "Second Front" strategy, the first such effort having died in the midst of the 1970 municipal election, at the height of the October Crisis.

This first effort, the FRAP, is perhaps best conceived of as a federation of neighbourhood-level political action groups, headed up by citizens working on local issues.[17] The planks in their platform were eventually to be adopted as public policy and will sound familiar to Montrealers: adopting a standard lease for tenants, setting up a housing renovation program and building social housing. Another of their top priorities is increased funding for public transport.

On October 3, 1970, the FRAP is ranking high in the polls. But on October 5, British diplomat James Cross is kidnapped by the *Front de liberation du Quebec* (FLQ) and a few days later, powerful cabinet minister Pierre Laporte is also kidnapped.

---

17. Pierre Belanger, *Le Mouvement Etudiant Quebecois: son posse, ses revendications et ses luttes (1960 - 1983)*, document produit par l'Association Nationale des Etudiantes et Etudiant du Quebec, 1984, http://studentunion.ca/aneq/Le mouvement etudiant quebecois - son passe, ses revendications et ses luttes (1960-1983) - Pierre Belanger-petit.pdf.

Enacting the War Measures Act, Canadian Prime Minister Pierre Trudeau sends in the army and Montreal falls under quasi-martial law. Hundreds of Montrealers are arrested and held without warrant, including two FRAP candidates in the middle of the election campaign,[18] in what critics, even the federal Progressive Conservative party leader, denounce as a serious breach of civil liberties. Police raid the homes of three FRAP candidates in the Saint Louis district, looking for links between FRAP and the FLQ.

On October 25th, under a siege-like atmosphere and despite the growing view that they should be postponed, Montreal conducts municipal elections and Drapeau is re-elected, winning every single municipal seat: FRAP does well in some neighbourhoods gaining 16% of the popular vote in the Saint Louis district, its best showing.

Somewhat ironically, this is the first election in Montreal's history with universal suffrage—the first time youth aged 18-21 are allowed to vote municipally—and the list of eligible voters nearly doubles from 380,068 in 1966 to 698,753 in 1970.[19] Drapeau wins the mayoralty with 92% of the votes cast, with 48% of registered voters participating.[20]

In May 1973, following the political failure of FRAP and the crushing of the 1972 Common Front, Quebec unions recommit to a municipal political strategy and form the *Comité régional inter-syndical de Montréal* (CRIM) with a mandate to found a new progressive political party in time for the next municipal election in November 1974.

Seconded to the job are two staff from Quebec's teachers' union and one rep from the *Conseil des syndicats du Québec* (CSN), Quebec's most socially progressive union. In early 1974, the team drafts a short document entitled *'Une ville pour nous'*, which defines the six main issues that will guide the new political party for the next decade: democratising Montreal's City Hall; housing; transport; parks and leisure; health; and the municipal budget.

A crucial strategic decision is taken by the three labour leaders to quickly broaden the foundations for the new political party by collaborating with established political formations, to the chagrin of some in the labour movement.

"Une ville pour nous"

Armed with its pamphlet *'Une ville pour nous'* the CRIM invited several groups to found the new municipal party: the Parti Quebecois, a

18. *Le Devoir*, October 26, 1970, 6.
19. *Le Devoir*, October 26, 1970.
20. *Le Devoir*, October 26, 1970.

provincial separatist party headed up by René Lévesque, a former journalist-turned political leader; the New Democratic Party, a federal social democratic party headed at the time by David Lewis, who cut his political teeth as a student in Montreal in the 1920s working with a Montreal municipal labour party,[21] and the *Mouvement progressiste urbain*, an anglophone anarchist group based in the Western part of Montreal.[22]

A careful analysis of this key moment in the founding of the party underscores the deliberate move by the three unionists to exclude community groups and citizen's committees from these initial meetings, to firmly root the strategy around a political party aimed at ousting control of the municipal government, rather than a popular movement.[23]

With only five months left before the next municipal election, and armed only with a thin document outlining a half-dozen planks in a municipal electoral platform, the MCM is formed and holds its first Congress.

The party is resolutely decentralised, with a popular, member-based Congress as its governing body, responsible for adopting the party program and electing members of the General Council; the General Council representing the Congress between annual meetings, and an executive committee and other committees. Finally, the MCM has local neighbourhood associations, which undertake actions, raise money, and forge resolutions and elements of the party program for approval at the annual Congress.

One neighbourhood is already well-organised, far ahead of any other, in 1974: the Saint Louis district. At the heart of the Plateau, just east of downtown Montreal, this district has a long history of left militancy, with a core of FRAP activists still livid from the 1970 municipal election, it already has a political machine preparing a run against Drapeau's party in the October elections.

The Saint Louis district, under the rallying call *Saint Louis, c'est chez nous*, joins the MCM as a local committee chapter. By far the most organised, radical and active district,[24] the Saint Louis district activists

21. David Lewis, *The Good Fight: Political Memoirs, 1909-1958*, (Macmillan of Canada, 1981), 457.

22. Pierre Gélinas, interview, July 22, 2016.

23. Jacques Godbout, and Jean-Pierre Collin, *Les organismes populaires en milieu urbain : contre-pouvoir ou nouvelle pratique professionnelle?* (Montréal: Institut national de la recherche scientifique, I.N.R.S.-Urbanisation, 1977), 201.

24. Geoffrey Ewen shows that the Saint Louis district of Montreal had long strong roots in radical critique of society: "On the other hand, in the growing Jewish immigrant community, socialism, both social-democratic and revolutionary, remained alive and vital. It was in the Saint Louis ward in the heart of the garment district that the Montreal Labor Party elected Joseph Schubert, a socialist, and a leading figure in both the Women's Circle and in the ILGWU, to city council in 1924. When Schubert retired in 1942, Communist Michael Buhay replaced him on city council. It was also in this area that Fred Rose would win the federal riding of Cartier for the Labor Progressive Party in 1943 and 1945. One reason that has been offered to explain why

will push party positions to the left over the coming months and years. Saint Louis, which also played a crucial role in fundraising for the MCM, was the thinking centre of the party, publishing a trilingual newspaper, and the activist heartbeat, organising actions on a regular basis throughout this period.[25]

Readying for the election of 1974

The founding MCM Congress adopts a party program largely reflecting the original CRIM draft *'Une Ville pour nous'* and finds candidates for every district, running a full slate against Drapeau's machine. Party candidates run the gamut of ideologies and experience, from single-issue housewives to university professors steeped in urban and radical theory: *"un parti heteroclite"*, according to one observer.

The party chooses Jacques Couture, a Jesuit-trained former priest with a fashionable moustache, to act as mayoral candidate, and the party runs under the slogan *Une ville pour tous*.

The electoral strategy is rooted in the platform, but the sentiment in the streets is "anything but Drapeau", at least in some parts of the city. One master theme is driven home during the campaign: bringing more control over neighbourhood development to residents at the neighbourhood level, les *"petites patries"*. While not that detailed, the principle of decentralisation of municipal power to neighbourhood councils is clearly articulated during the campaign, inside a vision of a city that protects human-scaled urban development:

> *La mise sur pied de conseils de quartier déviant l'instrument principal pour atteindre une revalorisation des quartiers. Il s'agit la d'une formule nouvelle qui a été utilisé à Winnipeg, Bologne et Grenoble, par exemple. C'est un peu révolutionnaire comme perspective, note Jacques Couture, tout en croyant que cette notion devra encore faire l'objet d'études.*

Couture frames Drapeau's vision of Montreal as one encouraging more cars, demolition and appealing to the *banlieux* and peripheral parts of the City, and entirely against the MCM vision, which is rooted in inner-city Montrealers' experience of their city:

> *Nous autres, nous sommes pognés à Montréal. On sent qu'il y a des valeurs humaines qui nous échappent. C'est complexe une ville. Tout ce qu'on sait, c'est qu'on demeure sur une rue, tu as des voisins, un environnement, de la chaleur humaine, une*

---

left wing political parties had so little success in Quebec after 1930 was that the francophone community did not benefit from the migration of a large number of politically conscious immigrants from Britain and Europe. Such immigrants made up as much as 95 percent of the CPC in the 1920's." Geoffrey Ewen, *The International Unions and the Workers Revolt in Quebec, 1914-1925*. Doctoral Thesis in History, York University, 1998.

25. Gélinas, interview.

collectivité. (...) On détruit l'âme de Montréal actuellement. Ce n'est pas unique à Montréal, ça.[26]

Free public transport—initially just for senior citizens: *"il faut être réaliste et prudent"*—is presented as a key strategy for preserving and protecting this inner–city quality of life, at the core of the MCM vision for the city:

« *On veut délibérément séduire, orienter et éduquer les Montréalais à utiliser le transport public. Pour ça, il doit être attrayant et économique,* » *de dire Jacques Couture. Aussi sa politique sera de diminuer le prix du transport, de l'abolir complètement pour les personnes âgées, ajoutant toutefois qu'il faut être réaliste et prudent avant de faire des promesses inconsidérées. [...]*

Sur l'automobile privée, le principe qu'il rétient est de décourager le transport par auto. Dans certains quartiers, comme le Vieux-Montréal, la circulation des autos pourrait être complètement éliminé...[27]

Et in Bologne, ego...

The Communist-led city of Bologna in Italy was a model for some MCM activists. In 1972, under a left-wing administration and after a prolonged neighbourhood-level consultation with its citizens, Bologna adopted a free public transport model and started systematically removing urban space from the automobile to create pedestrian-only zones and dramatically improved bus services: 200 new buses were purchased and reserve lanes were put in place.

Mass transit use doubled within the first year of implementation, and this city of 600,000 was heralded in 1973 in the New York Times as one of the best-managed cities in Europe,[28] and again later that same year in Newsweek magazine.

Importantly, Bologna also exercised its constitutionally-backed powers to merge the regional and local transport authorities into a single-minded entity, mandated to manage all forms of public transit in a coordinated manner. A similar approach was also proposed in the MCM's 1974 party platform.

These models were discussed and shared amongst the activist groups as the road to follow for Montreal.

The MCM wins 18 seats in the November election and gains 45% of the popular vote, in a surprising upset against Jean Drapeau and producing the first organised opposition to the mayor in many years.

26. *Le Devoir*, October 24, 1974.
27. *Le Devoir*, October 24, 1974.
28. Max Jäggi, Roger Müller and Sil Schmid, *Red Bologna* (London: Writers and Readers Publishing Cooperative (Society Limited), 1977), https://libcom.org/files/red_bologna.pdf.

January 1975: the campaign for free public transport

Meeting early in January 1975, the newly elected MCM councillors get to work unrolling a strategy forward.

The minutes of a January 9 caucus meeting record the striking of the *Personnes agées* committee which will spearhead efforts to organise the free public transport campaign, composed of three elected councillors: Ginette Kerouac, Phydine Tremblay and Marcel Morin.

On February 13, the caucus adopts three offensive strategies, one of which will focus on free public transport:

Le seul type de lutte qui mérite notre considération à ce stade c'est une lutte offensive que le parti pourra entreprendre ensemble. Deux critères fondamentaux doivent gouverner notre choix—nous devons pouvoir réaliser notre but et nous devons pouvoir utiliser la lutte pour conscientiser le monde à la nature du système et à la justesse de notre approche.

We get tantalising glimpses into some of the moments that unfold in the weeks following the launching of this MCM campaign, indicating that the movement is growing, and growing very rapidly:

On March 11, 1975, the free public transport for seniors campaign is launched publicly by the MCM, under the leadership of the former mayoral candidate: *"Operation Ville plus humaine: transport gratuit pour les personnes de troisiéme age."*[29]

On March 27, progress is reported on petition campaigns that are running in the churches and the metros. Archive documents include a detailed campaign strategy document with dozens of church parishes identified, hand-written notes of key contacts and team leaders, a map of the metro with targets identified, and talking sheets for organisers.

On April 3, four councillors are dispatched to lobby suburban mayors to the east and west in support of the campaign for free public transport for seniors.

On April 10, during a radio phone-in show, Radio CKVL, the station received 275 calls and 167 asked for a copy of the free public transport petition.

On, April 11, Jacques Couture is interviewed on the popular *Parle Parle Jase Jase* about the free public transport campaign.

On Saturday April 12, a rented regular city bus, packed full of activist senior citizens, careens through the streets announcing the inauguration of free public transport for seniors.

In mid-April, the councillors report back on their suburban mayor

---

29. Kenneth George, *Bilan de la campagne et stratégie pour la réunion du 16 avril 1975*, document interne, daté 15 avril, 8 pages, archives de la Ville de Montréal.

lobbying efforts: *"une lueur d'espoir existe tant qu'à l'adoption du principe de la gratuité pour les gens 3e age,"* they report.

By April 14th, over 140 civic groups are publicly supporting the campaign, the minutes report, including the *Ligue de sécurité publique.*

The play on City Hall

On April 16, armed with a petition signed by 75,000 citizens collected during a marathon campaign over six weeks, and supported by over 150 civic groups, the MCM councillors moved a motion in favour of free public transport for seniors at the *Commission de transport de la communauté urbain de Montreal* (CTCUM) meeting. However, the MCM councillors are in minority position.

After observing that many other cities already offer free public transport for their senior citizens, including several in Canada, the MCM spokesperson presents the following counter-arguments against the most common protests, according to draft notes found in the City of Montreal archives:

Wouldn't it cost too much? Reply: based on transit authority calculations the cost would represent only 1.2% of that year's operating budget. With an anticipated subsidy from Quebec, this cost should drop to 0.6% of the MUC's annual budget, or just over 1M$, something a few additional efficiencies in the system would pay for.

Why seniors? Why not other groups in need? Reply: seniors are on fixed incomes 'until the rest of their days', while those on social assistance are living a temporary setback; seniors over 65 will live on average another seven years, while those on social assistance "have a future ahead of them"; seniors are feeble, while other groups can ride a bike, hitch-hike, walk or take a car, while seniors do not have these options; finally, seniors should be prioritised for free transit because they have worked their whole lives already and made contributions to society: we owe them this respect. Also, the draft states, free public transit is not a priority for those on social assistance, who are busy fighting the water tax, rent hikes and unemployment, while for seniors, free public transport has been a top priority now for eight years.

We already have a reduced fare for poor seniors: isn't that the best policy? Reply: free public transport for all seniors would replace an existing fare reduction that was already in place for some seniors. At that time, 65% of seniors receiving a special additional income assistance subsidy from the provincial government were also eligible for a reduction in bus fares from the transport authority. Making fares free for all seniors would simplify the administration. Also, the material differences between these two low income groups of seniors is negligible, the MCM argued, when compared with other groups in society: dividing seniors into two low income groups and treating them differently doesn't in the end, save much money and creates unnecessary divisions in society: in fact, creating categories of poverty is a form of discrimination.

Income redistribution is a provincial policy area, not municipal: it's their job, not ours, no? First, as a principle at the root of democratic and efficient government: "problems should be addressed where they occur, if they are under the jurisdiction and competency of the government concerned." The MCM argues that because it is Montreal's seniors that are affected and public transit is a municipal responsibility, and we have the financial means to solve the problem, we must solve it. Yes, senior's ability to afford mass transit is a social problem. But in 1972, when the CUM initially reduced fares for seniors, they accepted the responsibility, they took the first step towards free mass transport. The most immediate level of government concerned should address the problem.

Drapeau's right-hand man and chair of the transport commission Lawrence Hanigan postpones the vote for two months to allow for the deliberation of the motion.

On June 18, the CTCUM meets again to decide whether to accept the fare change. Mayor Drapeau is in the room. The moment is tense. City Councillor John Gardiner is designated spokesperson for the MCM.

It is worth quoting an account that appeared in the MCM's summer newsletter, in an article signed by Dida Berku, published shortly after the meeting:

> Finally, we discussed how to continue the campaign for free public transport. Having passed the first phase of presenting the signed petitions to the MUC council on April 16th, 1975, the (MCM's General Council) had to decide how to carry through with its declared intention, which was to get free transport for senior citizens by January 1st, 1976. The decision that was taken was that the MCM was pledged to **total gratuity** [emphasis in the original] by '76 and that the councillors should vote accordingly at city hall in the event the administration introduced a half measure.
>
> At the June meeting of the MUC council, when the administration introduced its "eight bus tickets for one dollar" proposal, our councillors immediately prosed (*sic*) an amendment calling for complete gratuity by Jan.1, 1976. Drapeau ruled this amendment "unacceptable", provoking a long procedural wrangle. Thus the council was not able to pronounce itself on the question of free transport.
>
> When the vote was called, our caucus, with one exception who walked out, chose not to oppose the reduction, despite the mandate from conseil general. Their reasons were that the public might misinterpret such a vote

as opposition to a reduction and that possible opposition by some suburban mayors might have scuttled the reform altogether.

This incident illustrates that there is still an important need to clarify the relationship between the different instances of the party – executive, conseil, caucus, districts, members. Hopefully this will be aired and discussed in the coming months of preparation for the November party congress, and resolved at the congress itself.

The MCM councillors lost this battle and Drapeau came out as a friend of seniors, having simply extended his watery and bureaucratic partial fare reduction to some seniors. This early test of the party caused a major rift between the elected caucus and party membership which would continue to plague the MCM for many years to come.

As Marc Raboy puts it, writing in 1975:

> The election victory created a new political situation, not only in Montreal, but within the MCM itself. Before, it was easy enough for the party to state publicly that it would place the accent on mass public participation in all aspects of the decision-making process, beginning with the internal functioning of the party itself. But afterwards, the reality was that there were 18 elected councillors, overnight media personalities, with a precise, ready-made role to play within the existing political process. Immediately, tensions began to emerge between the "caucus" and the other party structures (executive, general council, local district associations, active membership at the base).

This first test, over the handling of the free public transport campaign, opened a fracture in the party.

The student movement is mobilizing

During the 1973-74 school year, partly in reaction to judicial and police repression during a five-week strike, the student movement briefly adopt a broader anti-capitalist and pro-worker strategy, called the *l'organisation politique de masse* (OPM),[30] but this is quickly replaced by a more traditional campus-based student union federation model, out of which is born the *Association nationale des étudiants du Québec* (ANEQ),[31] which will dominate the student movement for nearly 20 years. (ANEQ is a pre-cursor to the CLASSE, which played a crucial mobilizing role during the 2012 student uprising, symbolised by the red square.)

ANEQ gets broad support from unions and left-wing movements in Quebec at its launch in March 1974, and by September of 1975, has already cut its teeth in fights against obligatory aptitude tests and changes to the loans and bursaries program. At its founding in March

---

30. Belanger, *Le Mouvement Etudiant Quebecois*, 68.
31. Re-baptized some years later using inclusive language as ANEEQ.

1975, ANEQ represented 75,000 students or roughly half of the post-secondary student population in Quebec at the time. Concordia and McGill, the two large anglophone universities, have observer status and will be voting in the fall of 1975 on whether to join.[32]

In the autumn of 1975, at the *Université de Montreal*, students in sociology and geography strike and protest for greater control over the curriculum taught in the classroom. Thousands participate in marches. The university tries to break the movement by proposing a modest "pilot project" in Sociology along the lines proposed by the protesters, while brutally suppressing the movement with arrests, injunctions and threats of a year in jail and massive fines. Six students are plucked from the protests and punished, three of them student leaders.

October 1975: the public transit rate hike

On October 1st, the Montreal Gazette publishes an article that blends caustic wit with apparent fiscal inevitability: will public transit users face a fare hike? Seems likely, the article suggests. The article sketches out the budgetary crisis facing the CTCUM, pointing out that there hasn't been a rate hike in six years, and blaming strike settlements and plummeting revenues.

On October 2nd, the fare hike is officially announced in the daily newspapers: a 42% hike, raising the price per ticket from 35 cents to 50 cents per ticket, slightly less if you buy tickets in bundles. Existing rebates to seniors and children are not affected. Overnight, Montreal becomes the most expensive public transit system in North America, tied with New York City. Much of this fare hike is attributable to debt financing for the recent metro extensions, including out to the Olympic Stadium.[33]

Hanigan claims the fare hike is timed for the Olympics, and is intended to rake in extra revenues from tourists. He also blames the rate hike on the strikes and subsequent salary increases for bus drivers.

A *grogne* is perceptible immediately in Montreal: letters pour in to the newspapers, telephones light up during phone-in shows, parts of civil society spring to the defence of low-income Montrealers and the students leap immediately to action. Most users of public transit are low income.

CEGEP Maisonneuve, with a long and vibrant history of student

32. Belanger, *Le Mouvement Etudiant Quebecois*, 84.
33. Bernard Descôteaux, "Avec un budget de 7.7 millions: La CUM n'évite pas une hausse de la taxe foncière," *Le Devoir*, October 16, 1975, 1.

activism that continues to the present day, immediately calls a general assembly:

> *Dès le lendemain, la SOGÉÉCOM tient une assemblée générale. À cette occasion, on refuse le principe de tarif étudiant, jugeant la chose comme un privilège, et on revendique la gratuité du transport en commun pour tou(te)s.*[34]

The City of Montreal archives include an unsigned letter calling for a strike of the bus system on October 6, encouraging residents to hitchhike and drivers to join in. *"Nous n'avons pas besoin d'un syndicat. Nous sommes déjà réunis dans un même syndicat, simplement parce que nous employons tous le même service de transport,"* the letter writer observes.[35]

Urban planning and architecture professors from Montreal's universities damn the rate hike in the newspapers, noting that it is always the poorest that are punished by rate hikes and that this hike, which discourages people from taking public transport, leads the city in the wrong direction, towards more automobile use, more congestion, more parking, more demolition of buildings, more pollution, more noise, with the result being the ongoing dehumanisation of Montreal.[36]

An article in *Le Jour*, a progressive daily paper that competes with *Le Devoir* for readership and shares a nationalist editorial line, announces that a common front has been formed to oppose the fare hike, led by the MCM, unions and popular movements, soon to be called the *Comité de lutte des usagers contre la hausse des tariffs*. The article notes that the newly formed *Le Monde a bicyclette*, a bike lobby group, also joins the common front, and helpfully reminds readers that in Hamburg (1969) and in Italy (1975), popular movements of citizens have successfully rolled back transit rate hikes.

An October 11 article explains in detail how the ticket system works. Tickets are treated like cold hard cash: the CTCUM manages a heavily guarded distribution system, they carefully collect and burn used tickets, and they are introducing new designs with anti-counterfeit and fraud devices. The article ends with the following comment:

> Until today, the difference between (a fare paid with) cash and a ticket has been just six cents. Starting tomorrow morning, however, the difference will rise to 11 cents. "We prefer people to ride with tickets," Mr. Bouvrette [representing the CTCUM] said. "It's less handling for us...."

On October 15, the MCM crosses swords with Drapeau at the City Council meeting, aiming to block the fare hikes via a resolution. While

34. *Société générale des étudiantes et étudiants du Collège de Maisonneuve* (SOGÉÉCOM), "Histoire", https://sogeecom.org/histoire/.
35. City of Montreal archives, newspaper files, undated.
36. City of Montreal archives, newspaper files, undated

hundreds of students and others demonstrate noisily outside, MCM councillors take turns attacking Laurence Hanigan on various grounds: foisting the fare hike on users to get better terms on United States capital markets for the metro extension, not consulting council, bringing the hike in too quickly. The police expel a dozen protesters from the gallery for disrupting the council meeting, shouting *"vendus"* and *"bourgeois capitalists"* at Executive Committee members.[87]

Under the catchy slogan, *MUCTC plays robbers, we pay coppers*, the Loyola Student Association (LSA) launches a civil disobedience campaign to block fare boxes by paying in pennies. Fare boxes at the time didn't automatically count change, so it was impossible to tell how many pennies were going in the box. In addition, the fare box rapidly filled up, making it impossible for anyone to continue paying fares, before too long.

Hanigan's move: 50 cents for the property owners, too

On October 16, a front-page headline in La Presse shouts: "The CUM ready to hike tax by 50 cents per 100$ of the municipal evaluation" (author's translation), a whopping 43% increase from 1.16$ to 1.66$ per 100$ evaluation. The lion's share of this increase is dedicated to rising police costs, but public transit expenses are also rising significantly, the article states.

That same day, ANEQ announces they will join the rapidly growing movement against the fare hikes. A petition is started, calling for a student-card and reduced rates for all students. A rift opens immediately in the movement: some students want to push for a student fare, others want free public transport for everyone.

A wide range of creative and playful actions are launched by student groups as the month marches on. Students are jamming fare boxes with pennies, or hopping turnstiles. Some pay with cans of tomatoes.[88] Transit workers are turning a blind-eye, one article reports, but the union has not yet officially taken a position on the hike. The penny strategy rapidly goes viral, with broad-based citizen participation in the action.

According to Patrick Timmons, LSA rep to ANEQ, the purpose of this civil disobedience campaign is both to "disrupt regular operations of the service and to demonstrate support for other groups, such as the MCM and the Parti Québécois, fighting the fee hike".[89]

37. *La Presse*, October 16, 1975, page 3.
38. Gélinas, interview.
39. *The Georgian*, October 21, 1975, 3.

The editorial line of the student papers affects how the events are covered. Some papers give voice to student spokespeople who explicitly supporting a broader social movement that has formed, and not just focussing on gains for students alone.

On October 17, CEGEP Maisonneuve students launch a massive information campaign in Hochelaga Maisonneuve, a working class French neighbourhood on the east side of Montreal:

> *Des journées de débrayage s'étendront sur quelques jours entre le 17 octobre et le 23 octobre. On diffuse largement dans le quartier en faisant du porte à porte. On invite alors la population à une assemblée publique au collège le 22 octobre et à la manifestation du 23. La SOGÉÉCOM produira alors 100 000 tracts qui seront distribués dans Hochelaga. Elle produira aussi 10 000 macarons et 50 000 autocollants...* [40]

Students are hopping the turnstiles in the metro in increasing numbers, and encouraging others to do so on a massive scale. One report describes students carrying a happy old lady over the turnstiles so she doesn't have to pay.[41] Police are mobilized to block the students, but the students are too quick, disappearing into the underground system and reappearing elsewhere to continue their action, like a circus side-show game of Whack the Groundhog.

Low-income workers get a wage freeze

On the 20th of October, 1,7 million workers in Quebec wake up to news that a promised minimum wage increase, expected November 1, will be postponed. This is nearly half the working population of Quebec. Inflation is at 12% annually.

On the 21st of October, the minutes of an MCM caucus meeting held Wednesday evening at the *Centre communautaire Saint-Urbain*, reflect the mood of a rapidly growing movement. City councillors Arnold Bennett, John Gardiner, Nick Auf De Maur, Jean Roy, Paul Cliche and others are present, some come late, and three councillors are absent. The second item on the agenda is *"Proposition Cliche au sujet de la participation à la marche contre la hausse des tarifs du transport en commun,"* followed by a third item: *"100 millions de plus pour les Jeux Olympiques"*.

John Gardiner gets caucus agreement to ask the Sunday Express to give equal time to the MCM, after they provided Laurence Hanigan with a column in the paper. Paul Cliche explains his proposal, and the following resolution is adopted unanimously (author's translation):

---

40. SOGÉÉCOM, "Histoire"
41. City archives, newspaper clippings, undated.

Proposal to ensure the concrete involvement of MCM activists in the campaign to boycott the CTCUM fare increase.

Whereas the MCM, via one of its working committees, issued a public call to the population to boycott the fare hike, unjustly decreed by the commissioners of the CUM;

Whereas, as a result of this public call, a common front of popular associations has been formed (students, membres of the Parti Quebecois, "Save Montreal", etc.) and that various demonstrations have already taken place;

Whereas, a major demonstration will take place on Thursday evening on 23 October as part of this campaign;

Whereas, it is imperative that all militants of the MCM actively participate in this campaign so that students, workers and other activists are not left to fight alone after the public call has been issued;

It is proposed by Paul Cliche, and seconded by Gaètan Lebeau

1) That the MCM councillors take part in the demonstration on Thursday night and are ready to boycott the increase in tariffs, despite any arrest and legal procedure that may be taken against them;

2) That the executive of the MCM be promptly invited to adopt similar position by Thursday evening;

3) That the three caucus delegates to the General Council of the MCM immediately take the necessary steps, in accordance with Article 2 or 3 of Chapter 4 of the Statutes, to convene an emergency meeting of this governing body of the party so that its members:

(a) hear a report and the recommendations of the organizing committee of the campaign;

(b) take a stand in favour of the active boycott of the increase in tariffs in the same spirit as the first part of this resolution and that an explicit recommendation to this effect be made to all the district associations;

(c) recommend to the next Congress of the MCM to take a stand in favour of boycotting tariffs in the same spirit as Parts 1 and 2 of this resolution and that an explicit recommendation to that effect be made by the Congress to all members of the party.

Jean Roy then proposed that after the demonstration, the councillors would meet the east entrance of the town hall to go to the Champ-de-Mars metro station.

Councillors Jean Roy, Robert Keaton, Arnold Bennett, Nick Auf Der Maur and Ginette Keroack advise the caucus that they will participate in the "Save Montreal" movement. The others should participate in the one that will leave Lafontaine Park.

A glimpse inside the student debate, October 22

On October 22, students gather in the *Saint Louis de France* church basement at yet another general assembly.[42] The room is packed full of hundreds of smoking students, mostly daytime students from UQAM

42. UQAM's institutional newspaper, the voice of the administration, provides a peak into the complex proceedings of the student movement at the time. *L'UQAM, journal institutionnel de l'UQAM*, 28 octobre, 1975.

but also dozens of students from other universities and reps from ANEQ.

As portrayed in the article, the debate focuses on a struggle between the local UQAM student association, trying to get on its feet, and ANEQ, the national student organisation, trying to mobilise students for a larger fight: Do we build a local union, a base here at UQAM, or do we focus on national issues to build a broad-based movement?

An ANEQ representative puts forward a proposition: "The position of ANEQ is to mobilise students against the price hike in the metro and bus. Not yet, the unification of struggle with the unions." ANEQ's immediate strategic goal should be a special bus pass and reduced bus fare for students.

Later, to resounding echos of *Vive l'ANEQ*, another student strains into the microphone: "*Lutte? Toujours! Négociation? Peut-etre! Capitulation? Jamais!*"

The meeting is still going strong at midnight, "*dans une atmosphère bleutée de fumée de cigarettes*".

Students complained at the microphone that UQAM was built without any rooms larger than 200 students, the only one in Canada without big rooms. A hat was passed around to raise 150$ for the fee-rental for the room.

Just two days before the demonstration, ANEQ finally agrees to merge its proposed rally for a student card with the one being organised by the MCM, *Sauvons Montréal* and other members of the *Comité de lutte*, in favour of free public transport.

October 23: a mile-long demonstration descends on City Hall

Reports of anywhere between 15 and 20 thousand people marched on City Hall on October 23, 1975 to protest the fare increase and to call for free transit for seniors and students, but the reports vary widely. The *Montreal Gazette*, a suburban middle-class English daily, reports that 15,000 *students* marched on City Hall. *Le Devoir*, a nationalist and progressive French daily paper, has a somewhat more nuanced analysis on its front page:

> C'est à l'appel de l'Association national des étudiants du Québec (ANEQ), du Comité de lutte des usagers contre la hausse des tariffs, et de Sauvons Montréal que cette manifestation a été organisée. Il faut souligner que ce sont les deux premiers groupes surtout qui ont travaillé à l'organisation de la manifestation. L'ANEQ et le Comité de lutte devaient tenir deux manifestations différentes, à des heures différentes, mais à la dernière minute, l'ANEQ s'est ralliée.[43]

The student rally left Lafontaine Park with about 3500-4000 students,[44] other student formations from a handful of other schools joined the rally at City Hall, totalling maybe 2-3000 additional students, and the total rally estimates are 15,000 (police estimate as reported in *Le Devoir*) and 20,000 (organisers said).

Police guard the Metro stations on the evening of the demonstration, October 23rd. Source: *The Georgian.*

Le Devoir observes that contrary to common practice, no star union figure or politician spoke to the assembled masses. Rather, Pierre Gélinas spoke to the crowd, a young MCM organiser. He is quoted as saying that transport was just one of the crucial urban struggles, housing is another important one and that we must unite and fight if public transport is to be free.

Gélinas played a key role in rallying students to the movement, a demonstration that came together in just two and a half weeks. The few days just before the rally were torture, as he lobbied and cajoled different groups to participate: decisions had to be made collectively. Even ANEQ was still waffling, just two days before.

"*C'était effrayant*," he recalled. Party nerves.

Gélinas recalls the moment climbing the podium with MCM city councillor John Gardiner, and looking out over the masses of people

43. Bernard Descôteaux, "Marche à 15,000 contre le ticket à 50¢," *Le Devoir*, October 24, 1975, https://news.google.com/newspapersid=XDYgAAAAIBAJ&sjid=mVIEAAAAIBAJ&pg=5142,2458753.
44. According to *Le Devoir* and the Concordia *Georgian* newspapers.

that had gathered in front of City Hall. *"J'étais stupéfié. John était pas loin derrière moi (...) on était aux anges,"* he recalled.

Some observers have called this rally the largest mobilisation in Montreal's history, up to that point. Gélinas points out that this may be the first major demonstration that was truly and uniquely Montreal based. Where other demonstrations on language or national identity or common front strikes might draw demonstrators from the Montreal region or beyond, the size of this demonstration was even more remarkable because it focused strictly on a narrow Montreal issue.

Who attended the October 23rd rally?

The *Montreal Gazette* brushed the rally off as composed entirely of students, impetuous renegade youth getting their jollies out protesting and breaking the law: a typical and remarkably durable editorial line for this newspaper.

But who, really, was in that historic crowd? For Gélinas, one of the key organisers of this event, and acting as the interlocutor between the various student associations and the MCM, the crowd likely contained representatives of the following constituencies: unions, especially the three members of the CRIM; radical left-wing groups including the *Parti communiste du Québec*, the Marxist-Leninists, le *Parti des travailleurs du Québec*, Trotskyists, Maoists and others; *Sauvons Montreal*, a mostly anglophone network pushing for the protection of Montreal's built heritage, housing stock and parks,[45] US draft dodgers (of which there were many in Montreal at the time), housing militants from the Milton Park struggle, the ANEQ-led student constituent in addition to many other student groups; the *Parti Québécois*, a young provincial separatist party with a well-organised network capable of mobilising many hundreds at short notice; and the federal social democratic New Democratic Party.

For Gélinas, perhaps half the demonstrators were students.

The MCM tries to keep the momentum

On October 29, the MCM's *Conseil general* adopts many motions on free public transport, including, that:

(a) the MCM encourages direct action by all its working groups in the fight for free mass transit (2 against, 6 abstentions, motion passed)

(b) members of the *Conseil general* of the MCM be prepared to actively

---

45. Martin Drouin, *Le Combat du Patrimoine à Montréal (1973-2003)*, (Québec: Presses de l'Université du Québec, 2005), 43.

boycott any increase in transit fares, and this at the risk of any arrest or legal procedure that may be suffered, and that a recommendation to do the same be sent to all local associations;

(c) that the MCM is a political party and so will use this movement to its advantage to get elected, by (1) getting the name MCM out front on this fight (2) explain the MCM program on public transit (3) get the party position out in the public as much as possible, using especially the mass media.

As early as a week after the historic march on City Hall, evidence is mounting that the movement is crumbling. On October 30th, thirty students are arrested at the Peel metro station for jumping turnstiles, marking the first report of arrests. Despite repeated calls for their continuing participation in the movement, ANEQ refuses. Accounts of this moment are found in various documents, both from the time and in reflections published much later.

Yves Mallette, an ANEQ leader writing at the time, blames the MCM and others for stealing the spotlight which caused the coalition to fall apart:

> Mais plusieurs groupes soi-disant progressistes comme le Comité de lutte des usagers contre la hausse des tarifs, l'organisme Sauvons Montréal, le RCM (Rassemblement des citoyens de Montréal) et les groupuscules de la go-gauche ont été beaucoup plus efficaces que la police pour nuire à cette lutte. Voyant que, sur le terrain, nos actions mobilisaient les gens, ils ont tous tenté de récupérer le mouvement. Par exemple, nous avions proclamé la désobéissance civile sur les marches de l'hôtel de ville de Montréal à la fin d'une manifestation. Le lendemain, gros titres dans les journaux annonçant que le RCM proclamait la désobéissance civile... Et dans les textes, les porte-parole du RCM ne faisaient jamais allusion aux actions menées par les étudiants. Ils ne nous invitaient jamais à leurs réunions. Tous ces groupes agissaient en bébés, jalousant la capacité de mobilisation des étudiants et la sympathie qu'ils s'attiraient dans la population. Le problème, c'est qu'ils avaient une bien meilleure couverture de presse que les étudiants. De plus, ces groupes nous accusaient à tort de ne pas vouloir engager une lutte unitaire contre la CTCUM, refusant de comprendre que nous respections trop les syndicats ou groupes populaires pour parler en leur nom. Comme représentants étudiants nous mobilisions les étudiants et tant mieux si les autres se joignaient à la danse. Et ce n'est pas uniquement les étudiants qui prenaient le métro et l'autobus gratuitement, mais ces étudiants faisaient monter gratuitement tout le monde. Par exemple, nous prenions de vieilles dames et nous les soulevions par-dessus les barrières. Elles trouvaient ça très drôle et elles économisaient le prix d'un billet.
>
> ... Si je me suis attardé un peu à l'exemple de la lutte contre la hausse des tarifs du transport en commun, c'est qu'elle illustre bien l'impact des groupuscules de la go-gauche dans ces années-là qui ne réussissaient jamais à organiser quoi que ce soit de concret sur le terrain, mais qui tentaient toujours de récupérer les luttes mises de l'avant par d'autres, quitte à saborder le mouvement... au grand plaisir des policiers et du pouvoir en place.

Unfortunately, Yves Mallette does not go into any detail on how the *go-gauche* scuttled the movement. The fact remains that this movement very rapidly lost momentum and has disappeared from the public radar by January of 1976.

Meanwhile, in Quebec City

In Quebec's capital city, the left-leaning Parti Québécois moves a motion on November 13, 1975 to censure the centrist Liberal government for failing to adequately support senior citizens by reducing transit fares, especially in the Montreal region.

The motion reads:

> *Que cette Assemblée blâme le gouvernement pour avoir omis de mettre en œuvre une politique globale d'aide au transport en commun susceptible de permettre un service adéquat à un coût abordable et d'empêcher les récentes hausses de tarifs, notamment dans la région de Montréal, sans pour autant taxer encore davantage les budgets déjà trop grevés des municipalités.*[46]

The debate ensues, during which many barbs are launched and the debate boils down to a handful of broad observations about who should pay for what, and what are the priorities of government.

Marc-André Bédard, speaking in favour of the motion to censure, argues that the Liberal government keeps building roads for cars, ever more cars, that there is ever more urban space devoted to cars. In downtown Montreal, he states, it costs more to build an underground parking space for an automobile than it does to build a home for the average family. Where will it end? Montreal will end up like Los Angeles or New York. "We shouldn't wait until our city, sick from the automobile, dies from it before discovering that we took the wrong road" (author's translation). In fact, he argued, we need equal space for cars and mass transit: *"au moins des places égales au transport en commun et à l'automobile"*.

Berthiaume, representing the ruling Liberal Party majority, responds that the Parti Québécois wants to tax the people from the countryside, who are already economically weak, to pay for the residents of the city: *"(le PQ) voudrait taxer les gens de la campagne, qui sont déjà économiquement faibles, pour payer pour les gens de la ville."*

Sequel: The *Commission des transports du Québec*

The *Le Devoir* article published the day after the historic rally on City Hall points out the upcoming pressure points in the movement.

46. 30e législature, 3e session (18 mars 1975 au 19 décembre 1975), Le jeudi 13 novembre 1975 - Vol. 16 N° 60, Journal des débats, http://www.assnat.qc.ca/fr/recherche/recherche-avancee.html?rch=Travaux&zn=3&mcl=transport en commun 1975&pdd=1975-01-01&pdf=1975-12-31&sle=1079.

Montreal's city councillors and the mayors of the region could overturn the decision at their next meeting on November 14, an unlikely event, given that the opposition MCM councillors were the only members to oppose the hike. No suburban mayors would support a roll-back of the rate hike, the article states.

The second pressure point, also faint hope, would be to take the matter to the *Commission des transports du Québec*, a quasi-judicial body responsible for settling transport disputes.

The MCM did pursue this route, and so did at least three other groups representing civil society, but to no avail: the effort failed. Nearly a year later, the MCM issued a press release denouncing the decision of the CTQ to maintain the fare hike.

The aftermath: 1976 and beyond

Addressing an assembly of trade unionists in April 1976 with a calm voice, MCM Councillor Michael Fainstat denounces the Olympic Games as one of the greatest scandals in the world.   Given the ballooning Olympic Stadium deficit, estimated by this point at nearly one billion dollars, the City of Montreal could have built over 120,000 units of subsidised housing or provided free public transport for everyone for 10 years.[47]

Drapeau blamed the ballooning Olympic deficit on inflation. Fainstat hardly needs a calculator to show how absurd this is: inflation could account for 44% of the cost overruns, not 430%.

The MCMs 1976 Congress represented a major turning point for the young party. At that crucial meeting, roughly one third of the party planks adopted aim at deep, long term structural changes that will correct social and power inequality in Montreal. The MCM tries to shake off its internal contradictions and situate itself squarely and solidly as a municipal socialist party.

Between 1976 and 1978, the MCM attempted to rid itself of divisiveness and internal inconsistencies by adopting a more overtly socialist stance. The 1976 Congress adopted a plan to bring together politicized citizens to resist the way capital was transforming their city, through the mobilisation of active popular support.

Ironically, the 1978 municipal election was a disaster for the MCM and it seemed as though the people of Montreal, who had recently experienced the coming to power of the Parti Québécois at the provincial level, did not wish to risk further change by rejecting the stability and authority of the Drapeau machine.[48] Several of its dissident

---

47. *La Presse*, April 14, 1976, d20.

members that had left the party campaigned actively against the MCM as having swung dangerously to the left, which didn't help the campaign either.

In the 1986 campaign, the MCM removed free public transport from its platform in the months leading up to the Montreal municipal election, softening their position to one that limited the financial contribution from transport users to one third of transport operating costs. The call for free public transport is deemed "too risky" at that political junction so they put the emphasis on more popular themes, such as cutting the bureaucracy, better gender representation, and culture.[49]

Author's note: This chapter is based on preliminary research into the events of 1975, and is an extract from a larger work, to be published in 2018.

48. Tim Thomas, "Municipal parties and governments and their effectiveness as vehicles for participatory democracy," Université McGill, Programme d'études sur le Québec, 1994, https://www.mcgill.ca/qcst/files/qcst/TimThomaspdf.pdf.
49. Serge Belly, "Les partis politiques municipaux et les élections municipales de 1986 à Montréal et de 1989 à Québec", *Politique*, no. 21 (winter1992), 27, http://id.erudit.org/iderudit/040711ar.

Hasselt: One City for All

Michael Brie

A surprising election victory

In 1994, Steve Stevaert,[1] the owner of several restaurants, put forward his candidature for mayor of the Flemish-Belgian city of Hasselt; to everyone's surprise, he won the election. Stevaert was forty years old.

During the preceding ten years, Stevaert had represented the social democratic *Socialistische Partij Anders* (sp.a) in Limburg's provincial parliament and had been a member of Hasselt's town council. In 1995, he was elected to the Flemish Parliament, reflecting his rising importance as an active local and regional politician.

Stevaert's candidacy for mayor of Hasselt was triggered by the increasing levels of traffic in the town, which he believed threatened people's quality of life and the local economy. In his view, car and truck traffic was destroying this beautiful medieval town, that had existed for more than 800 years. But the city also had a large public debt. He pushed a vision of the city that called for a cost-effective use of tax revenues coupled with new investment in public services. Second, signalling the end of a post-war euphoria associated with cars and motorways, he opposed new infrastructure for automobiles and proposed instead a city for people.

---

1. In Europe, it is not unusual to have overlapping political mandates, as these positions are often part-time and even unpaid.

During his campaign, he established broad alliances between municipal and regional political levels that proposed new ways of linking social, environmental, local and regional economic and cultural interests. He brought together trade unions, both in public and private enterprises, local and regional entrepreneurs and owners of the local shops and restaurants, ecologically concerned citizens and those who demanded social equity. He called for free public transport, building a base from which the new middle classes and the traditional working classes—and suburban and inner-city residents—bridged their differences. At the centre of his campaign, of his vision, was transport—always a contentious issue during a municipal election campaign—but Stevaert's surprising election result demonstrated that local elections could be won with a vision that opposes 'car-friendly' cities.

Before we continue, let us sketch out the urban context of Hasselt, so we know what we are talking about. Hasselt is the capital of the province of Limburg, with a population of 75,000 residents, expected to rise to 100,000 by 2030. Limburg has around 860,000 inhabitants and covers an area of more than 2,400 km2. Hasselt lies roughly in the middle, a town encompassing over 102 km2.

Situated at the juncture of supra-regional trading routes, Hasselt has been a centre for trade for hundreds of years. It now has a university with around 6,000 students. Regional industry began developing in the town in the 19th century, and during this period Hasselt was especially famed for its production of juniper schnapps.

The town is of particular importance to the province as a commercial centre, with a surprisingly large volume of people—150 000 souls, or twice the actual population—travelling to Hasselt every day to do their shopping. Moreover, almost 40,000 school pupils and students from surrounding communities attend school or university in Hasselt daily. Although the town is only the 21st largest in Belgium when it comes to population size, it is ranked 4th in terms of service provision. A large number of commuters also journey to Hasselt every day for work: around 22% more people work in the town than live there.[2]

Many of these people come to Hasselt by car. To accommodate these daily rivers of steel, rolling noisily in from all directions, several highways have been built around Hasselt, and in response, the town now has both an outer and an inner ring road.

Importantly, Stevaert's candidacy for mayor was triggered by the

2. Marc Verachtert, "Free Public Transport. Hasselt from the beginning to the end" (PowerPoint presentation, Summer School on Free Public Transport, Tallinn, Estonia, 2013), 4, http://www.tallinn.ee/eng/g10210s64057.

planned construction of yet another (a third), ring road. His election campaign particularly focused on preserving and expanding Hasselt's special character as a regional hub for education, services and industry, but not by inviting more cars. On the contrary, he aimed to improve the quality of life and attractiveness of this centuries old town. As a social democrat, with political experience at the regional level, Stevaert's campaign combined social, regional, economic and environmental issues into a dramatic new vision of urban development. Traffic calming measures, the expansion of pedestrian zones, increased space for bicycle and, in particular, free public transport—combined into a new vision of the city—was to finally bring an end to urban development's subordination to the private automobile.

At the centre of his political campaign, and in this new integrated vision of Hasselt, was free public transport, which would aim to reduce car trips into the centre and allow the city to breathe again. It is to this topic we now turn.

Public transport in Hasselt

In Belgium, local and regional public passenger transport receives a relatively high level of subsidies. This reflects the recognition that public transport is an essential service, as it enables people to participate in public life and provides them with access to work, education, shopping, health facilities, government authorities, culture, and so on; this is particularly the case with people on low-incomes. The ability to enjoy real social and cultural rights is dependent on public transport.

This initially high level of subsidies put the introduction of free public transport in Hasselt within financial reach of the local government. In the case of Hasselt, the regional government paid 89% of these costs, while the local government covered the remainder of the operating costs, an annual investment of approximately €250,000 (US$300,000) in 1997.[3]

Prior to 1997, Hasselt's public bus network served only 1000 people daily and often ran buses that were nearly empty, representing just a tiny fraction of the modal share. Under the mayor's leadership, and by eliminating the price barrier to public transport and scrapping the proposed new ring road, passenger volumes on public transport jumped dramatically. The number of passengers per year went up from 350,000 to almost 4.5 million, or an increase of nearly 13 times. Among the new users of public transport were, most importantly, many

3. Verachtert, "Free Public Transport," 12.

previous car drivers, but also a sizeable portion of cyclists and pedestrians now choosing the bus.

The regional government owned the transport company that provided the town's bus service. Thus, agreements had to be made on how to redistribute the higher costs incurred through the provision of free public transport. At the same time, although the plans to build a third ring road had been scrapped, the accompanying cost savings did not directly benefit the town. These locked-down financial arrangements—the garrisoning and rabid defense of capital budgets for automobile infrastructure—make the development of local transport solutions more difficult, or at least more vulnerable to forces at a higher level: they are also patently unfair. This was certainly the case in Hasselt, as would become clear around 15 years later. In short: although something may make economic sense, it does not necessarily lead to cost savings for public budgets. Furthermore, even when a local policy does produce higher revenues and/or lower expenditures, this often affects unrelated budgets or completely different budgetary items: Hasselt is also a good example of this problem.

Moreover, certain costs, such as declining health expenditures from improved air quality, more exercise, and lower levels of stress—now that people have better levels of mobility—are rarely directly linked to specific projects, nor are they noticeable at the treasury, and rarely even make it into the political debate.

Free public transport – 'just the cherry on the cake'

The introduction of free public transport in Hasselt in 1997 made the town famous overnight throughout Europe. However, it is important to note that the policy of 'free rides' for all on public buses was implemented in the context of wide-ranging urban development and should in no way be reduced to simply the abolition of charges for urban public transport. As Stevaert's head of cabinet pointed out in an interview, 'the free bus makes the headlines, but it's just the cherry on the cake'.[4]

Steve Stevaert's motto was *Hasselt für alle*—One city for all!, and the achievement of this motto could only be delivered via a reinvention of the urban transport system. Once the planned third ring road had been stopped, Stevaert's team pushed back against the domination of the automobile even harder. Instead of expanding the second ring road, the inner ring road, which runs close to the medieval city wall, was actually

---

4. Elisabeth Wehrmann, "Stadt ohne Fahrschein" in *Hasselt—Stadt ohne Fahrschein* ["City without a ticket" in Hasselt—City without a ticket] (2007), 4, www.zukunft-ennstal.at/pdfs/HASSELT.pdf.

narrowed from four lanes to two and greened, effectively restoring the inner ring road to what it had been during the 19th century: a promenade.

At the same time, free parking for cars and bikes was established on the outer (second) ring road; the car parks were guarded by long-term unemployed people. Free buses transported people from these areas to central sites in the town. Three main transfer points were established at this outer ring, all of which were suitable for people with disabilities. A bike lending system was also established, and Hasselt's town centre was turned into a zone for pedestrians and cyclists, the keyword being 'walkability'. Two thirds of parking spots in the town centre were repurposed, leaving only 500 parking spaces for the private car.

Clearly, free public transport in Hasselt was just a piece—albeit a crucial piece—of a broad range of measures aimed at reimagining the city centre and strengthening social cohesion and solidarity in the urban community. For every child born, a tree was planted during festive events held three times a year. Young people aged 16 or above were offered the opportunity to undertake paid work for the town during their summer holidays and, thus, learned to accept responsibility for their town's public spaces and community affairs.[5] Gradually, the streets in the town were pedestrianised, and large areas remain car-free today. The higher levels of expenditure that this led to were partly recovered through substantial increases to parking fees in the town centre (mid-2000s: €10/US$11.90 for half a day). Furthermore, shops were only able to take deliveries at selected times or by bicycle and the speed limit for cars was reduced to 30 km/h. Finally, measures were also introduced to make public transport more attractive by adding new buses, creating a very dense network of bus stations and a close, coordinated link to regional transport, together with restrictions on private car use.

While these measures were mainly introduced to free up the town centre from car traffic, it would be wrong to assume that they resulted in lower levels of mobility. In fact in some cases, people who do not drive cars were able to travel more often, to hospital or to the market, for example.[6] At the same time, these measures made the town more attractive and led more people to move to Hasselt. Among those who adopted public transport, 16% had previously travelled by car, but it was not only car drivers who switched to public transport: 9% of bus passengers had previously travelled on foot. Moreover, although 12% of passengers had formerly journeyed by bike, the number of cyclists in the town actually increased. This also led roads in the town to become

5. Wehrmann, "Stadt ohne Fahrschein," 5.
6. Verachtert, "Free Public Transport," 12.

quieter and safer, and many people who had been restricted in their mobility could now travel free of charge.

After 1995, and as part of the renegotiations conducted with the regional transport company *De Lijn*, Hasselt was no longer merely responsible for 11% of the costs of bus transport, but for 25%. Clearly, the adoption of free public transport was neither cost-neutral for the town nor the region, at least if we only take the direct costs into account. During this period, the number of buses also had to be increased, given the enormous increase in ridership (as noted earlier, public transport use jumped from 350,000 in 1997 to 4.4 million in 2012).[7] In 2012, buses began leaving the transfer points every five minutes, not only effectively eliminating waiting times, but also meaning that public transport was now the fastest means of urban transportation, in some cases.[8]

The costs incurred through the provision of free public transport over the years amounted to approximately 1% of the town's budget. However, these costs were more than compensated for by the higher revenues that resulted from the town's increased attractiveness. In 2012, Hasselt spent around €1.75 million (US$2.08 million) on the project, which equates to around €0.06 (US$0.07) per inhabitant per day or €23 (US$27.37) per person per year.

During the 15 years in which free public transport existed in Hasselt, one thing remained unchanged: 90% of households continued to own a car. Today, an average of 2.8 trips are made by car per day in Hasselt. Just 3% of the population travels to work on foot; 10% uses a bike, and around 7% opts for public transport. Accordingly, almost 80% of the population still uses cars.[9] Clearly, even the provision of free public transport was unable to break the centrality of the car. As such, the project mainly took on the role of converting Hasselt into a largely traffic-calmed zone and increasing the town's attractiveness. These, of course, are permanent achievements, but the project was unable to achieve real environmental and social change viewed through a shift in people's approach to mobility.

An experiment ends

After the 2012 local elections, the advocates of free public transport—the Social Democrats (sp.a) and the Greens—were still able to form a government. However, this time they formed a coalition with the

7. Verachtert, "Free Public Transport," 9.
8. Claudia Zimmermann, "Magnet für die Region" in *Hasselt – Stadt ohne Fahrschein* ["Magnet for the region" in Hasselt – City without a ticket] (2007), 7-8, www.zukunft-ennstal.at/pdfs/HAS-SELT.pdf.
9. Verachtert, "Free Public Transport," 17.

Christian Democrats, a party that had campaigned for the re-introduction of (albeit low-priced) tickets. By this time, Belgium's policies of austerity and the associated shift of expenses from the national and regional levels to the municipalities were intensifying the constraints on public finances. In addition, *De Lijn*, the company operating the bus service, sought to radically reduce its share of the costs. From now on, 15 years after the introduction of free public transport, Hasselt would now have to find €2.8 million (US$3.33 million) instead of €1.8 million (US$2.14 million) a year to continue funding the service. Hasselt's free public transport system ended on January 1, 2014. Most people living in the town now pay €0.60 (US$0.71) per journey. Nevertheless, in the Flemish region of Belgium, young people up to 19 years of age, as well as retirees and people on very low-incomes, are still entitled to travel for free, in accordance with Flemish law.

If we look back on this time, the implementation of free public transport in Hasselt between 1997 and 2013 was part of a largely successful, wide-ranging process of urban redevelopment, in particular of the town centre. Consequently, and as a mark of its success, the free transport component no longer seemed necessary. When the project came to an end, there was no return to traffic jams in the town centre. The cherry might have been gone, but the cake remained. Second, the project was tied to political and human constellations that were no longer as strong as they had once been: the social democratic and green parties had lost their influence, and the project's initiator, Steve Stevaert, had left office. As such, the dynamic that had been pushing for a broad socio-ecological transformation no longer existed. Free public transport was merely viewed as one policy among many others. Third, both the crisis and austerity changed regional and national power relations and led to new perspectives: the vision of a socio-ecological transformation was no longer influential. Fourth, over a period of fifteen years, traffic movements in the town centre had changed dramatically: pedestrians, cyclists and public buses now dominate the townscape. Still, these changes were not enough to put an end to the dominance of the automobile. Private households continued to spend a considerable portion of their income on cars. As such, the abolition of free public transport did not seriously affect many of these people. Additionally, the reintroduction of fares for public transport has not affected the attractiveness of the city centre, which continues to thrive as a car-calmed oasis with a vibrant local service industry.

Political projects such as the one mounted by Stevaert are reliant on a careful discursive framing, on the ability to garner support for alternative approaches and to gain supporters from a broad range of stakeholders, while also counteracting the opposition. But importantly, Stevaert did so without marginalising economic interests and budgetary questions. Leveraging his business skills, he managed to provide free public transport even within the constraints of a tight municipal budget. Too often, social and ecological activists ignore the problems of local or regional budgets and taxes, and they tend to see entrepreneurs—like Stevaert—more as an enemy than as a possible partner in alliances. Successful political projects, like the one in Hasselt, can only be built up via cross-class and cross-milieu alliances, with solutions that enhance the economic development of the city and that are feasible within the budget constraints of cities, communities and regions. As Stevaert emphasised, "the point is to promote the interests of the middle class while at the same time continuing to act in a manner that is socially and environmentally responsible".[10] In short, the strength of Stevaert's project lay in the fact that it reconciled often irreconcilable interests and approaches.

In Hasselt, memories remain of a vision demonstrating that mobility in public spaces can be made free of charge, and that this can contribute to social justice and improve both the quality of life and the attractiveness of a town. Only time will tell whether we will see a return to this vision in Hasselt, and Belgium as a whole.

---

10. Cited in: Wehrmann, "Stadt ohne Fahrschein," 5.

[8]

Tallinn: Estonia leads the way with Free Public Transport

Allan Alaküla

What follows is an exchange between Allan Alaküla, representing Tallinn at the European Union, and Taavi Aas, acting mayor of Tallinn, in which the mayor outlines the history and achievements of the city of Tallinn with regards to their free public transportation initiative. The exchange was conducted in English in June 2017 and lightly edited for clarity.

How did Tallinn come to the idea of free public transport?

In the urbanist community, the idea of free public transport is not new and the experiences from Italy and France go back to the 1970s. But as there is no universal definition for free public transport, the reasons for doing it vary as well.

In Tallinn, the free public transport idea was raised initially by the Greens and Social Democrats (SDE) in local elections in the previous decade. But the Greens remained under the electoral threshold and SDE remained in opposition. Free public transport was promised later by conservatives in Tartu, the second biggest town in Estonia, but when they joined the city government there, the promise was forgotten.

To some extent it is fair to admit that in Tallinn, the Centre Party took the idea from Tartu, saying that "in Tartu they only promise, but in

Tallinn we do." The objectives for free public transport in Tallinn were however much deeper and wider.

First of all, it was meant to ease the social aftermaths of the 2008-2010 economic contraction (a total reduction of 17% in Estonia). While Tallinn's public transport was subsidised as usual, above 70%, the main problem for passengers became ticket prices, which had already been frozen. Continuing this heavily subsidised public service which became unaffordable would have turned into a drastic waste of public money. This was the soil of the idea of granting free mobility for all.

It was however also presumed that free mobility would stimulate the local economy, enhancing consumption of local goods and services. People would go out more in the evenings and weekends and spend more money for entertainment, sports, culture, food, and drinks.

And regardless of the state of the economy, Tallinn's city centre remained packed with cars. Providing free public transport was meant to become an alternative for private car users. The aim was to contain and possibly also decrease the number of cars in the city centre.

What steps were made towards free public transport by authorities, political parties, civic society, inhabitants?

The idea was proposed for public consideration by mayor Edgar Savisaar in January 2012. Soon after, the city government initiated a local referendum on the issue, which took place March 19-25 the same year. The plebiscite question for the residents of Tallinn was: "Do you wish for free rides in Tallinn's municipal public transport network?" With voter participation at 20% of those eligible, 75% said Yes, and 25% said No.

Interpretation of the referendum result by the city administration was not limited only to the direct question, but was used as a mandate for wider improvements of public transport. Immediately, in the summer of 2012 separated/exclusive bus lanes were expanded through the city centre. Sharp increases in parking tariffs were also envisaged. The referendum gave political parties and civic society an opportunity to profile themselves on the free public transport issue.

A straightforward opponent of free transport was the Reform Party. Social Democrats did not like having the referendum but favoured the idea. Conservatives kept a low profile as they recognised that the idea was stolen by the Centre from their election manifesto in Tartu.

Strong media coverage, although predominantly sceptical during the referendum campaign, informed and involved residents in decision-making. 20% is the biggest participation rate in history of the six local referendums held in Tallinn since 2002.

What were the main problems in implementing free public transport?

In retrospect, we can admit the precautionary measures taken by the administration were partly overkill.

Fiscally, the plan to cover all ticket revenue loss from the existing budget was extremely conservative. Although there was presumed to be some increase in the number of taxpayers, none of us predicted that the amount the city would earn from implementing free transport for residents would almost double the amount we lost.

For some tram lines, an alarm button service was contracted with a private security company—to face presumed growing vandalism in the night-time. Today, it is evident that with growing number of passengers in night-time and weekends, the opposite happened—vandalism naturally decreased.

And overall, the city administration, which was accused of strong populism, had the courage to promise only maintaining service quality levels. There was no guarantee for better service issued. And even this approach was courageous in the context of the time—according to mainstream media coverage we were nearing doomsday with complete and immediate collapse of the public transport system. Today, it is evident that service quality has risen substantially, in all aspects which are monitored.

And at the end of the first month of implementation, in January 2013, the minister of finance from the Reform Party at that time, previously one of main opponents to the idea, admitted in public that free transport may be not be the worst idea from a driver's perspective too, as traffic from his green suburb to Tallinn centre became smoother.

What were some of the first results?

Changes in public transport usage remained modest. The city was ready for up to 15% increase in trips, but the real increase remained under 10%. Mainly due to the context, where all residents over 65 already had free rides, and student discount levels made service affordable for them.

Traffic in the city centre decreased initially by 15% but this change was partly explained by major road repair works. Permanent decrease of traffic in the city centre does not exceed 6-7%, but simultaneously traffic has slightly increased around the city centre (by about 4%). This is in large part a side effect of the widening of on-street paid parking areas and a raising of the parking tariffs: now 24/7 in Tallinn Old Town, the parking charge is 6 euros (US$7.20) per hour, and in the centre, €4.80 (US$5.75) per hour.

Why was the decision taken to enlarge free public transport?

Expansion of free rides, from municipal public transport to trains, was envisaged by the city already in early spring of 2013, but as the trains belong to national authorities, negotiations were not easy and the agreement was enforced only from late October 2013, from the very next day after local elections, where the Tallinn government remained firmly into the hands of the Centre Party—the initiator of free public transport.

Were there problems with enlarging the scope of free public transport?

The main problem for the city was fiscal, as the city pays the national train company according to real usage by Tallinn residents. For budgeting, it was critical to estimate the growth of passenger flow. We presumed, with big reservations, that the usage may double as a maximum (for trains, there was no free transit for seniors before, and the student discount was not meaningful). We were wrong—already at the end of the first month of free train rides, Tallinners' usage tripled, and after six months it stabilised at a level of seven times higher.

As train trips make up less than 2% of municipal public transport trips in Tallinn, it is still bearable for the city budget. However, one trip by train costs the city remarkably more compared to a trip made by municipal public transport.

The case with trains provides a clear example, where service quality alone does not matter, and affordability is even more important. Instead of outdated old coaches, new commuter trains (Swiss made by Stadler) were brought into operation in 2013 midsummer, with no change in usage, until the agreement with Tallinn made the difference in October of the same year.

What are the current debates around free public transport (authorities, political parties, civic society, inhabitants)?

I would say we have no debate in public about the continuation of free public transport. We have local elections coming up in October 2017 and there is no party or movement who promises a return to paid public transport. None. Even the previous main opponent, Reform Party, keeps silent on that issue.

People, and parties hunting for their votes, see free public transport as a new and desired normality.

And upcoming plans and developments?

Tallinn is completing, in 2017, a full renovation of tram tracks and a renewal of the fleet. A new extension of the tram to the airport opens in August and, next, an extension to the passenger harbour is in its planning phase.

As the Centre Party formed the national government in November 2016 and took the prime minister position, they also made a commitment to make all regional public transport, which consists of the county bus lines, free for all users in autumn 2018. A step which was fully inspired from the successful implementation of free rides in Tallinn.

If that happens, Tallinn will have to expand free rides in the city to everybody, regardless of residency. While the county around the city becomes free to everybody, the city cannot limit free rides only to its own residents.

So, Estonia may become the first free public transport country.

Does Tallinn also act as an example abroad?

More and more so. If initially we learned from others, we now note new cities who admit that Tallinn served as an inspiration for them. The most recent, and biggest example is Dunkerque, France, which is starting free public transport for all users in autumn 2018. With a population of 200,000, Dunkerque´s free public transport area will be the largest in France (after Aubagne´s 100,000) and the second biggest in Europe (after Tallinn).

Do you have recommendations for others?

There is no universal definition for free public transport yet, so the objectives of this policy can be very different.

Our universal advice would be to look around for other cities experiences, speak more to the practitioners and believe less the theoreticians. Free public transport is definitely a courageous policy but it has also provided a large number of successful examples from cities of different sizes, climatic conditions, cultural backgrounds and ideological approaches. So, we do not see any reason to exclude free public transport from policymaking options.

The most universal feature of free public transport seems to be the fact that people like it everywhere that it has been implemented.

9

Eight Contradictions in Tallinn's Free Public Transport

Wojciech Kębłowski

The particular case of free public transport (more precisely, fare-free public transport) in Tallinn is important for at least two reasons. First, it is the largest and most renowned program of this kind worldwide. Second, ever since the introduction of free public transport, Tallinn has declared itself the "capital of free public transport" and the central node in the international network that promotes this policy. The Tallinn municipality has regularly organised free public transport-related events, gathering researchers and practitioners from home and abroad. As well, it has sent its officials to various sites of fare-free programs across Europe and in China. One could therefore argue that by inquiring into the fare abolition program in the capital of Estonia—asking why, how, where and for whom this policy has been implemented—may provide a good understanding of free public transport itself.

Rather than provide a chronological or systematic account of Tallinn's free public transport—which would likely turn this chapter into an overly academic or technical report—I prefer to focus on the various contradictions that have shaped the fare abolition in Tallinn.

1. The rides are "free" ... but not for all

First of all, the key fact regarding Tallinn's free public transport is that the free rides are available only to passengers that are officially residing in the city. At the same time, visitors and commuters to Tallinn continue to pay full fares. The price of the single fare has doubled since the fare abolition, increasing from €1 (US$1.20) to €2 (US$2.40).

2. "Free" transport system ... but with tickets and controls

Tallinn's free public transport has therefore introduced a division into those passengers who have access to "free" tickets and those who do not. Paradoxically, both groups need a ticket to use public transport. The right to use the service basically means the right to top up a personal electronic card (which costs 2€) with a year-long "zero ticket," renewable annually. Consequently, although Tallinn's public transport is "free," the ticketing system is still in place, and "free" rides must be validated every time one boards public transport – failure to do so has been judged illegal by Estonia's Supreme Court. Even though the number of controllers has been reduced, ticket controls have been maintained.

3. A "policy that makes no sense" ... yet works?

The idea to abolish fares was developed in opposition to local transport experts. As one of them told me, "free public transport in Tallinn makes no sense". Supposedly, it does not allow for increases to the quality of public transport, and therefore it is not an incentive strong enough to encourage car drivers to use buses, trams and trolley-buses. As the mayor recalls in the interview, the introduction of free public transport was expected by some of the local commentators to trigger a collapse of the transport network, or at least to significantly deteriorate its quality. None of this happened. While initial studies, based on data for first three months after the abolition of fares, showed that the modal share of public transport increased by only 1.2%,[1] this estimate was later corrected, showing that the share of trips made in public transport increased by 8%.[2]

4. A crucial transport instrument ... supported by unreliable data.

However, it is extremely difficult—if not impossible—to precisely identify to what extent the increase of the modal share of public

1. Oded Cats, Triin Reimal, and Yusak O. Susilo, "Public Transport Pricing Policy – Empirical Evidence from a Fare-Free Scheme in Tallinn, Estonia" Presented at the *93rd Annual Meeting of the Transportation Research Board*, Washington, D.C., 2014.
2. Oded Cats, Yusak O. Susilo, and Triin Reimal, "The prospects of fare-free public transport: evidence from Tallinn," *Transportation* (2016): 1-22.

transport mentioned above, and the continuous improvement of Tallinn's public transport, occurred *because* of free public transport, or *despite* it. First, different data sources on traffic flows, passenger volumes, and the modal split—and how each of these aspects has been affected by the introduction of the program—have been neither reliable nor comparable. Second, fare abolition was preceded by major improvements in the public transport system: new buses and trams were purchased, out-of-way bus lanes were designed, electronic tickets were introduced, and an electronic information system was implemented on vehicles and at bus stops. Third, major road works preceded the introduction of free public transport, constituting an important anomaly in the city's transport system. This is why, as a local transport researcher told me, "there were so many changes at the same time that it is difficult to compare [data] across years". We do not really know how mobility in Tallinn worked before free public transport, and therefore we cannot really tell what happened after it was introduced—whatever figures are being provided to support or refute the effect it had on mobility should be approached with extreme caution.

What we can argue, however, is that free public transport strongly contributed to the promotion of public transport, putting it in the centre of the public debate, and gathering strong support for its development. Nonetheless, local transport experts bemoan that Tallinn's public transport still largely follows the same routes as during the Soviet times, and needs a thorough re-design. It remains to be seen whether free public transport makes this task any easier.

5. A bold step ... that was largely unprepared and improvised?

The lack of comprehensive and accurate methods of collecting mobility data indicates a wider contradiction that underpins Tallinn's switch to a "free" public transport system. On the one hand, it is discussed as the most important—for better or worse—political decisions taken by the Tallinn municipality in the last two decades. It seems a bold step towards changing the logic behind transport, conceptualising it as a public service to (nearly) all, rather than as a market commodity. On the other hand, however, this step appears to have been taken in an improvised, rather than planned manner—not only due to the lack of reliable data, as discussed above. There is no mention of fare abolition in the draft of Tallinn's mobility plan, which still awaits official approval, and would constitute the city's first document of it's kind since the collapse of the Soviet Union. In the years preceding the introduction of free public transport, the municipality of Tallinn received a European

Union subsidy (through the CIVITAS program) to implement a state-of-the-art electronic ticketing system—a move that largely contradicts the later decision to provide "free" tickets. Furthermore, as the mayor recalls, the financial strategy behind it was simply wrong—rather than lead to significant expenses, free public transport turned out to have generate new revenue. Similarly, when the service was expanded to embrace the train system within the Tallinn borders, the estimates were, again, largely inaccurate.

6. "Tallinn has won, but others have lost"

Local officials in Tallinn take pride in demonstrating that despite having drastically reduced the revenue from fares, free public transport has proven to be not only financially sustainable, but it has actually allowed them to obtain additional funds. The reason behind this paradox is simple: free rides are not available to all users of local public transport. By offering it only to the registered inhabitants, Tallinn has attracted new residents, and the city's population increased from 415,000 in 2012 to 440,000 in 2016. Even though it may be difficult to establish what exact share of this increase could be directly attributed to free public transport, most registrations were done in the months preceding and following the fare abolition, which points to free public transport as the key reason behind this "migration". However, according to the Tallinn municipality, among the "new" residents as many as 60% already lived in the city. Has the remaining 40% actually moved to Tallinn? It is unlikely. The process of changing one's official address in Estonia is fairly easy and can be done online, and there exists no formal way for the authorities to verify whether one actually lives at the declared address. Put simply, to officially reside in Tallinn, one does not actually have to live there.

The fact of having attracted 25,000 "new" residents is critical for the financial sustainability of free public transport. In Estonia, local municipalities can collect a part of personal income tax. According to the Ministry of Economic Affairs and Communications, on average this means a revenue of €1,000 (US$1,197) per resident. 25,000 souls, thus translates to €25 million (US$29.93 million) of revenue, which allows the Tallinn municipality to largely cover the cost of fare abolition, estimated at €12.8 million (US$15.32 million). As a local official confessed to me, thanks to free public transport, "Tallinn has earned [...] a substantial addition of funds to invest in public transport" and could "fill the budget". This, however, results in reduced tax revenue for municipalities outside Tallinn. A plethora of small rural communities that surround the city have seen a share of their residents "leave" for Tallinn. The geography of this process is highly uneven: some municipalities have offered additional public services that convinced their residents to "stay," while others have no financial capabilities to compete with the country's capital city. A mayor of one of such municipalities told me that:

> By having attracted new residents and having raised new revenue from their personal income tax, [...] Tallinn obviously won. But if you look more globally, this means that this money is not going to another municipality. And the municipalities surrounding Tallinn are suffering because of that. [...] People who live in [suburban] municipalities and work in Tallinn, they use [suburban] infrastructure, their kids go to [local] schools and kindergartens, [...] but their money goes to Tallinn. So Tallinn has won, but others have lost.

7. A transport policy ... that is not about transport.

The dynamics between Tallinn and the rest of Estonia show a major contradiction of free public transport: although presented and discussed as a transport policy, the main motivation behind it, and the key impact it has made, has little to do with transport.

First, it has clearly worked as an element of competition between the city and its suburbs. In the midst of this competition, key mobility issues in the Tallinn agglomeration have not been addressed. The city's most urgent transport problems are not to be found in its centre, but at its borders, since as many as 90% of commuters to the city use the car. Free public transport made this matter more complicated than before, deepening the division between Tallinn and its suburbs in terms of public transport accessibility. Tallinn's separatism has, however, lead to quite progressive ruptures in the Estonian mobility debate. Free public transport emerged in clear opposition to Estonia's largely neoliberal approach to transport—seen in the abolition of tax on individual cars, and privatisation of inter-city bus service. Openly mocked by right-wing politicians several years ago, today fare-free policy is planned to be expanded nationwide onto the network of regional short-distance buses.

Second, free public transport has worked as an element of social policy, directly addressing mobility inequality in Tallinn. As a result of fare abolition, the share of trips made by public transport has increased among the unemployed (32%), residents with income lower than 300€ (US$359.17) per month (26%), the elderly (60-74 years old, 19%), and the youth (15-19 years old, 21%). This data could be interpreted to show that Tallinn's public transport allows people across social classes to get better access to the city. Here seems to lie one of its major achievements, which is highlighted even by some of the critics of fare abolition.[3]

8. A political strategy … yet no political transformation

As explained above, free public transport was developed in opposition, rather than in co-operation with local transport experts. Instead of being prepared by closed bodies of technical "experts," it was conceived by politicians who proposed an open and direct vote on it, thus taking a political gamble. This re-politicisation of transport can be seen as a welcome approach, for it questions the usual domination of de-politicised, technical narratives that surround mobility, and it puts the transport question on the political agenda.

However, the referendum on free public transport was highly controversial. The voting lasted for seven days: during the last two days, the municipality suspended fares in public transport. While this move was officially explained as an attempt to provide better access to polling stations, it can also be interpreted as a rather unwelcome influence over the voters – the very idea upon which they were meant to decide materialised before the decision was actually taken. Whether we assess its turnout as high or low, the trouble is that the referendum was paradoxically conceived as a way of limiting the debate on fare abolition. While the mayor is right to point out that this debate was influenced by the national and private media that often presented a critical view of fare abolition, the municipality-owned TV station and press continuously offered an overly positive and uncritical stance on free public transport. Having produced a result that was undoubtedly favourable, the referendum put all discussion about this policy to an end. This means that despite being conceived as an explicitly political strategy, free public transport was prepared and implemented in fully top-down fashion. There was no effort to launch a participative process that could engage the users of public transport as well as its workers. Some of the bus drivers told me that while they enjoy working in a fare-free network, they were never consulted about the idea of abolishing fares, and were simply told to accept it. Whatever the impact of Tallinn's free public transport may be, this policy never attempted at changing the power relations underpinning transport in the city; instead, it could be argued that free public transport is meant to solidify them.

8. This issue goes beyond the question of improving accessibility to stimulate the local economy – despite the mayor's declarations, there exists no strong evidence that fare abolition helped to achieve this: Cats et al., "The prospects of fare-free public transport," 2016.

10

Planka.nu: Jumping Turnstiles in Sweden

Anna Nygård

History

Stockholm, September 2001. The left had been hit hard by repression after the global mass protests that culminated during the EU summit in Gothenburg in June that year. Many activists had been injured or imprisoned and even more had been disillusioned or lost their faith in the anti-globalisation movement and its methods. The summit protests had become ritualised and no longer created any major discussion or attention around the political issues. The targets of the protests were faceless global institutions like the International Monetary Fund, the World Bank and the European Union. Their connection to the activists' lives was unclear and had very little to do with the daily life and relations to family, neighbours and co-workers. There was a need for local, day-to-day activism and organisation.

The galvanising moment occurred at this time: the Stockholm County Council raised the public transport fares yet again, and this act sparked protests. SUF Stockholm, the local Anarcho Syndicalist Youth Federation, initiated a fare strike and it immediately gained a lot of attention.

In 2001, not every non-profit organisation had a website and even text messaging was considered a novelty. By using these trendy communication tools, SUF Stockholm managed to create a massive hype around their campaign. They named it *Planka.nu* which roughly translates as "fare-dodge.now" and their demand was free public transportation, owned by all citizens together and controlled by the workers in it. Instead of the unfair fare system, they advocated a tax increase to cover the costs of operation and necessary expansion of the public transport system.

The name "Planka.nu" can be read as a request but it is also a website address. In the early 2000s more campaigns with the same kind of name appeared—*maska.nu* (on workplace activism) and *jagvillhabostad.nu* (which translates as iwanthousing.now)—and some even talked about a "dot-now movement". (The island state of Niue, of which .nu is the country code top-level domain, must have been happily surprised over its sudden popularity).

Unlike most other extra-parliamentary left-wing organisations at this time, Planka.nu chose to accept interview requests and used traditional media for their communication. This, even though the articles that were published were often far from supportive to Planka.nu's cause.[1] Their own low-budget marketing consisted, in addition to the website, of tens of thousands of black and white oblong stickers that were spread rapidly over the city. On the stickers, below the website address and the logo with the characteristic turnstile jumping person, was the following slogan: "You have nothing to lose but your fines."

Source: Planka.nu.

Three things need to be stated regarding Stockholm. First, it is very segregated, where the inner-city is dominated by people more well-off, and the suburbs connected to the centre by public transport are dominated by poorer people. This creates a situation where many

---

1. A search in the media database Retriever, available in Swedish libraries, gives only 5 matches for the search "Planka.nu" in 2001. Retriever contains articles from about 460 Swedish magazines and newspapers, but it doesn't store articles published online and it doesn't show any matches for TV or radio. During the early 2000's many newspapers refused to mention Planka.nu by name, instead they hinted about the organisation "you-know-which" that is promoting cheating in the public transport system. However, in 2010 the same search generated 103 hits, peaking at 114 hits the year after, in 2011.

people don't have access to everyday necessities without using public transport.

This leads us to the second thing that needs to be stated: fare dodging was a common practice in Stockholm before Planka.nu was started, but was at that time seen as an individual problem. By creating a collective identity and practice, and proposing a solution to the problem of expensive public transport in a segregated city, the fare dodger became a political subject that could no longer be ignored.

The third thing is that the company running the public transport system in Stockholm is a politically managed organisation, but they are using independent contractors for its operation and maintenance. This means that public transport is characterized by profit interests, which is reflected in both personnel policy and customer service. All services provided by public transport company, *Storstockholms Lokaltrafik* (SL), from driving buses to cleaning platforms and checking tickets, have been contracted out to the lowest bidder, the company that promises to carry out the assignment at the lowest cost. The metro, for example, is run by Hong Kong based MTR. Since they took over in 2009, there have been continuous scandals and protests. The company was sued by one of the trade unions organising public transport workers for transferring the job of a member who had been working as a train driver for 35 years, to a post as a cleaner.[2] And MTR has become notorious for controlling their employees to the extent that even toilet visits have become a matter of conflict.[3]

Instead of asking for free public transport, Planka.nu found a way to just take it, or at least make it very cheap. The methods—fare strike and direct action—have origins in the labour movement and were inspired by the 1970s autoreduction movements in Italy.[4] The protestors in the autoreduction or self-reduction movement refused to pay the unreasonably expensive bus tickets they needed to get to work and back home again. So, they made their own tickets and paid only as much as they considered fair. The bus company responded by cancelling the buses, but since it meant that the workers didn't come to work, it did not take long before the fares were forced down to affordable levels.

2. "Facket stämmer MTR som kör tunnelbanan" [Union sues MTR which runs the subway], *P4 Stockholm*, March 1, 2013, http://sverigesradio.se/sida/artikel.aspx?pro-gramid=103&artikel=5459655.
3. Charlotta Andersson, "Facket protesterar mot MTR's personalpolitik" [The trade union protests against MTR's personnel policy], *SVT Nyheter*, February 11, 2015, https://www.svt.se/nyheter/lokalt/stockholm/facket-protesterar-mot-mtr-s-personalpolitik.
4. Eddy Cherki and Michel Wieviorka, "Autoreduction movements in Turin, 1974," in *Autonomia - Post Political Politics* (semiotext(e), Intervention Series #1, 1980), Text from www.classagainst-class.com. Slightly edited by libcom.org for accuracy, https://libcom.org/history/autoreduction-movements-turin-1974.

The method spread to other parts of society and the fare strike also succeeded in influencing electricity and food prices.

The Strike Fund

To make it possible for people to participate in Planka.nu's fare strike they created a solidarity fund, "P-Kassan" (The P Fund), where all members contribute 100 SEK (€10.46/US$12.46) per month, and if someone gets caught, the fine is covered by the fund. A prerequisite for this to work is that the fine given to fare dodgers that get caught by ticket inspectors is no real fine in legal terms. There is a special law that regulates the "additional fee" in Swedish public transport, and the fine is in practice a very expensive ticket and not a criminal punishment: fare dodgers who are caught do not get a criminal record or lose driving points. Fare dodging fines are therefore not equal to fines for speeding on the roads, for instance, and from here on we will refer to it as the additional fee.

In 2001, the monthly ticket pass cost 500 SEK (€52.38/US$62.59) and the additional fee was 600 SEK (€62.86/US$75.11). At the time of writing, 2017, the monthly SL card costs 830 SEK (€86.96/US$103.91) and the additional fee has been increased to 1,500 SEK (€157.15/US$187.78), but members of P-Kassan still pay the same 100 SEK as 16 years ago. There has been no adjustment for inflation for participation in the solidarity fund.

The P-Kassan can make a big difference in the everyday life for someone who cannot afford to pay either a ticket or an additional fee; but from a wider view, it is at the same time problematic since it can legitimize the system by ensuring that the additional fees get paid. Even though the very act of fare dodging questions—and protests—the fare system, it isn't very subversive to pay the additional fees. Especially if it leads to more people accepting the additional fee from the inspectors instead of avoiding it.

Another problematic situation occurs when the members of the P-Kassan also pay for a monthly card but at a reduced price, by lying about their age: a kind of half-measure protest against the unfair fares. The whole idea of the fare strike and fare dodging as a questioning of the system disappears if it is just used as a method of getting a cheaper ticket. If fare dodgers would start to refuse or deny the additional fee, P-Kassan would no longer be needed, or even have a *raison d'être*, however the fund is still a vital part of Planka.nu's existence.

P-Kassan is administered weekly, and it provides an economic basis for political activities around the free public transportation topic. The number of members has usually been around 500 per month, at most a little over 1000. In the summer, membership rates generally go down a bit, increasing again when the school semester starts. Since most transit users pay monthly, and sometimes miss a day or two, there are always gaps between memberships, reducing the total numbers at every count.

But still, it is a very small percentage of the total number of fare dodgers in Stockholm that are insured by P-Kassan. In 2013, 3%[5] out of the 786,000 daily commuters[6] traveled without a valid ticket according to SL. Higher fines, more ticket controls, and fare increases have always led to more members in the solidarity fund, which means that there have been more funds to draw from in bad times, when there are many people receiving fines. Usually, only a handful of the members get busted weekly, but this varies over the seasons, and is sometimes affected by temporary control drives at strategic spots. P-Kassan has enabled Planka.nu to always have some sort of activity, even during periods when less people have been engaged in the campaign. The main strength of Planka.nu's fare strike is that it is a powerful tool and at the same time it shows today how society could look tomorrow.

In the beginning, Planka.nu's actions consisted mainly of mass fare dodging actions, where many people at once pass through, or over, the turnstiles, with the purpose of collectivizing the struggle and transforming what had previously been isolated, individual actions—in the absence of alternatives—into a political tool. Sometimes they were not more than a handful, but at other times there were hundreds of fare dodgers crossing the barriers together. At most of these actions, the gates have already been opened, either on the initiative of the public transport company (SL), or on the advice of the police to enable the political action to go smoothly (or at least quickly pass). At times where this hasn't been the case, the activists have opened and set up the turnstiles themselves with stickers, cable ties or plastic wrap, so that fare dodgers can slide in easily. The fear of disturbing the flow of public transport, either on the part of the public transport company (SL) or the police, has enabled other people, who didn't plan to participate in the actions, to safely pass through the gates without risk of being squashed.

Another recurring action from Planka.nu is to warn fellow travelers about ticket inspections, either physically, by standing in the subway with a sign when there is a mass inspection at the exit gates, but also

5. Aron Andersson, "En miljon plankningar varje månad" [One million fare-dodges each month], *Metro*, March 2, 2013, https://www.metro.se/artikel/en-miljon-plankningar-varje-månad-xr.
6. Storstockholms Lokaltrafik (SL), *Årsberättelse 2013* [Annual Report 2013], http://sl.se/globalas-sets/rapporter-etc/sl_arsberattelse2013.pdf.

using various technical warnings systems. Already in the first year of the actions, text messages were used. By signing up to a text message list, travelers all around Stockholm could warn each other of ticket inspections and avoid the additional fees. The service however became so popular that the system collapsed due to overload after only a few weeks. In more recent years people have been using social media for this purpose instead of text messages.

It is important to underscore that Planka.nu is a political movement with a specific goal, not a ragtag group of ruffians or cheats. All actions made by Planka.nu are documented and are publicly available, and Planka.nu has also regularly published instructional films on the web, showing how to pass through the turnstiles and barriers in the public transport system of Stockholm. Planka.nu has also targeted commercial advertising in the public transport system, both by argument in articles and debates, and by direct action by removing ads or replacing them with art. Again, the actions are political: the revenues generated from granting surfaces for advertising represents only a few per cent of the total operating revenues of the public transport system—almost half of it is today tax financed and the rest is from ticket sales—while commuters are force-fed with commercial messages. Planka.nu is incorporated as a non-profit, but has a horizontal management structure, no formal leadership, and is run entirely with volunteer labour.

Controlling language: learning from Orwell

A few years after SUF had started Planka.nu in Stockholm, sister organisations with the same name were started in Gothenburg, Östergötland and Skåne. *Pummit*, which means "planka" in Finnish was started in Helsinki, and then came Planka Oslo in Norway. *Planka* does not mean anything in Norwegian, but since Swedish and Norwegian are so close, the word is understandable for Norwegians. The Norwegian word that was previously used for fare dodging sounded too negative according to the Norwegian activists that founded Planka Oslo, so they chose to adopt the Swedish word instead.

Many people in the Swedish debate still refuse to talk about fare dodging using the verb *planka*, because it is a neutral word; instead they use compound words starting with thief or cheat. Coining their own terms and creating concepts have been an important strategy for Planka.nu as a way of taking control of the debate. Right-wing rhetoricians like to complain about the high tax burden, but Planka.nu has chosen to talk about the "fee burden" instead: instead of referring to tax havens they use "tax bunkers". Another term Planka.nu has insisted on using is "squash barriers" to refer to the fare gates, simply because it is a commonly occurring problem that the gates to the public transport system in Stockholm squash commuters regardless of whether they paid or not. The older generation of gates with simple turnstiles is almost entirely replaced today; and squash barriers has become an established term to describe the newer kind of gate with glass doors.

In arguing for free public transport, the fact that "free" is a controversial word is something that Planka.nu has experienced repeatedly. "There's no such thing as a free lunch" is a liberal mantra, and in a way, that is correct. Running public transport costs money. But so does screening movies at the cinema, yet it is still sometimes possible to go to the movies without paying anything at all. With *free tickets*. A company giving out free samples is also not something that is usually questioned, and in Sweden there is hardly anyone today who is upset over the fact that children have access to free dental care or free medical care. The word free in this context is thus used to describe something that is free of charge.

Planka.nu has been met with quite some opposition and the organisation has been reported to the police more than once, accused of conducting illegal activities, but so far there is no indication that the campaign or its initiators will be charged with either committing crimes or inciting others to commit crimes. None of the reports have led to prosecution, but rather have contributed to creating additional publicity for the organisation and the issues they are pursuing. In discussions, when Planka.nu's critics get tired of talking about public transport, they often ask the rhetorical question: "What else should be for free?" This shows how the topic opens into a broader discussion about society and its priorities, and hopefully also alternatives for a future society. Advocating free public transport leads to broader political questions about taxation, tax evasion, unfair wealth distribution and the fairness of user-fees in general.

Idea and development

Planka.nu started as a response to a price increase but there has always been an awareness within the organisation of the risks of becoming too much of a reactive movement. By setting their own agenda, promoting free public transport instead of just protesting fare increases and introducing new words and concepts, Planka.nu successfully established itself as a well-known organisation and managed to amplify the voices of both fare dodgers and regular commuters.

Planka.nu protest; sign reads "for a free public transport". Source: Planka.nu.

Planka.nu's principles—and the tactics that flow from them—have always been rooted in "build from below". What started small and local at (and under) the streets with stickers and home-printed flyers grew to be part of an international movement with solid theoretical grounds. In one of the first, very simple, leaflets from Planka.nu, they listed their arguments for free public transport: just, climate-smart and equal. There wasn't too much thought behind it at the time, it just felt kind of obvious.

But over the years Planka.nu has built a firm theoretical ground to stand upon. The reasons for introducing free public transport are many. In recent years, much of the focus has been on environmental and climate aspects. In many cities, reducing fees has increased use of public transport and decreased the numbers of motorists. But there are also social effects on the city with a free public transport system, which are just as important. The question is not only about numbers, and not just technical, regarding income or carbon dioxide levels, but about what kind of city we want to live in. Do we want to live in an open, accessible and social city where people's human relations can thrive? Or a closed and bordered city, a surveillance city, where barriers are used by the police and security agents, a city with internal border controls and random patrolling control-guards in the central districts?

In some cities, free public transport has been implemented for senior citizens[7] because they are known to be a group short on money and are easily isolated if unable to use public transport. Seniors also use the system during off-peak hours. But there are many others in the same situation: unemployed, students and single-parents, to mention just three. In the same way as the sidewalk is a necessity to make the city accessible for pedestrians, and the elevator is crucial for workers and citizens to access the upper floors of tall buildings, we need to recognise public transport as a fundamental system for accessing all parts of the city. As a right to the city.

Public transport is the lifeblood and bloodstream of the city; it maintains the economic system and enables social interaction. Ticket-funded public transport means that a millionaire will pay the same amount as someone who is homeless: a meaningless amount of money for the millionaire, a significant percentage of their daily income for the homeless. Funding public transport from income tax fixes this inequality: the rich pay more and public transport users with low and medium incomes pay less. Since there would be more people sharing the total cost, most public transport users would actually benefit from making it fare free.[8] Unemployed people and students who don't pay taxes would also benefit.

Studies that map travel patterns show clear differences in how men and women travel. Men usually travel longer distances and with fewer stops, often just back and forth to work. Women travel short stretches with many stops: from home to preschool, on to work, by the pharmacy or the optician, to the preschool again, via the grocery store, the neighbour who borrowed a pair of rubber boots last week, and home again. Women often work part-time, have lower income and are more dependent on accessible, affordable public transport. Women as a group would benefit from a fairer system to finance public transport.

Always innovating, ever creative: keep it fun!

An attitude that has become typical for Planka.nu is the approach "how hard could it actually be?" and from that, all sorts of possible (and impossible) projects have been taken on with a happy face. And this is good advice to activists in all cities.

In 2007, Planka.nu published their first report after concluding that report writing could not be too difficult. They called it *Highway to Hell*[9]

---

7. Frida Andersson Johansson, "Här åker seniorer gratis buss" [Here, seniors ride the bus for free], *Senioren*, May 24, 2016, http://www.senioren.se/nyheter/har-aker-seniorer-gratis-buss/.
8. Gustav Gelin, "Nästan alla skulle tjäna på nolltaxa i kollektivtrafiken" [Almost everyone would benefit from free public transport], *ETC Stockholm*, January 27, 2017, http://stockholm.etc.se/inrikes/nastan-alla-skulle-tjana-pa-nolltaxa-i-kollektivtrafiken.
9. Planka.nu, *Highway to Hell?* [in Swedish], http://cdn.planka.nu/wp-content/uploads/2008/11/plankanu_highway_to_hell.pdf.

and it was an attempt to criticise and bust the myths surrounding the construction of a gigantic highway project in Stockholm. The report was well received and circulated quite broadly, partly thanks to the climate action group *Klimax* who took the report to the Swedish Transport Administration. They occupied the lobby and demanded a written comment on the report while they were playing the song called *Highway to Hell* on a boom box.

Planka.nu wrote more reports, one on the costs of the gates in the Stockholm public transport system and another on the benefits of free public transport. In 2009, they published a report called *Trafikmaktordningen* initially translated into *The Traffic Hierarchy*[10] and later *The Traffic Power Structure*. Like the previous ones, it was about ten pages, printed and stapled into a small booklet, but this theoretical molotov against the car industry and the current mobility paradigm in society required more space. *The Traffic Power Structure* became a series of articles on Planka.nu's website, and in 2011 they were reworked into a small book with the same title, published by *Koloni förlag.*[11]

The Traffic Power Structure describes the hierarchy among different modes of transport. The automobile comes out on top, and underneath are public transport, cyclists and pedestrians and at the very bottom those in need of mobility aids such as a walker or a wheelchair. The book shows that mobility and class are tightly linked. Not only does mobility depend on economic resources, with the rich having better access to mobility than the poor, obviously; but at a deeper level, the current mobility paradigm contributes directly to the increase of economic and social injustice. Resources, and particularly public resources, are allocated unequally to different modes of transport, and this (mis)allocation reinforces inequality. An obscene percentage of public money is poured into enabling the automobile, and with aging post-war infrastructure that must be fixed for safety concerns, this percentage is growing rapidly.

Working on *The Traffic Power Structure* led Planka.nu into sometimes slightly unexpected debates, such as those surrounding feminist snow-clearing, gasoline prices and environmental racism. These debates also led to the discovery of some fundamental paradoxes in our society. There is a fixation on mobility in the globalized world and we live in a high-speed society. Those who can, are traveling as often as they can and as far as possible to enrich their lives. Paradoxically, they travel to these

---

10. Planka.nu, *The Traffic Hierarchy*, 2010, http://cdn.planka.nu/wp-content/uploads/2010/06/plankanu_the_traffic_hierarchy.pdf.
11. Planka.nu, *Trafikmaktordningen* [The Traffic Power Structure] (Korpen Koloni Förlag, Sweden, 2011).

sandy beaches to escape the sadness of everyday life – to escape from the unavoidable soul-destroying daily commute...in their automobile!

The labour market increasingly requires available, flexible and mobile workers. At the same time, more and more scientific reports are showing that the daily commute—enforced traveling—makes people sick and unhappy. Another: studies on what makes people happy in life show that spending time with friends and family is what we value the most, and commuting (by any means of transport) makes us sad and stressed. Finally, the transport sector has an enormous impact on the climate with emissions that cause global warming, and yet the number of people forced to relocate due to climate-related causes is constantly increasing.

Considering these paradoxes and contradictions, Planka.nu has come to focus on accessibility rather than mobility as they contribute to debates about future traffic plans and city planning. By thinking both locally and globally at the same time, we can forge a more sustainable way of life where one doesn't have to travel much to attend a good school, experience interesting events, or relax in nature at a city park or suburb.

The idea of accessibility is based on a more just and less segregated city structure, where schools, health centres and other public services are not operated under a profit-motive and forced to compete. Society in our neo-liberal times ranks individual freedom of choice higher than anything else. This has given us political reforms that force people to choose their health centres or schools, instead of trusting that there are equally good medical and learning institutions everywhere in the city, leading to an increase of forced commuting.

> But just as much as this is a question of mobility, it is also a question of class. By recovering our local centres we can stop the current development where quality is segregated to inner cities. By introducing a principle of proximity for public services we are in extension making the overall quality of them better. Instead of making it possible for the better-off to pay extra and commute to a better school, a revitalisation of proximity makes everyone organise for improvement where they live. In simple words: by letting the middle class in the residential area share schools and other public services with people from the blocks of rental apartments we are guaranteeing a raise in quality for everyone.[12]

Successful (and maybe unsuccessful) projects

Planka.nu has always sought broad partnerships and cooperated with different groups from diverse backgrounds, and one of the most enduring partnerships is with the network No One Is Illegal. During

12. Planka.nu, The Traffic Hierarchy, 11.

the years Planka.nu has been active in Stockholm, they have witnessed how the police have systematically cooperated with ticket inspectors to find undocumented migrants. Because Swedish law does not allow ID checks on the street without reason, the police use this opportunity to identify people in public transport, where its barriers become border controls in the middle of the city. An undocumented migrant can't easily use the public transport system without paying since being caught without a ticket means you will have to show ID, and if you are unable to show the right papers there is a high risk the controllers will call the police. In 2012, Planka.nu revealed that police, dressed up as cleaners or craftsmen, were performing so called inner border controls in search of undocumented commuters. The revelation received a lot of attention and the operation became widely criticised as racial profiling.[18]

It did not take long after Planka.nu was founded before people started contacting the organisation with questions that were not about just fare dodging or free public transport. Many times, it was just regular commuters who had been poorly treated or even beaten up by SL staff or security guards in the public transport system. They had been in contact with SL's customer service but were not helped or even listened to. Sometimes someone asked for legal advice on how to report a guard that had been physical/violent or on how to appeal against an additional fee. The Planka.nu activists that did not have legal competence themselves, therefore made sure to establish an ombudsman for public transport that would deal with this type of question. The role of the Public Transport Ombudsman is usually appointed to one or more law students that are helping Planka.nu in their spare time to support people with legal advice, such as before a trial linked to a public transport related incident.

In winter 2005/2006, a conflict occurred in Stockholm's subway after a union safety representative, who had been criticizing deficiencies in safety, was fired. The conflict led to a political strike which was supported by a group that called themselves *United Commuters of Stockholm*, together with Planka.nu. They opened up the public transport barriers and they gave other commuters the opportunity to place their ticket money in the workers' strike fund instead of paying the fare to SL. Because of Planka.nu's roots in the labour movement it has always been both natural and important for the organisation to take a stand and express solidarity with workers when there have been conflicts between employers and employees in the public transport sector. Also, the

18. "Outrage over Stockholm cops' 'racial profiling'," *The Local*, February 21, 2013, https://www.thelocal.se/20130221/46330.

deterioration of working conditions for public transport staff almost always means security risks for both employees and travelers.

When in 2008, SL stated that they were going to replace the turnstiles with the modern and "fare dodging proof" squash barriers, members of Planka.nu managed to film themselves while fare dodging through the same type of barriers – in France. The film was then distributed to all politicians in charge of the decision and was featured on both of the biggest local news channels on TV: SVT ABC[14] and TV4 Stockholm.[15] Despite the media attention and the warnings that buying the new barriers would be a total waste of money, the squash barriers were installed. This story is one of many examples of how Planka.nu manages to draw attention to their campaign, but also of how they are rarely listened to by decision-makers in their home town.

March 1st: Free Public Transport Day

On March 1, 2008, Free Public Transport Day was celebrated for the first time. The holiday, that Planka.nu made up simply because they thought it should exist, occurs annually on the first Saturday of March. The first year, it was launched with a demonstration inside the Stockholm metro system, and since then it has been commemorated with demonstrations, actions and parties in many cities all over the world. Since 2010, Planka.nu has also been awarding the Free Public Transport Award to individuals or organisations that have done something notable for the cause of free public transport during the past year. The award is given out in connection with the celebration of Free Public Transport Day and has been awarded to schoolchildren and activists, as well as to academics and cities. The creation of these rather grand phenomena are good examples of the drive and "doing by *doing*" attitude that has often characterized Planka.nu's activities.

A regular pleasure for activists in Planka.nu is to ad-bust and mock the recurring campaigns against fare dodging run by SL. When SL announced a competition online, where the public was invited to upload their own design for the SL travel card, Planka.nu was quick to participate with a bunch of innovative designs. Among them was a graph showing the price increases of the monthly card and another one with the word *plastkort*, (plastic card) written on magenta pink background

14. "Planka.nu om nya Spärrar på SVT ABC Lokalnyheter" [Planka.nu about new barriers to SVT ABC Local News], YouTube video, 2:06, from a news clip televised on SVT ABC, posted by "starchild666" November 25, 2008, https://www.youtube.com/watch?v=HXNiP9kjcoU.
15. "Nya spärrar stoppar inte plankning - TV4 Lokala Nyheter Stockholm" [New barriers do not stop fare-dodging - TV4 Local News Stockholm], YouTube video, 1:39, from a news clip tele-vised on TV4 Stockholm, posted by "Planka.nu Stockholm" February 10, 2010, https://www.youtube.com/watch?v=dw_CZrWJVDM.

using the same font Planka.nu was known for using. By mobilising their many thousands of social media followers, and encouraging them to vote, the designs critical of SL went straight to the top of the voting chart. SL managed to suspend some of them *ad hoc*, by creating new rules that prohibited designs that promote fare dodging in the competition, but they failed to completely stop the criticism, so a drawing showing a soft toy rabbit squashed between the gates ended up among the top three entries, and the design could be purchased in SL's web shop for several years. This episode is a great example of the impact that can be achieved with relatively little effort if you have a large network and know how to exploit the benefits of social media. The campaign, which was intended to gain publicity for SL, was completely hijacked and the surrounding discussion came to be about free public transport instead.

Over the years, Planka.nu has been contacted by many people with different ideas and proposals. Planka.nu often says yes to all kinds of requests, and has also made it a point of honour to work in unexpected and sometimes unholy alliances. This has resulted in debates against political opponents, interviews by schoolkids and collaborations with musicians and artists. Many times, the results have been good, but sometimes the outcome has been rather strange, like when a group of trade school students wrote their thesis on Planka.nu's organisational structure with references to literature on terrorist networks. But on principle, Planka.nu will always refuse collaborations with people who are interested in developing a solidarity legal fund for car drivers who speed, inspired by P-Kassan, for example, or an early warning system for traffic speeders.

Current activities and plans

In addition to ongoing work and the weekly administration of the solidarity fund, Planka.nu is currently working on the distribution of their manifesto, *The Traffic Power Structure*. The book was recently translated into both German and English. Planka.nu activists are travelling and giving lectures on their experience and theories when invited. They are also writing a new book on their history and activist experience, mocking the latest SL campaigns and taking part in current political debates regarding traffic issues, climate justice, mobility and migration.

The same highway project that Planka.nu wrote about in their report *Highway to Hell* ten years ago is now under construction but the protests against it continue. In August 2016 Planka.nu was one of the groups that arranged a protest camp against the highway construction. The protest was inspired by *Ende Gelände*[16] and culminated with an action where about a hundred activists, including both experienced environmental activists from all over Sweden and ordinary citizens from the local area, shut down the construction work for one day.

Sixteen years have passed since Planka.nu started, and public transport in Stockholm is more expensive than ever. The repression against fare dodgers has increased, infrastructure investments still prioritise car traffic despite the fact that climate threats can no longer be ignored, and the issue of tax financing of public transport seems to be dead on a higher political level. But elsewhere, both in Sweden and in other countries around the world, things are moving. In Paris, public transport was made temporarily fare free in December 2016, as an attempt to reduce emissions.[17] It is now a well-known fact that free public transport is an efficient tool to reduce car traffic. The capital of Estonia, Tallinn, implemented fare free public transport in 2013 and changed their city slogan to "The Capital of Free Public Transport".[18] Several smaller cities have also implemented some form of free public transport.[19] Across the Atlantic, *Movimento Passe Livre*[20]—a Brazilian sister organisation to Planka.nu—are mobilising hundreds of thousands of people to their protests, demanding fare free public transport for all.

The growing global movement gives strength to the local struggle and instead of getting carried away with theory and nostalgic over previous days of glory, the activists of Planka.nu Stockholm are determined to stay focused on their core activities in the near future. SL has recently promised to double the amount of controllers[21] but as a spokesperson from the company stated in the New York Times a couple of years ago: "These hard-core dodgers, I think we will never reach them."[22] Previous years have shown that the harder SL tries, the stronger the union of fare dodgers becomes; and eventually they might win, even on their home ground.

16. *Ende Gelände* is a German climate justice initiative. Since 2015, they have used annual mass protests, direct actions and civil disobedience to protest coal mining and the fossil fuel industry.
17. Henry Samuel, "Smog forces Paris to offer free public transport," *The Telegraph*, March 14, 2014, http://www.telegraph.co.uk/news/worldnews/europe/france/10698580/Smog-forces-Paris-to-offer-free-public-transport.html.
18. See chapters 8 and 9 in this volume for further discussion of free public transport in Tallinn.
19. See chapter 1 for a discussion of different forms of free public transport that have been inmplemented in cities and towns around the world.
20. See chapter 12 for more detail on the MPL.
21. Babs Drougge, "Klart: SL fördubblar biljettkontrollerna" [SL doubles ticket checks], *Mitt I*, July 26, 2017, https://mitti.se/nyheter/klart-fordubblar-biljettkontrollerna/.
22. Matt Flegenheimer, "Fare Dodging Is an Organised Rebellion in Stockholm, and It's Winning," *New York Times*, May 17, 2014, https://www.nytimes.com/2014/05/18/world/europe/fare-dodging-is-an-organised-rebellion-in-stockholm-and-its-winning.html.

11

Challenging the Impossible: Toronto

Herman Rosenfeld

Toronto's public transport system, in a nutshell

Toronto is Canada's largest city, with a population of 2.7 million, and over six million in the Greater Toronto Area (GTA). The public transport system is the third largest in North America (after New York City and Mexico City). It is made up of four subway lines, 11 streetcar routes, and over 140 bus routes.[1] The city transit system is run by the Toronto Transit Commission (TTC), which is responsible to the Toronto city government. There are also public transport stops for the regional system, called GO, which in turn is managed by the regional transit authority, Metrolinx, responsible to the province of Ontario. Suburban regions and municipalities also have their own operators. Compared to them as well as GO, the TTC carries by far the most passengers.

While massively used, the Toronto transit system is chronically underfunded—absolutely, and in comparison with other transit systems. The subsidy per rider was 90 cents (€0.62/US$0.74) in 2016, below the North American average of around $2.50 (€1.71/US$2.05).[2]

The subsidy is key, for public transport operations can never be fully

---

1. Toronto Transit Commission (TTC), "General Information," https://www.ttc.ca/Routes/General_Information/General_Information.jsp.
2. TTC, "2016 TTC and Wheel-Trans Operating Budgets: Impact of TTC Budget Committee Recommendations," https://www.ttc.ca/About_the_TTC/Commission_reports_and_information/Commission_meetings/2015/November_23/Reports/2016_TTC_and_Wheel-Trans_Operating_Budgets_Report_Nov_23_201.pdf.

paid for by fares. But, the Toronto "fare-box ratio"—that is the percentage of operating funds that come from fares—is around 70%, also the highest in North America. This is due to the low levels of government subsidy (from both the city and the province). In 2015, fare-box revenues totalled $1.109 billion (€760 million/US$910 million).

Not surprisingly, fares have risen in recent years, from $2.10 (€1.44/US$1.72) per ride in 2006, to over $3.00 (€2.06/US$2.46) in 2017. The city has a senior and student fare, at a 30% reduction from the full cost of a monthly fare—and a $2.00 (€1.37/US$1.64) individual fare. There are plans for a new low-income fare, but it is set at the current senior fare level and is due to be brought forward in stages, beginning in 2018, initially covering social assistance recipients, and eventually covering all people on low-incomes. The funding for the low-income passes is far from being assured. The demand raised by the transit movement is for free fares for social assistance recipients, and $50 (€0.62/US$41.02) monthly fares for those on low-incomes.

Toronto's transit system is also uneven in its outreach to different class fractions and neighbourhoods. In the downtown core of the city, rapid public transport is dense, but in the so-called inner suburbs—formerly independent municipalities, amalgamated into the larger city of Toronto—there is an over-reliance on buses and private cars. Due to socio-economic trends associated with neoliberal urban development, many of these areas are home to an increasing concentration of poor and low-income people, often from racialised communities. In other parts of the GTA (and in most parts of Canada, except in the largest cities), transit reliance is much smaller in proportion to the overall population. The vast majority of commuters drive private cars.[8]

For a number of decades, there was little investment in new public transport, but in the past few years, the province and the city have reintroduced plans to build, both downtown and in the inner suburbs. But there have been bitter fights over the form of new transit and funding issues. These are often related to divisions between those who are dependent on private cars, and those who use buses (the latter which are sometimes overcrowded, slow and unreliable); those for whom public transport is the primary form of mobility and those who rarely use it; and those for whom the cost of transit is minimal, and those who find it too expensive.

3. See, for example, J. David Hulchanski, *The Three Cities within Toronto: Income Polarization Among Toronto's Neighbourhoods, 1970–2005* (Toronto: Cities Centre Press, 2010), http://www.urbancentre.utoronto.ca/pdfs/curp/tnrn/Three-Cities-Within-Toronto-2010-Final.pdf.

The Free Transit Toronto movement

Free Transit Toronto is a movement dedicated to introducing the idea of free public transport in the city of Toronto. It was part of a larger political experiment called the Greater Toronto Workers' Assembly (GTWA), launched in 2009. The GTWA brought together much of the Toronto socialist and anti-capitalist left, and attempted to bridge the differences between the different components of the working class, in a project to challenge neoliberalism and the limits of social democracy.[4]

One of the projects of the Assembly was to develop a campaign that could mobilise major working-class constituencies, and fight for a demand that could push towards a key structural reform—and involved other necessary radical reforms. As well, we wanted to build a movement around a challenge to neoliberal urban practices and structures: privatisation, radical cuts to collective public goods, attacks on unionised labour, precarity, racialised, gendered and deteriorating housing patterns, etc. We also wanted to craft a campaign that was "ours," and could help to build and consolidate the Assembly project.

We wanted to work within a framework inspired by the "Right to the City" movement[5] contributed by David Harvey (based on an original book by Henri Lefebvre[6]) which emphasised a different vision of urban life shaped by public and collective services for the people who live and work there, not the neoliberal urban vision of the corporate headquarters, offices and condo developers. Finally, we wanted to sponsor a campaign that raised fundamental questions about capitalism.

There was a debate over a period of a few months about which campaign to adopt first, and after a series of discussions, we chose a free transit campaign. There was dissent. Some argued that this was too radical a demand and wouldn't find any real traction. Others argued that the transit workers union would never support a campaign to eliminate fares and they didn't want the union to come out in opposition to the campaign. In any event, we decided to build our own campaign for free transit: Free Transit Toronto.

We were inspired by the successful example of the Los Angeles Bus Riders Union's effort to organise working class people to demand affordable and accessible public transport, and larger efforts to actually apply a radical and anti-capitalist perspective to struggles over a central

4. Herman Rosenfeld, "The Greater Toronto Workers Assembly: A Hopeful Experiment," *New Politics* 13, no. 3 (Summer 2011): 51.
5. David Harvey, "The Right to the City," *New Left Review* 53 (September-October 2008): 23 – 40; and chapter 14 in this book.
6. Henri Lefebvre, *Le Droit à la ville* [The right to the City] (Paris: Anthropos, 1968).

component of peoples' lives, the public transport struggles in Berlin, San Francisco and elsewhere.

Building the campaign—creating a footprint

As we began, we realised that we knew a lot more about fighting for decommodified public services in general than how it might be applied to public transport. In an environment where there were important new and rather fierce political debates about how to expand a public transport network that had not seen any appreciable investment in the previous 20 years, and where there had been steadily increasing fares, we were way behind the curve when it came to understanding the concrete issues involved in actual Toronto public transport, and the TTC.

We started reading up on the history and then-current contextual realities of Toronto transit issues and debates, while we concentrated on getting the principle of free transit "out there". Public transport, we argued, needed to be treated as a fully funded public service, such as Medicare and the public library system—without user fees. We organised a series of public rallies, introducing our campaign (all in the student-heavy downtown communities where we were in our comfort level), and produced pamphlets and fact sheets about the principles underlying free public transport, with examples of international cities that had either completely free, or partial fare-free service.[7]

We engaged in some extremely creative tactics to popularize the idea of free public transport. We boarded subways and buses (as paid users) and performed street theatre vignettes, creating a playful context to speak with passengers about free public transport, handing out literature and listening to transit users' responses to the points we raised. We found that they, for the most part, thought that the idea was interesting, new, fresh—but utopian. People asked us how we proposed to raise the funds for such a project; how to address other concerns about public transport, such as getting decent service; how to get reliable public transport into the inner suburban areas where many low-income working-class people live. Many encouraged us to push for lowering fares, in the short run.

We created displays for use at transit stops, shopping areas, schools and public meetings of various kinds. We were able to get noticed on various alternative media outlets (university, community, etc.) and we produced more in-depth materials, addressing many of the issues raised by transit users in our outreach work.

7. See examples in chapters 1, 4, 5, 7, 8 and 9 in this volume.

In that first period, we attracted a number of future activists—some older, some younger—who were intrigued by the idea of free public transport, and who were committed to the idea of fighting to decommodify public services. Most were either students or people attached to the labour or environmental movement. We all grew together in building the movement.

We also participated in a number of international sessions where we exchanged experiences with others engaged in free public transport campaigns, one in Stuttgart, Germany in 2010, and another conference specifically on free transit movements in Toronto in 2013.

We also produced a number of longer pieces of literature on free transit, and its necessary interrelation to a larger, eco-socialist analysis of urban life. A call for decommodifying public transport can only make sense in relation to a larger urban agenda, one that includes massive funding through progressive taxation from higher levels of government, as well as the city. This requires major changes to existing political and administrative institutions. Building public transport on the scale required to make it work, calls for challenging existing patterns of urban geography and car dependency. It would mean nationalised financial institutions and government willingness to borrow on a scale comparable to the mobilisation of the wartime era. The dominance of existing elites, such as private developers, financial capital and the beneficiaries of the P3 (Public-Private Partnerships) craze would have to be challenged. New capacities to build, manage and plan, which require both expertise and popular participation, would have to be developed.

The dominant economic activities currently operating in our city would have to be transformed and replaced, with popular service provision, production of ecologically necessary materials, and other popularly-determined activities. Housing would have to be affordable, public and co-operative, and developed and shaped by working peoples' needs. What is known as 'gentrification' would have to be replaced by designs of livable and exciting city life, not based on wealth. Land municipalisation as well as rent controls would all be in the mix. Finally, there would have to be democratic forms of planning and input, so people of all incomes and neighbourhoods would have input on mobility levels and public transport planning. Many of these issues were integrated in our materials.

One of our most successful actions was a demand for free public transport on days when the city declared heat or cold alerts. Low-income people needed to have access to cooling or heated shelters, and public transport was essential in those instances. In partnership with a coalition of social activists working for low-income passes—the Fair

Fare Coalition (FFC)—we organised a protest at a central four-stoplight corner/intersection in the city centre, and marched with a cardboard replica of a subway car—courtesy of the FFC. It received lots of publicity, being covered by local TV and radio outlets, and introduced the ideas of low-income passes and free fares during extreme hot and cold weather into the larger discourse about public transport.

Source: Herman Rosenfeld.

Hitting a ceiling—branching out into the movement

At a certain point, the Free Transit campaign hit a ceiling: our educational work did not bring in new members—the relatively small group that had organised around the campaign remained the same, with activists coming and going around it. It was seen more as a novelty, rather than a growing campaign. As well, we had no success in building links with the transit union or with dissident movements/members inside the union. We never had a confrontation, but the leaders were cold to our message, although the individual drivers and TTC workers we encountered in our activities were always friendly.

A new direction

Around that time, in 2012, a small number of activists floated the idea of trying to build around another Toronto public transport users movement, called TTCriders, which, at the time, was a mostly paper group, that solicited petitions against fare increases and did educational work around the need to build a Light Rapid Transit (LRT) network across the city. It was tied to the Labour Council and the Toronto Environmental Alliance, but did little organising and had no membership infrastructure. These activists working to build it were supportive of our movement and encouraged us to work with them.

After a series of meetings, we decided to help to build TTCriders as a democratic and mass-based organisation, and influence its structure, program, direction and larger orientation, all the while maintaining the independence of our Free Transit Campaign.

We engaged in the initial debates over the structure of TTCriders, and in particular helped to argue for an emphasis on lowering fares, increasing the reach of new public transport to working class communities across the city and improving the quality and accessibility of public transport. These were not "motherhood" issues: there were those who argued against lowering fares (either calling for freezing, or ignoring the issue), in the name of accepting the limitations of what's 'possible' in the medium and short term, reluctant to identify with working class interests and needs. We were not alone in arguing for the kind of organisation that concentrated more on activism than lobbying. The new TTCriders attracted young and energetic participants, and in particular, was led by an extraordinarily talented politically independent activist, a woman who helped pull it together.

Most of the Free Transit Toronto people were central in helping to build TTCriders. During this period, we combined our efforts in producing independent materials, power-point presentations at activist movement spaces (fighting municipal cutbacks, Popular Summit activities, etc.), and discussing and planning strategic approaches to our work in TTCriders and the broader transit movement.

Combining the long and short-term

In the following years, TTCriders grew, as did our participation in it. We continued to argue for and help develop collective rallies and mass actions; opposing P3s and privatisation (an approach increasingly embraced by the political and economic elite in the city); emphasising work in, and building in, lower-income and ethnically diverse working class communities; building across different components of the working class; intervening in a particular way in the critical debates of the time (for example, how to grow, how should ordinary working people shape or participate in these processes, and gentrification).

In the process, we struggled to find a way to both shape and build the larger movement on the one hand, and, on the other, maintain our independent voice and influence and grow as an independent Free Transit movement. Much of our energy and small resources went into building the campaign for low-income fares (with the critical ideological underpinnings of arguing for a public transport system that acts as a public right, rather than a paid service for "customers"); emphasising building in communities and within the working class, rather than giving deputations, lobbying and developing relationships with elected political decision-makers (all of which are certainly necessary) and, as part of TTCriders, fighting for adequate funding from the city, province and federal governments.

In 2016, another Toronto network, the Fair Fare Coalition became part of TTCriders and—with this renewed energy—organised a more ambitious campaign for low-income passes. After a series of consultations with low-income organisations and individuals, it developed demands for free public transport for people on social assistance, and $50 (€0.62/US$41.02) annual passes for people on low-incomes. We then organised a number of large protests at city hall, demanding and eventually winning a commitment to develop a low-income fare. It is extremely modest, will not cover all low-income users who need it, and will not be applied in a timely manner. But it is a major step forward, and our work helped to inspire, shape and win it.

On the other hand, much of our independent activity was reduced, in favour of shaping the orientation of TTCriders and the Fair Fare Coalition. We started to work on our website, stickers calling for free transit, and producing a blog, but most of the independent work became subsumed into our TTCrider work.

In March 2015, children under 12 were given the right to ride free—a move unilaterally enacted by the conservative mayor. While it was done as a way to mitigate the city government's unwillingness to raise taxes to pay for transit, it was an important step forward, which introduced a limited experience with free transit.

Ongoing challenges and openings

The GTWA dissolved in 2016, but the Free Transit Campaign continues to operate as Free Transit Toronto. We continue to meet, and still face the ongoing dilemma of how to build an independent movement for a de-commodified public transport system, all the while organising in the short and medium term for better, cheaper and accessible transit, in the context of a larger public transport movement.

Clearly, this challenge is not unique. In an era where there are no socialist political parties—hegemony on the left remains within social democrats and various anarchist orientations—an organisation fighting for free transit is working without political support. There are almost no reference points within working class institutions and communities that argue for the kinds of massive changes that free transit would need to become a reality—and that it could initiate. There are movements around housing, tax fairness, anti-poverty, and the environment, but they remain separate from a larger political orientation that is left of social democracy. Individual activists with more radical perspectives work across the city, but the focus remains on short-term, incremental improvements that accept the larger signposts of the status quo.

It would be fair to say that within the social democratic community in the city (city politics in Toronto are officially "non-partisan") there is a left wing. Some of its members do call for the kind of taxation instruments that could provide resources for expanded and more affordable public transport. But these people are far from the majority within the social democrats, and refuse to build a more radical program around reduced transit fares, massive new funding for public transport, restrictions of private car use, not to mention their hesitancy to initiate or support more radical actions in support of necessary reforms.

Moreover, while there has been a good deal of support from the progressive grouping of social democratic-oriented city councillors for low-income passes and some of the main demands raised by TTCriders, there has been no support for the idea of fare-free transit. Issues of funding to pay for free transit and transformation of the tax base are very difficult things for even the most progressive city councillors to consider. The lack of a truly radical or socialist voice at city hall (even with 44 city councillors) is key here.

Examples of this dilemma are not hard to find. In a recent strategy discussion for TTCriders, we debated whether we should demand funding for a proposed "relief" subway line, or oppose it. The "relief" line would take the pressure off the main subway artery to the downtown business district—which would relieve overcrowding for the tens of thousands of people coming to work from both the affluent suburbs, and less affluent areas. Those who opposed it argued for funding a much-needed light rail line that would serve a current transit desert in the inner-suburban, working class neighbourhoods. The debate was framed in terms of what we can "afford" to pay for, given the current funding plans from the city, province and federal government, rather than what we "need" and could afford, if we challenged the current deficit obsession, and the austerity model it entails.

In the current political moment, challenging austerity seems "impossible". Indeed, the greater the success of neoliberalism, the more everything else seems impossible. This needs to be challenged, but it requires a longer-term perspective, and a commitment for deeper and more fundamental change. Both the relief line and the expanded version of the LRT network are possible and necessary—as is our collective responsibility to fight for alternatives to gentrification of lower-income working class neighbourhoods, as part of the battle to win new public transport.

But in this kind of environment, Free Transit Toronto is a building block to move beyond the current political limitations. We will continue to weigh-in on key political struggles involving public transport—within and independent of the larger transit movement; propose and organise for developing public capacities to plan, develop and build transit (as opposed to P3s); argue for progressive tax reforms and a commitment to replacing car dependence with public transport with all that it entails for funding, job creation and transformation of the structure of the city; challenging the elites that run the city's economy—from the financial interests, to the private development industry; and working to root the transit movement in working class communities, where new leaders can be developed to argue for free transit, and a larger alternative urban vision.

Keeping alive that vision, all-the-while fighting to defend, enlarge and deepen public transport, remains our principal challenge.

[12]

Greece: Automobiles or Public Transport?

Georgios Daremas

Introduction

Public transport is undergoing a dramatic crisis in the contemporary capitalist world. The main culprit for its material decline and its socio-cultural devaluation is the antagonism it experiences by the ever-growing trend of private car use in both developed and developing countries. The consequences of such a grand shift in the modes of citizens' physical mobility are numerous economic, political, social and environmental effects detrimental to social life, but most important is the restriction in the universal right of mobility that affects certain 'disadvantaged' social categories that are effectively denied their inalienable right to free movement.

This chapter, part of a larger study, documents the shifting patterns in modes of mobility across the public space and the systemic bias in favour of private forms of physical mobility.[1] It takes up the case

1. This chapter draws from a broader research-in-progress that assesses the impact free public transport schemes have on their users and the broader community within which they operate. Using the method of participatory research, it aims to excavate the hidden possibilities a free local public transport scheme activates in foreshadowing the contours of an alternative emancipatory mode of living. The possible prefiguration of a mode of life where participants have mitigated their competitive individualism in favour of a communal existence, in which the social existence of the other is the valuable condition of possibility for the self-realisation of one's own individuality. Through in-depth interviews and focus groups, it explores whether

of Greece, where a forceful paradigm of private car use has only just recently been entrenched, following its integration into the European Union, promoted by both the state and dominant commercial interests. Against this dominant trend that stratifies citizens into 'privileged' and 'under-privileged' and denies the right to mobility to sizable groups and/or 'eats away' increasing portions of income of a great number of people who have suffered considerable diminution of disposable income due to a long (seven years) period of imposed neoliberal austerity policies, it explores a series of alternative 'experiments' in free public transport introduced by a number of municipalities in the vicinity of Attica, Greece where the great majority of the national urban population is concentrated. It concludes with some provisional results of the research-in-progress study of the social perception of such newly introduced experimental schemata of freely provided public transport.

The crisis of public transport in the contemporary capitalist world and the right to free mobility

Private use of cars for individual transportation dominates the mode of physical mobility worldwide. To make it possible, constantly expanding road networks and highway infrastructures are built and upgraded, subsidised by public money contributing most often to state indebtedness in order to finance this 'freely offered' public good. The scale of intervention in road construction by the states is so massive that the 'web of road arteries' is highly visible from satellite images of the planet taken from afar. In this sense, global road construction is a 'terra-forming' practice that amounts to a human 'hubris', an expression of the capital-led imperative to subjugate the natural habitat no matter what the adverse consequences may be for the future of the planet and humanity's chances of survival.

To grasp the magnitude of change and the consequent private mobility explosion that has happened in the post-war period in Europe, it suffices to note that over the period 1970–2014, car use in the EU-15 increased over 165%, with the modal split of passenger transport increasing from 74.5% of passenger-kilometres by car in 1970 to 82.8% in 2014.[2]. The change is even more dramatic for Greece, where the annual passenger-kilometres traveled by car have increased from under

social subjects experiencing life under a multiplex socio-economic, political and cultural crisis can envision a realist utopia, a collectively self-determined world shaped by relations of equality, justice, social solidarity and a non-exploitative treatment of the natural habitat.
2. Across the EU-28, private car travel is now approaching 5 trillion passenger-kilometres per year. European Commission, *Statistical Pocketbook 2016: EU Transport in figures* (Luxembourg: Publications Office of the European Union, 2016), https://ec.europa.eu/transport/sites/transport/files/pocketbook2016.pdf.

10 billion in 1970 to nearly 100 billion in 2014.[8] Such increase has been attributed "to income and population growth as the main driving forces behind increasing vehicle ownership and use".[4]

These two 'driving forces' supposedly accounting for the explosion of private car use obscure and 'naturalise' car use since they do not explain why mere 'population growth' did not accommodate its mobility needs through the use of public transport systems, or why 'increase of income' should have been spent on 'vehicle ownership' and not otherwise. It is a widespread ideology in science, in public policies and in the lay public to presume that car ownership and use is a 'natural state of affairs' expressive of the 'growth' of the standard of living and the affluence exhibited in our contemporary civilisation. Cars are expensive commodities to own and use, their consumption sustains one of the largest, if not the largest, industries worldwide. Car ownership has become a socially recognisable marker of class status and its attendant prestige hierarchy not only for the car owners themselves but also for those who are deprived of the means to own and maintain a car. Car ownership is part and parcel of an idealised mode of commodified social living (promoted ferociously by global advertising and the mass press) reflecting the (neo) liberal market-based credo that an individual's self-centred conduct, to the degree s/he obeys 'the rules of the game', contributes in the aggregate to social prosperity and to the public benefit.

What is left unaccounted for in this 'justificatory' ideological discourse is that the trend towards monopolisation of public mobility through a mode of private use to the detriment of the use of public transport networks[5] creates a two-tier system of 'first class' and 'second class' citizens. From this emerges a class polarisation between the 'privileged' who can afford a car and the rest of the 'underprivileged' social categories who cannot afford to own or use a car (the poor, the unemployed, the under-employed, the precariat, persons with special needs, the socially conscious objectors to 'private automobility'). Car ownership has turned into a prevalent index of social inequality in late capitalism. By 2014 there were 491 cars for every 1000 EU-28 inhabitants.[6] The resultant class discrimination between those who have

3. European Commission, *Statistical Pocketbook 2016*.
4. Stephen Marshall, and David Barrister, "Travel reduction strategies: intentions and outcomes," *Transportation Research Part A: Policy and Practice* 34, no. 5 (2000): 321-338.
5. For instance, "[i]n the early 1960s the public transport system in West Germany accounted for as much traffic as personal motorized transport – thirty years later its share had fallen to below 20 per cent". Michael Brie and Mario Candeias, *Just Mobility: Postfossil conversion and free public transport*, Translated from the German by Alexander Gallas, (Germany: Institute for Critical Social Analysis, Rosa Luxemburg Foundation, 2012), 5.
6. European Commission, *Statistical Pocketbook 2016*.

and those who do not have a car demotes the latter to needy 'imprisoned' (choice-less) users of second-rate underfunded and inefficient public transport while public money is poured lavishly into infrastructural support for private car use, thus constituting a head-on affront to the democratic principles of social inclusiveness and universal provision of public service catering to the right of free movement for all citizens.

This situation often consolidates a self-fulfilling vicious circle. The deterioration of public transport services on offer (crowding, longer waiting hours, shortened running schedules, exposure to 'soft' criminality) pushes growing segments of the population into privatised 'escape' solutions offered by the second-hand car market, while at the same time condoning, socio-symbolically, the car owners' lifestyle as the appropriate consumer route for the exercise of their right of freedom of movement thus reproducing and reinforcing the existing *status quo* of privatised mobility.

Car owners are trapped in an unresolvable contradiction. On the one hand they live their fantasy of personal 'freedom' secluded in their automobile microcosm but on the other hand they suffer mundanely ever-increasing traffic congestion, longer hours driving to and from work and visiting entertainment venues, exposure to heightened aggressiveness by other suffering drivers, over-exhaustion by driving itself, sizable costs for fuel, insurance, car maintenance, licence taxes and for parking space,[7] and last but not least susceptibility to car accidents. The total death count and the number of infirmities and permanent crippling caused by car use annually, in all major civilised countries, suggests without much exaggeration that the car is a 'weapon of mass destruction' in peacetime. 1.25 million deaths by automobile worldwide. 85,000 people dead by automobile accident in Europe last year, roughly the size of the city of Maroussi in Greece (to be discussed below) or twice the size of the town of Dover in England. Every year.

Nevertheless, the sum-total of human casualties and the physical, psychological and social infirmities sacrificed to the 'Moloch of Asphalt' appears merely as an abstract statistic. Likewise, for the tremendous problem of 'air pollution' directly linked to automobiles, spewing a cocktail of over eighty different poisonous gases and particulate micro-elements that cause countless but invisible deaths, and whose occurrence is registered only probabilistically through big data analysis and thus lack the image of death in 'flesh and bones'. As for the images of death created by road accidents that parade every now and then through

---

7. For the UK, car use expenses amount to 'about a third (!) of their net monthly earnings'. Brie and Candeias, *Just Mobility*, 2012, 7.

the television screens, they may cause a momentary death anxiety to the average car owner, almost instantaneously to be 'repressed' into his/her unconscious, substituted by the relief that s/he is still alive and activating the rather typical egoistic response of 'live and let the others die'.

The crux of the problem is that the impact of private car ownership/ use is not treated as an ongoing societal problem, as one of the modern malaises of a materialistic society that requires explicit policies on the part of governments to address. There is a 'conspiracy of silence' woven around the deleterious effects of private car mobility precisely because the fractions of capital, both industrial and financial, associated with the production and circulation of the automobile commodity, command excessive political clout, sufficient to influence, if not to determine outright, the design of the policies adopted by governments.

This economic-political collusion between the interests of the car industry and its associated branches of production (manufacturers of parts), fuel suppliers (the oil and petrochemical industries) and commercial service providers (wholesale and retail dealerships, car repair businesses) and other peripherally contributing sectors (telecommunications and information technology sectors) *with governments,* has for long been established in countries with an important domestic industry of automobile production like Germany, France, Italy, Japan, the US, Canada and lately China and India. But it can also be traced in countries which do not have any car industry of their own but are merely net importers of automobiles produced elsewhere. This happens because income spent on consumption of cars is the second major expenditure (after housing) that the average citizen in the western world will ever make during his/her whole lifetime. Most often this considerable expenditure is financed by borrowed credit which means that the car owner becomes indebted for a number of years, if not for longer periods of his/her productive life (through car replacements) and thus entering a relationship of economic-social *dependency,* a restriction of his/her freedom for the sake of which s/ he is motivated to obtain a car in the first place, living in order to work to pay off the value of his/her coveted commodity (and this life-commitment to acquire and enjoy one's own car explains why the car is often perceived as an extension of one's own self). Unlike housing, cars lose 46% of their value within the first three years, according to the trusted non-profit consumer advocacy group Consumer Reports.

The 'conspiracy of silence' over the deleterious impact of a social life organised around privatised car mobility is overdetermined by the salience of the advertising industry which is the fundamental source of financing for the commercial mass media systems that provide news information and entertainment to the great majority of citizens-consumers throughout the globe. In the U.S. alone, three of the top ten advertisers in media are car companies, rivalling only cellular phone companies in total purchasing power of advertising in the U.S. media.[8] Since the car industry, and its associated commodity products and services, is one of the largest advertisers worldwide, the mass media networks which themselves are profit-seeking capitalist corporations tend to avoid all information or critical interrogation that could possibly generate 'displeasure' to their regular major advertising clients.[9]

The political submission of pro-market governments to the capital imperatives of the automobile-industrial complex is most often dissimulated by the political 'rationalisation' that the financing and deployment of public policies supporting the development of the highway and road infrastructures is a form of 'democratic' responsiveness to demands and wishes coming from civil society and in particular from the 'middle classes' (a nebulous but convenient category that tends to cover nearly everyone) which expect policies conducive to their 'way of life' regardless of adverse effects to the society as a whole. At the same time, the 'middle classes' are regarded by the political elites as their 'privileged' electorate clienteles whose electoral support is the *conditio sine qua non* for gaining and/or maintaining political authority.

In many cities, this plays out politically as the suburbs dominating political transport choices that favour the automobile, while forcing inner city residents to choke in pollution and ride an underfunded mass transit system. So, the dominant privatised mode of living of the middle classes in its *public* life is reflected back to them *via* a 'populist' rhetoric of the governing elites that promotes privatisation as the substance of the public benefit *per se*. In spite of the 'democratic' pretence, the illegitimate decision-making power afforded to the 'special interests' of the automobile-industrial-complexes, behind 'closed' and through 'revolving' doors, suggests that the condition of 'post-democracy'[10] rather than knocking at the door is already sitting cosily on the chesterfield. Such corruption of the normativity of democratic life implies that any project for the socio-ecological transformation of social life must address head-on the impinging de-democratisation and spoliation of the public norms of common existence in the capitalist world. In short: democratic life needs a defibrillator.

8. Bradley Johnson, "How Nation's Top 200 Marketers Are Honing Digital Strategies", *AdAge*, June 27, 2016. http://adage.com/article/advertising/top-200-u-s-advertisers-spend-smarter/304625/
9. In the recent Volkswagen scandal of the company's deception about the level of pollution emissions of its cars, the company threatened French television media that it would withdraw its advertising campaigns and thus gained a 'gentle' and quickly by-passed treatment by them.
10. Colin Crouch, *Post-democracy* (Cambridge, UK: Polity, 2004).

In contradistinction to the 'enclosure' in a private microcosm that the car owner autistically enjoys, public transport in any of its forms is a moving terrain that *socialises* the individual by bringing him or her into living contact with numerous other fellow citizens. It is distinctly possible to flirt with the person sitting across from you on the bus or the train. This is much less likely, even in heavy traffic, with the person you can see in the next car. Even the mere social co-presence of other travellers allows oneself to live the formative experience of being not only with other human beings but of distinguishing and comparing his or her own self from the others and each other from any other.

This originary social sensibility rests at the base of any authentic 'tourist' experience whose goal is to get exposed to foreign cultures and mingle with the locals. This is one of the reasons that visitors in another city or place choose to travel by public transport and for sightseeing even if they could afford to hire a private means. Being in a public means of transport multiplies the chances of social encounters and impromptu social interactions as well as in cases of emergency of acts of solidarity. This primitive bond of sociability, of exposing oneself to unknown others and vice versa is a humane social capability that tends to emasculation in the current culture that privileges self-centred isolation (even in public places) in one's car, home or portable virtual environment.

The public-private interface of transport in Greece

Greece is a net importer of private and public means of transportation. An effort to develop the manufacture of a plain jeep model during the 1980s failed, despite state subsidised procurement to private contractors to secure a supply of vehicles for the national defence forces and for civilian use. Such endeavours require long range planning strategies that clash with the logic of a clientelistic state that is hostage to the volatility of electoral cycles and the vagaries of a bi-partisan political system that celebrates policy discontinuities whenever each opponent conquers political power.

The rapid though distorted economic growth of the recent decades gave birth to a considerable expansion of the 'middle classes' and strata, both in the private and in the state sectors and led to the development of an extended suburbanisation process reflecting the increase in the standard of living and at the same time reinforced by 'internal migration' to the greater Athens area due to ample employment opportunities offered by the labour market. These two structural changes were conducive to the development of a rampant consumerist culture, triggered also by the introduction in the late 80s/early 90s of a national commercial mass media system, especially commercial television and a mass market lifestyle magazine sector that 'indoctrinated' Greek citizens on the merits of consumerism.[11] At the core of this newly discovered consumerist cornucopia was the offer of private locomotion through car ownership. To a certain extent, this grand-scale relocation to the suburbs necessitated a turn to car ownership since no effective alternative means of public transport existed (a single metro train line provided service to extremely limited areas) and the contemporary public bus system with its proverbial inefficiency did not respond to the drastic changes in the socio-geographic dispersion of the population. Certainly, despite the generation of such massive new social need for physical mobility, no organised public voice was raised to demand politically the establishment or expansion of the public transport system, and the accommodation of the new social need was left to private 'market-mediated' solutions. The massive shift to private automobility resulted in the aggregate boost of the trade deficits year in year out over the last thirty years. Parallel to this rapid expansion of car ownership, governments launched over-ambitious programs to develop highway and road infrastructures, financed through public debt and procured to particular capitalist construction interests that overcharged on their construction contracts and garnered surplus revenues through perennial renegotiations of the procurement contracts.

The automobile culture has attained such a dominant place in everyday life that it has devalued all alternative means of transportation and locomotion. Ownership of a car is not simply an expression of the rampant consumerism that pervaded the consumption habits of a society undergoing rapid economic growth and 'modernisation' but a symbolic marker that one has 'succeeded' in life and has entered a much-desired middle- or upper-class status. The signification of the car as a sign of class status has resulted in the establishment of a rigid symbolic hierarchy of status order that defines for many people both the 'meaning of life' and his/her station in life. Because of that a lot of people ended up heavily indebted, owning luxury cars they could not have afforded in the first place. This is the case in Greece, in this context but also true elsewhere, at other times and in other contexts in cities around the world. The predominance of the automobile culture was deliberately promoted by the political elites as a kind of 'bribing

---

11. For the introduction of commercial television in Greece and its impact on politics and society, see: Georgios Daremas and Georgios Terzis, "Televisualization of Politics in Greece", *Gazette: The International Journal For Communication Studies* 62, no.2 (2000): 117-131.

off' of electoral clienteles. A provision of a pseudo-affluent privatised lifestyle (each a king or queen within the private boundaries of his/her automobile) in exchange for political submission to the powers that be. Concurrently, since automobile ownership is a property asset, its widespread ownership generated a lot of new tax revenue for the state, through licence fees, luxury excise taxes, increased insurance taxes pegged on the value of the car, fuel charges on gasoline exceeding 60% of the pump price and a unique personal income tax assessed against the car's value (the size of its engine in cc) regardless of the owner's declared income. Unfortunately, no portion of this sizable annual tax stream originating in private transport was earmarked to subsidise public transport: it all went to general revenues. The government could have siphoned a significant portion as a dedicated tax to support small-scale energy production from renewable sources or to convert the operating basis of the public transport systems from fuel-based to renewable energy sources and thus facilitate an ecological transition to a less harmful, sustainable model of public mobility. It could have dedicated this revenue to a free public transport system and an increased public ecological awareness about which Greek society is relatively unaware. A missed opportunity.

The onset of the 2010 public debt crisis and the adoption of the bail-out memoranda imposing severe neoliberal austerity measures, have resulted in a historically unprecedented 'great recession' amounting to the loss of 27% of the GDP by 2015 and a stagnant economy thereafter. The economic collapse, with the drastic cuts in salaries and benefits in the public sector, the steep decline in the wage level of the private sector, the cut-backs in pensions, the rapid rise of a sizable precariat due to the deregulation of the labour market, the shrinkage of the petty-bourgeoisie resulting in innumerable bankruptcies of small-medium enterprises and of self-employed entrepreneurs, the exorbitant rise in unemployment to 27% by 2014 (having declined slightly to 23% under the current Syriza government) has confronted Greek society with an unimaginable and unprecedented crisis and a bleak future on the horizon.

Car owners themselves have been trapped in a dead end. Many were forced into fire sales, losing most of the value spent (a major portion of their life savings). Another significant number unregistered their licence plates to avoid the annual state fees thus becoming deprived of the use of the car. A third segment, that kept their car (often family households and persons whose car is a professional tool or a necessary accessory to their job), have cut down on the distances travelled and overall use. The consequence of the reduction of cars in circulation and in use, is the overburdening of the mass public transport systems that are called upon to service the new swarms of commuters. Nevertheless, such a needy turn has not led to an increase of revenues for the public transport operators but a worsening of service provisioning.

Free public transport mistakes

In the midst of the recent economic crisis, brought about by austerity, the Ministry of Labour signed an agreement with the public transport companies that permits free use for all registered unemployed persons. But the tight ministry budget does not allow for timely reimbursements of cost coverage and this augments the economic deficits of the public transport companies. This necessary and socially just policy for the unemployed has produced an unintended adverse side effect. It has ballooned the so-called phenomenon of the 'free rider'. Given the absence of ticket control, most commuters pretend to be unemployed thus avoiding invalidating their tickets with a consequent huge loss of revenues for the companies. This egotistical mentality is beneficial in the short term for the 'free rider' but socially harmful in the long term for society and for themselves since it leads to the collapse of the public transport system.

Let me be clear here. The 'free rider' phenomenon that occurred at this juncture in Greece is ill-fated not because the tactic is unjust, but because it is not accompanied by a meaningful larger social and political project. It is a tactic without context. It is to this subject that we must now turn.

In general, any meaningful project for an emancipatory socio-ecological transformation must address the issue of values. Without a popular espousal of pro-social values, aimed at harnessing individualistic self-seeking beneficial conduct that externalises the costs upon society, any emancipatory project is doomed to failure. With continually increasing budgetary deficits, the public transport companies cannot provide the public service the public itself demands. According to the 2016 budgetary accounts published in the official government newspaper, the combined deficits of the two public companies (STASY S.A and OSY S.A) are estimated to be €77.27 million/US$91.08 million (revenues of €330 million/US$388.97 million, expenditures of €377 million/US$444.36 million). These huge operational deficits are reflected in the deterioration of service provision. The number of drivers has been reduced from 4016 in 2014 to 3440 in 2016. Despite a fleet of 2139 buses, only 900 buses are fully operational.[12] This has resulted in fewer and less frequent bus itineraries and hence to longer waiting hours (sometimes more than an hour), and congestion and disgruntlement of the commuters. In these conditions of undignified public mobility, sociability turns into its opposite and the others' presence is experienced as a nuisance instead of a boon.

Reclaiming the commons: towards a more robust free public transport model

The idea of implementing local transport services freely accessible by the residents of a town or municipality is relatively new in the Greek social context. The major reason for its absence till recently is owed to the over-centralised character of the administrative structures of the state institutions. Both the administrative structures of the regions and of local administrations are effectively subordinated to the general government without any degree of relative autonomy vis-à-vis the decision-making policy of the Ministry of the Interior, responsible for home affairs. The PASOK government (under the Greek version of a social democratic party) in the late 90s introduced a modernising administrative reform program with the Kapodistrias Law in 1997 and then, in May 2010, passed in parliament a more radical administrative reform, the Kallikratis Law, that is still in force today. The law enforced a compulsory unification of adjacent municipalities and communities reducing the total number of the new administrative units to one third of the previously existing ones. It delegated far greater civil and administrative responsibility to city municipalities, though without transferring proportionate funds and sources of revenues to support local administration in its new responsibilities.

Municipalities had to become more active in identifying new sources of income and participating in state-funded programs. One such program inaugurated a year before the major overhaul of local administration was the program 'Syn-Koinonia' (it means literally 'moving society' or transportation) run by the Ministry of the Interior and it subsidised free public transport on the municipal level. One of the few beneficiaries of the program was the municipality of Xylokastro, located in the mountainous Northern Peloponnesus which ran a free public transport service from January 1, 2009 until February 28, 2010 (for 14 months) when the program ceased abruptly due to financing difficulties at the onset of the crisis.

What is significant is the operational model of the local transport program because it will be imitated later by other municipalities in the greater area of Athens, the capital of Greece. Public transport systems

12. Weekend Newspaper *Imerisia*, October1-2, 2016, 61.

tend to have high fixed costs (especially rail systems) but variable costs are relatively small.[18] So, rather than incurring the cost of purchasing the buses and employing drivers the municipality leased the services of a regionally operating private provider. The problem with this type of public-private partnership is that as easy as it is to start, it is also equally easy to discontinue if financing for the deal is not forthcoming, as happened in the above-mentioned case.

The longevity of a free public transport (FPT) program requires a certain initial resource commitment on the part of the municipality so as not to be jettisoned at the first difficulty. Furthermore, if the program is wholly 'owned' and run by the municipality rather than outsourced to an external provider, then there is greater flexibility to adapt the program to the changing needs and priorities of the municipal residents.

Even more importantly, a self-operating transport scheme allows for the possibility of democratic participation of both municipal users and non-users in the planning and implementation of the scheme. This can occur either through participatory budgeting and local popular assemblies or through municipal stakeholder deliberative bodies. Thus strengthening the local social bonds and socially transforming the community of users into a self-acting communal body, instead of being passive receivers of services offered by the municipal authorities.

The longevity of an FPT program is not a guarantee by itself that it will elicit citizens' involvement and grassroots democratic participation. Apart from the development of a self-grown participatory culture, it requires a left-oriented political power at the helm of the municipality that actively promotes citizens' involvement. In the absence of such 'trigger' the provision of 'free public transport' becomes a mere routine practice, a taken-for-granted service that well-meaning patronising mayoralties offer to their electors in exchange for their electoral support, as was attested by the case of the Maroussi municipality, an example to which we will now turn.

This municipality, made famous in the English-speaking world by Henry Miller, is located in northern Athens. Maroussi is one of the largest municipalities in the country population-wise (72,333 inhabitants according to the national census of 2011), and extends over 13 square kilometres, having one of the highest population densities in Greece (5536 residents per km^2). It is a rich middle-class borough with many corporations from the health, financial, telecommunications and retail trade sectors having their home base there. It launched an FPT program in December 1997 and thus has a twenty-year history in operation. It

13. Barry Ubbels, Marus Enoch, Stephen Potter, and Peter Nijkamp, eds., Unfare *Solutions. Local Earmarked Charges to Fund Public Transport* (London, UK: Spon Press, 2004).

offers free commutes not only to municipal residents but also to visitors. This is part of a strategy to upgrade the city as a commercial and business centre that has been successfully deployed. It started with one bus line and after ten years it succeeded to cover 93% of the city's area through five local bus routes that operate daily from 5:45am to 11:45pm. The municipal enterprise that manages the program possesses a fleet of 23 midi thermal buses (Euro II) of 15 seats each and two buses powered by natural gas (CNG) of 33 seats each. Daily, the buses conduct 160 itineraries covering 1200 km, and transporting around 18,000 passengers. In terms of its scope and efficiency, the program is perceived as successful and contributed not only to successive re-elections of the mayor but also to catapult him to national prominence, and to his election as president of the national federation of municipalities.

In the last two or three years, there has emerged a growing trend of various municipalities, not only in Attica but in other cities of the country, to initiate pilot FPT schemes or even to announce the launch of full-scale programs. Two main reasons account for such upsurge in offering free local transportation. The first reason, as we saw in the case of the Maroussi municipality, is the promotion of the municipality itself as a business and commercial centre of attraction and at the same time motivating the local citizens themselves to shop locally thus enhancing the local city market while also catering to the mobility needs of its inhabitants. In this category falls the popular tourist island of Kos whose municipal authorities recently announced (July 29, 2016) the pilot launch of an FPT program aiming to support the local market and economy—free public transport offered to all residents including visitors and tourists.

The second reason is the insistent demand by municipal residents suffering under the crisis to be provided with local means of public transport in order to obtain freedom of movement within their cities and thus access local public agencies, health services, workplaces and the entrance points/stations connected to the major public means of transportation in greater Athens. The economic crisis in Greece has made it imperative at the municipal level to provide free public transport. Such circumstances explain free public transport in municipalities like Ilioupoli (launched in May 2015), Koropi (August 2013), Glyfada (March 2016), Moschato-Tavros, Rafina-Pikermi (pilot launch in October 2016), Vari-Voula-Vouliagmeni (February 2017), and others. Some municipal experiments that started relatively early, like in Vyronas (2004) or even more recently like Papagou (2013), have faced considerable resistance and were compelled to scale down the programs.

Each municipality is a self-enclosed administrative unit. This means that even when municipalities share a contiguous geographical border (e.g. when traversed by the same highway, street or avenue) it is nearly impossible to collaborate on a common project (such as an inter-municipal free public transport program) that could increase efficiency and reduce costs while providing better public service. This politico-administrative isolation is heightened by the problematic relationship single municipalities have with the Attica prefecture, the higher level regional administrative body which commands a significant budget for local public works and projects but deals with municipalities on a one-to-one basis without fleshing out policies that promote inter-municipal collaboration.

Surely, to be successful and robust, a long-term free public transport model will require better coordination at all levels of the politico-administrative machinery and strong political will.

Conclusion

If the dictum that a socio-economic crisis is also a 'window of opportunity' for social change has any truth in it, then Greek society stands at a critical crossroads. Either Greeks will cling nostalgically to the memory of the 'good old days'—really not that long ago—reproducing the logic of seeking private 'solutions' to its common problems, or we will critically examine the misperceptions that led us to our current despair and 'restart' the arduous task of building a genuinely democratic society premised on egalitarianism, social justice and social solidarity.

A good start could be the reclamation of public space not as a neutral background for the deployment of one's own egoistic interests but as a collectively-designed participatory domain where institutional life is held accountable and the social quality of life—rather than the material standard of living—guides our decisions and practices. An important aspect of such re-appropriation of public space is the prioritisation of a democratically organised public transport system guaranteeing the freedom of mobility for all, above the capitalistically driven privatised commodity 'solution' securing automobility for the one and denying it for the other.

Brazil: From Dream to Nightmare

Paula Aftimus and Daniel Santini

Background

In June 2013, thousands took the streets across Brazil to protest yet another increase of bus fares announced in various cities, signaling an explosion of social mobilisation in favour of free public transport.

The protests were massive, and repression by the police, brutal. After each march, newspaper headlines all over the world showed not only the activists, many very young, but also the violence. The Brazilian police, behind black Robocop suits, big shields and a vast armory, frequently used tear gas and rubber bullets to disperse the crowds. In São Paulo, one photographer permanently lost his eye from a rubber bullet while covering the protest.[1] The violence took such a form that instead of frightening people, it made them angrier, and the protests grew larger after each act of repression.

Regular workers and whole families joined the students, now

---

1. The photographer Sérgio Silva remembers how he lost his eye: "I was trying to register the shock troops (riot police). They were shooting all around in an attack position exactly in the corner opposed to where I was. I took three pictures with one click. When I put the camera down, I felt the impact". The last time he could see with his left eye was on June 13th, 2013. He described the moment, in 2016 during a presentation of the book Ocular Memory ("*Memória Ocular*," in Portuguese), which describes how he has been trying to get the São Paulo state government to recognise its responsibility for his injury. His motto is "rubber bullets blind, but do not silence." For more about the book (in Portuguese), see: "Lançamento: Cidade em jogo e Memória ocular" [Release: City in Play and Eye Memory], *Fundação Rosa Luxemburg*, July 11, 2016, http://rosaluxspba.org/lancamento-dos-livros-cidade-em-jogo-e-memoria-ocular/.

demanding not only free public transport, but also new social policies in areas such as education and public health. Too big and too unsatisfied to be ignored, in the end the movement won a victory: the bus fares were not increased. In addition, it forced the Federal Government to make a public statement promising the implementation of new programs to attend to their other demands. Never before had the country seen such strong social mobilisation for free public transport.

The protests, led by the *Movimento Passe Livre* (MPL, or Free Pass Movement in English), didn't start in 2013, nor did they end that year. The movement had begun at least ten years earlier and continues to this day in different regions of Brazil. In Salvador da Bahia, in the northeast of the country, the emblematic *Revolted do Buzu* (Bus Riot) took place in 2003, and in Florianópolis, in the south, there was the *Revolta da Catraca* (Ticket Gate Riot) from 2004 to 2005. Even in São Paulo there had been large free public transport protests in 2006, 2010 and 2011. Officially, MPL was created in 2005, during the World Social Forum in Porto Alegre, in southern Brazil.[2]

Protest against bus fare increases, Rio de Janeiro, 2013. Source: Agência Brasil, June 14, 2013.

2. Sérgio Haddad (PhD) has recently published research on MPL's educational practices. Considering that MPL is a radically horizontal organisation – its members are not allowed to assume a leadership position if not to announce or share collective decisions – getting official answers is not exactly easy. Haddad observes that MPL is merely a consequence of a larger mobilisation for the right to access cities. His results are very useful to anyone interested in better understanding the movement and its perspectives.

The belief that transport is a social right—and should be free—is not an entirely new concept in Brazil. This idea, that inspired the nationwide protests and that is at the core of MPL's foundation, had already been the subject of discussion at the end of the last century. Shortly after the end of 21 years of military-civilian dictatorship (1964-1985), among the efforts to rebuild Brazilian democracy, there was an attempt to implement free public transport in São Paulo, Brazil's most populous city.

Free public transport in São Paulo

Like other metropolitan areas of Latin America, São Paulo is a huge city, that developed very quickly and without proper urban planning—in some areas, without any planning at all. In the 1950s, the city became the most populous in the country.[3] By 1960, there were 3,825,351 people living in São Paulo, while in Rio de Janeiro the population was 3,307,163. That was the year the political capital of Brazil moved from Rio to Brasilia.

By 1980, São Paulo had over 8.5 million inhabitants and, under the logic and policies of the regime, an urban transport infrastructure that was anything but democratic. Investments in transportation were made primarily to reduce traffic jams, facilitate speed and benefit private transport.[4] However, the urban highways that popped up everywhere—wiping out entire neighborhoods and forcing people further away from the city-centre—just fuelled the never-ending cycle of growth without urban planning, as well as massive traffic jams.

Obviously, the further away you live from your job, the longer it will take to get around, and under a government that does not invest in public transportation, having a private vehicle becomes a necessity. More cars generate more traffic that demands more highways. Asphalt and concrete take over, while people are pushed towards the periphery. It seems unstoppable. Inevitable. But is it?

According to the official census, there were almost ten million people living in São Paulo in 1991 (the last update, from 2013, shows over 12 million). In 1988, Luiza Erundina was the first woman elected as mayor in São Paulo, and it was during her administration (1989-1993) that

3. Animated infographic showing the evolution of the population in Brazilian state capitals is available in Portuguese at: http://www.oeco.org.br/blogs/oeco-data/27232-as-capitais-brasileiras-que-mais-cresceram-no-ultimo-seculo/.
4. For a deeper analysis on perspectives and possibilities for free public transport and a comparison between cities built for individual transportation and cities structured for collective public systems, refer to: Michael Brie and Mario Candeias, *Just Mobility: Post-fossil conversion and free public transport*, Translated from the German by Alexander Gallas, (Germany: Institute for Critical Social Analysis, Rosa Luxemburg Foundation, 2012), https://www.rosalux.de/fileadmin/rls_uploads/pdfs/Analysen/Analyse_Just_Mobility.pdf.

the subject of implementing a free public transport system was first seriously addressed. She nominated Lucio Gregori, a civil engineer and enthusiast of the idea, as her transportation secretary. They had one main idea guiding their urbanization plan: that a city, especially one the size of São Paulo, cannot function without good public transport infrastructure, and that the main beneficiaries of public transport networks are companies, industry and the large media organisations.

Therefore, they proposed what they called a Transport Fund, in which both the public administration and the private sector would transfer resources to finance the city's free public transport. Along with the Fund, they proposed a revision of all contracts between the bus companies and the city, along with other modifications, including changes to the tax system.

Their plan, however, never made it past the drawing board. The private sector was extremely unhappy, the corporate media led a strong campaign against the plan, and bus companies found the idea of changing rates and taxes an outrage. In the end, without a majority in the local chamber, the municipal parliament buried the proposal. Even inside her own party, PT—*Partido dos Trabalhadores* (Workers Party) —Erundina faced questions. Later, during several interviews she pointed to the transport issue as one of the most difficult, complex and challenging of her administration.[5]

The attempt to establish free public transport in Brazil's largest city may not have succeeded, but it did become a reference in the country for the mobilisation and development of public policies. Some ideas of the ex-secretary and engineer Lucio Gregori influenced real changes in the public system—he always advocated, for instance, that the cost of transport and fare prices be considered separately, which means that it would be necessary to subsidise the system to avoid increases in fares on account of fluctuations, like additional transit and operational costs. In some cities, working with private contracts, transport companies pass on business cost increases to their customers, the citizens who use the system. Gregori argues that the population should not have to pay to maintain the economic balance, arguing that managing the city transport system as a regular business would legitimize the notion that some people have the right to profit off the mobility rights of others. This concept influenced the public transport structure of several cities;

5. Erundina presented not only an analysis of what happened during her administration, but also some considerations about perspectives and challenges, to the site TarifaZero.org, in 2009. For her, the main point is to foment discussion about the topic and try to reach out to, and convince, the public opinion about not only the viability, but also the pertinence of free public transport. "'Ficou a Idéia'. Entrevista com Luiza Erundina" ["The Idea Remains". Interview with Luiza Erundina], *TarifaZero.org*, October 11, 2009, http://tarifazero.org/2009/11/10/ficou-a-ideia-entrevista-com-luiza-erundina/.

and in São Paulo, the municipality subsidises part of the costs, which reduces fare prices.

Gregori's idea is that to finance these subsidies, those that benefit most from the public transport system, meaning private businesses, are the ones that should pay. This idea, however, was never implemented. He also argues that the transportation infrastructure of a city is mainly a political matter, and therefore the decisions regarding the subject should not be based only on technical and numerical assessment, but on a social perspective. On top of that, Gregori emphasizes that the State must consider other costs in the equation, such as the pollution impacts of a car-based transport system on a city's public health system.[6]

Erundina herself became a defender of the concept that transport should be considered a social right. She became a congresswoman, was elected five times as federal representative, and in 2011 she presented a proposal to change the Brazilian Constitution so that transport would be recognised as a social right.[7] Strengthened by the impact of the 2013 demonstrations, she saw the proposal approved in 2015. Now the transportation issue figures among the main social rights that Brazil, as a democratic state, must guarantee to all its citizens, according to its constitution, together with the right to food, health, housing and education. It was a huge step towards establishing concrete changes to guarantee this right and a solid base for future demands. In 2016, at the age of 81, Erundina ran once more for mayor during the municipal elections in São Paulo, now representing the PSOL—*Partido Socialismo e Liberdade* (Socialism and Freedom Party). She placed fifth in the election.

The nightmare of 2016

To better understand the issues surrounding the implementation of social measures such as free public transport, it is essential to attempt to understand Brazil's complex political situation.

2016 was the year of the soft coup that resulted in the impeachment of President Dilma Rousseff (PT). More important even than the betrayal of her ex-ally, Vice President Michel Temer (*Partido do Movimento Democrático Brasileiro*, PMDB), Dilma faced the gradual erosion of her support base in a process that had begun during her first term as president. Elected for the first time in 2010, Rousseff never managed to handle the Congress as well as her predecessor, Luiz Inácio Lula da

6. Gregori explained his ideas on public transport during an interview with Daniel Santini (one of the authors of this chapter), in 2011, see: "Ex-secretário de transportes defende tarifa zero" [Former Secretary of Transport Defends Zero Tariff], *Outras Vias*, February 8, 2011, https://outrasvias.wordpress.com/2011/02/08/ex-secretario-de-transportes-defende-tarifa-zero/.
7. The Brazilian Constitution is available in Portuguese at: http://www.planalto.gov.br/ccivil_03/constituicao/constituicao.htm.

Silva. In 2012, she was given the first sign that negotiating with them wouldn't be simple: the government was defeated in a discussion over the new Forest Code. Not only did the changes the government pushed for not happen, but the *ruralistas* (right-wing senators and deputies that represent, or are themselves, plantation owners) got exactly what they wanted, which was the reduction of forest protection.

Rousseff's government was trapped between a conservative, gradually overconfident and rebellious Congress and flooded with complaints coming from different sectors of society, all somehow affected by the combination of austerity measures and the economic impact of pharaonic projects—such as the demonstration by Indigenous peoples against the Belo Monte Dam construction. So of course, having to deal with the 2013 protests did not do her any good. In 2014, Rousseff was barely re-elected. She received 51.6% of the valid votes, against 48.4% for Aécio Neves (*Partido da Social Democracia Brasileira*, PSDB), an advantage of just over three million voters out of the 105 million who went to the polls—the smallest advantage seen in a presidential election since the re-democratization of 1985.

To regain the people's trust, Rousseff promised social measures and political changes that she would subsequently not be able to keep. If Congress during her first term was a problem, this second time it was a nightmare. Also recently elected, the new Congress was older, richer and more conservative than ever. In an election where private campaign funding makes all the difference, the 513 elected MPs each spent an average of R$529,000 (US$169,266/€141,640) in their campaigns, 93% more than the average spent for those not elected. Only 51 women were elected, not even 10% of Congress. Among those elected and re-elected, 85% had previous experience in public administration. Trying to soften future problems, Rousseff went on to negotiate new austerity measures demanded by the main opposition parties. As a result, she got even less support from the streets.

The economic scenario, with commodity markets facing an international crisis that directly affected the Brazilian economy, also did not help. Neither did the corruption allegations involving the PT and almost every other party in the government, including Vice President Michel Temer's PMDB. The economic crisis, along with the corruption headlines, was the straw that broke the camel's back, fueling the massive mobilisations of 2016, this time much more conservative and without the concrete demands that were present in 2013. People—wearing the colours of the Brazilian flag—protested corruption as if it were merely a moral issue, demanding Dilma's exit but not any other structural or political change. Not once did the marchers mention private campaign funding, for example. The protests were so heterogeneous and the demands so unclear that one could see, in the middle of the demonstrations, groups defending the idea that only another dictatorship could "save" the country.

In this complex scenario, Rousseff suffered a political impeachment based on a highly technical matter—the way the government presented its financial information in previous years. Temer—as immersed in the corruption accusations, if not more so, than most PT politicians—took power with an even tougher austerity agenda. During his first months of governing, he resorted to repressive measures against social movements to advance his initiatives for reducing social welfare, including changes in labour legislation and the social security system. Facing this reality, NGOs and social movements—instead of pressing for advances in social and ecological protections—began to focus simply on trying to resist setbacks, and the issue of free public transport became somewhat dormant.

Steps back and—forward—in São Paulo

Let us return to São Paulo. Transport was one of the main topics during the municipal elections of 2016. The incumbent mayor, Fernando Haddad (PT), had dared to confront the historic infrastructure logic privileging private cars, and instead funded space for other forms of transport, such as bikes and buses. His administration built bike lanes all over the city, along with bus-only lanes along big avenues and highways. He also reduced speed limits and installed traffic-calming measures. In a city with a deeply rooted automotive culture, such changes angered many people. Drivers were shocked they could not go 90km/h in urban areas. Memes about the "Industry of Traffic Fines" spread alongside acidic criticism of Haddad.

These advances brought important changes, not only in infrastructure, but also in culture. Because of the bike lanes, many realized that it was perfectly possible to get around without a car in São Paulo, especially the city's middle class which benefited the most from this change (bike lanes were built mainly in the areas near the city-centre, where housing is more expensive). After all, São Paulo's poor already knew what life without a car is like. This sector of society saw its mobility improve with the bus-only lanes, and its quality of life improve with the reduction of speed limits.

Haddad's administration, however, was far from revolutionary, and resisted changes that it considered too radical. In June 2013, for example, the mayor initially opposed the demand for free public transport and did everything in his power to minimize mobilisations against both the state government, which regulates the prices of the metro, and city hall, which is responsible for bus fares. Instead of negotiating with the *Movimento Passe Livre* (MPL), Haddad aligned himself with Governor Geraldo Alckmin, from the conservative PSDB. As mayor, he questioned the viability of the movement's proposals, tried to reinforce the image of young irresponsible protesters and, at the same time, opened new negotiations with the student union, historically connected with his party (PT). Obviously, he could not foresee the size the mobilisations would reach. In the end, he had no choice but to revoke the fare adjustment: from R$3.20 (US$1.02/€0.86) back to R$3.00 (US$0.96/€0.80).

In 2015, however, both city hall and the state government announced a new fare increase, raising bus and subway rates to R$3.50 (US$1.12/€0.94). At the same time, Haddad announced free transportation for low-income students. Instead of continuing to question the viability of MPL's demands, the mayor began to present free passage alternatives: in São Paulo, free public transport policies were adopted, benefiting not only students but also retired citizens, people over sixty, people with disabilities and the unemployed.

Although these were important steps towards the universalization of the free pass, the MPL never viewed Haddad as an ally. Especially since in 2016, an election year, the price of the fares rose yet again—now to R$3.80 (US$1.22/€1.02).

During the election, Haddad's main opponent, João Doria Jr. of the conservative PSDB, knew how to take advantage of the tension around the transportation issue in the city. A playboy who presented himself as a successful entrepreneur and who in the past presented a TV show based on Donald Drumpf's "The Apprentice," Doria made good use of his fortune. Drawing on a strong investment in marketing, he deconstructed his image as a member of the elite and instead proclaimed himself "*João, o trabalhador*" ("John, the worker"), a self-made administrator who could manage the city as successfully as he manages his companies.

At the same time, his campaign constantly criticized Haddad's transportation policies, such as prioritising public transport, building bicycle lanes and reducing speed limits. With an eye on the frustrated drivers, he adopted the motto "Speed up, São Paulo". If elected, Doria promised to return the speed limit of some urban highways to 90 km/h. Although controversial – reducing speed limits in the city had resulted in a considerable decrease in the number of fatal traffic occurrences during the Haddad administration (2013-2016)[8]—Doria's promise received the support of many. Haddad, affected by the national crisis of the Worker's Party (PT), was criticized by both right and left during his re-election campaign. The MPL and other social movements were against him. Doria ended up winning the election.

Doria entered City Hall in a context of economic crisis and high inflation. This meant he had to handle the increased costs of the municipal bus system while trying to keep his promise not to change the fares. Such a promise, of course, was made to avoid further protests led by MPL in the first days of his administration. Combining a good marketing strategy with actions planned alongside the state government, his ally, he chose to maintain the current price of the bus fare. However, Doria implemented significant changes in other fares, such as the discounted combo of several tickets for those who regularly use the public transport system, and tickets that allow the combined use of subway, train and bus (called "integration tickets"). He also announced that he might review the free fares for people over 60, raising the minimum age to 65 years.

The first reaction to the changes came from the Court of Justice, which suspended the partial adjustment of the tariff, arguing that the measure was discriminatory and would affect mainly those who use the system most: those who truly depend on public transport to come and go in the city. The announcement also prompted MPL to announce and organise mobilisations in the city.

Public transport in Brazil

In Brazil, in all cities with more than 500,000 inhabitants, the population must pay to use the public transport system, which is not exactly cheap. Prices, according to the last update made by the National Association of Public Transport in July 2016, vary from R$2.70 (US$0.86/€0.72) in Teresinha-PI and Jaboatão dos Guararapes-PE, to R$4.00 (US$1.28/€1.07) in Sorocaba-SP. Considering two trips a day and twenty trips a month, a worker from Sorocaba, for example, would spend R$160 (US$51.20/€42.84), per month on transportation, or 18% of the minimum wage at that time, R$880 (US$281.58/€235.62). In 2017, the minimum wage was readjusted to R$937 (US$299.82/€250.88). However, many of the tariffs of several Brazilian capitals have also been readjusted.

8. We avoid the word "accidents" to describe road incidents like getting run over or being involved in a collision. An "occurrence" only becomes an accident after an investigation shows that the case is really an accident (i.e. that there was no intention, and no possibility to take actions to avoid it). When we consider that all incidents are accidents, we are not considering that, in some cases, the driver should be considered responsible. For further details on this semantic point (in Portuguese) , see: Daniel Guth, "Carros vs não-carros" [Cars vs. Non-Cars], *A Bicicleta na Cidade*, February 15, 2016, http://abicicletanacidade.blogfolha.uol.com.br/2016/02/15/carros-vs-nao-carros/?cmpid=comptw.

Some large cities provide fare reductions or free fares for certain groups, such as seniors, students and people with disabilities. Only a few small cities, all with a population under 50,000, have implemented fully free public transport (for all residents): Agudos-SP (population of 36,150), Anicuns-GO (21,195), Eusebio-CE (49,455), Itatiaiuçu-MG (10,563), Ivaiporã-PR (32,699), Monte Carmelo-MG (47,595), Muzambinho-MG (21,007), Pitanga-PR (32,841), Porto Real-RJ (17,663), Potirendaba-SP (16,401) and Silva Jardim-RJ (21,366).

Only one larger city has implemented a universal free pass policy: Maricá-RJ (139,552), a rich city that has a budget based on royalties from petroleum extraction. In December 2014, Mayor Washington Quaquá (PT) invested in the acquisition of new buses and announced free transport within the municipality. The new lines with the new buses, called "Vermelhinhos," were not able to serve the entire population and were instead limited to some areas and some schedules. Two private companies with long-term contracts with the city were able to continue operating, charging a tariff of R$2.70. However, the population could choose which buses to use and most people, of course, preferred free public transport whenever possible. The companies were not happy and did everything they could to cancel the new policy, including bringing a lawsuit against Quaquá's administration.

The first attempt by the two private transport companies to end free public transport in Maricá came in 2015, through a legal action established on behalf of the Union of the State of Buses. Their allegation was dumping: free bus lines meant unfair trade conditions. The court accepted the argument and suspended the buses, but the city was able to reverse the decision.

In October 2016, a new decision closed the lines, and the Quaquá administration, once again, promised to try to reverse the decision. In municipal elections, held that year, the issue of free buses became the centre of the debate. Among the promises of Fabiano Horta (PT), an ally nominated as a candidate by Quaquá himself, was a commitment that he would continue the policy of free public transport initiated by his predecessor. Horta won the elections.

Since 2013, tariff readjustments have become a delicate issue for mayors, to say the least. In Belo Horizonte-MG, the last mayor, Marcio Lacerda (*Partido Socialista Brasileiro*, PSB), announced that the price of the bus fare would increase from R$3.70 (US$1.18/€0.99) to R$4.05 (US$1.30/€1.08) in 2017, making it the most expensive among Brazilian capitals. The new mayor, Alexandre Kalil (*Partido Humanista da Solidariedade*, PHS), agreed to the measure and had to deal with three major protests during his first six days in office. In the past, the Public

Defender's Office had questioned not only the readjustment but also the way contracts are established with bus companies. As happened in São Paulo in 2013, the protesters in Belo Horizonte questioned not only the fare prices but also how the system was structured, demanding greater transparency and democracy in the decision-making process. Now, it is not only the MPL and other similar social movements acting, but also some civil society groups and organisations: the movement is growing broader.

In Brasília, a city that has also raised its transport tariffs, the National Bar Association (OAB), an organisation that represents public lawyers and advocates in favour of democracy, human rights and social justice, questioned the readjustments established in early 2017. Its president, Juliano Costa, argued that the variation was higher than inflation in the last 12 months and that an increase in the cost of public transport affects the entire economy. The Brasília government faces two lawsuits and several protests against the changes.

Why free public transport?

The arguments in favour of free public transport in Brazil are related both to social justice and to ecological issues.

Regarding inequality, a study presented by the Brazilian urbanist Pedro Guedes about Recife-PE, one of the main capitals in the northeast of the country, might help understand how mobility issues are connected to social disequilibrium and housing problems. In a deep data analysis presented at the State of the Map LATAM 2016, the Latin American Open Street Map conference that took place in São Paulo in November 2016, the town planner presented a situation that is common in many other cities in Brazil.

In Recife, due to gentrification, while job opportunities exist in central areas, many are forced to live on the periphery, or even in other adjacent municipalities, where houses are affordable but there is no work. This reality, of course, overloads the transport system, with people trying to get to the central areas in the morning and leaving for the outskirts at night. Among those who live in adjacent municipalities, 27% study and/ or work in the capital. In some cities, like Camaragibe-PE, the number goes to up to 50%—literally half of the city must travel every day to accomplish their daily activities.

The study also showed that, among those who live along the borders of the capital or in the greater metropolitan region, those everyday trips to work take between 40 to 85 minutes, each way. That means a total of up to three hours to come and go every day. In Brazil, according to the most recent research (from 2010) the average travel time was 32 minutes. In cities configured to privilege individual motorised transport, instead of facing the long trip on overloaded and expensive buses, those who can afford to, buy cars. In Recife, from 1998 to 2014, while the population increased 13%—from 1,390,000 to 1,600,000—the number of automobiles increased 95%—from 310,000 to 615,000. More cars in the streets means more traffic jams, and those who depend on the collapsed public transport system are the ones who suffer the most.

Pedro Guedes believes that to face the problem it is essential to consider free public transport as a way to encourage people to choose collective transport instead of cars. He insists that it is impossible to imagine urban solutions that allow efficient transport for all based on automobiles.

Rather, the solution lies in collective solutions that are faster than the automobile, especially at rush hour. In cities that put public transport first, as they did in Curitiba, Brazil with Bus Rapid Transit, the public transport system moves 70% of the population at rush hour, one of the world's most celebrated examples.[9]

As for ecological impacts, air pollution is perhaps the main issue, as it has an immediate impact on quality of life within cities and significantly increases public health expenditures. One of the main independent organisations that is dealing with the issue is the Institute of Energy and Environment (IEMA). Since the last decade, the institute has been warning about the risk of this type of transportation system in the city, which prioritises individual motorised transportation and only contributes to increases in the number of cars in the streets. In a recent study, the organisation pointed out deficiencies in the way that some cities monitor air quality.[10] Many cities do not even have proper equipment to establish baseline conditions and actually map the situation.

IEMA Director André Luís Ferreira argues that air pollution and related problems should be discussed not only by the environmental departments in public administrations, but also by others such as the transport departments.[11] Air pollution primarily affects children and elderly people, and, in cities like São Paulo, in the winter, when the air

9. See, for example, "How Curitiba's BRT stations sparked a transport revolution – a history of cities in 50 buildings, day 43," *The Guardian*, May 26, 2015, https://www.theguardian.com/cities/2015/may/26/curitiba-brazil-brt-transport-revolution-history-cities-50-buildings.
10. IEMA, *1° Diagnóstico da rede de monitoramento da qualidade do ar no Brasil* [1st Diagnosis of the air quality monitoring network in Brazil] (IEMA, 2011), http://www.energiaeambiente.org.br/2014/08/1o-diagnostico-da-rede-de-monitoramento-da-qualidade-do-ar-no-brasil/.
11. According to the 2011 IEMA report on air pollution and automotive transport in Brazil, freight transport is primarily by trucks burning diesel; for further details see: Daniel Santini, "Controle de emissões não basta" [Emissions control is not enough], *O Eco*, February 28, 2011, http://www.oecocidades.com/controle-de-emissoes-nao-basta/.

is dry and the dispersion of toxic substances is more difficult, public hospitals are always full of people who are having trouble breathing. Pollution also increases the risk of heart diseases while reducing life expectancy of the whole population. Facing the problem means prioritising investments in policies that value public transport and discourage the use of private automobiles.

To change the paradigm of mobility in Brazil is quite a challenge, mostly because it is also a cultural matter. Cars symbolise individual success, independence and liberty, while for many, public transport is something to be avoided, if you can. Investments in bridges, larger highways, tunnels and sometimes bizarre adaptations like elevated highways to allow the circulation of more and more cars, usually have great public support. The automotive industry's propaganda has a key role in this collective imaginary, and the still huge deficiencies of Brazil's public transport networks do not help. To this day, the administration of public transport is a very shady, centralised and obscure business, even in the capitals.

The crucial importance of open data

Some of the problems are so prosaic that they seem unreal. Torsten Grote, a German free-software activist living in Brazil, encountered difficulties when trying to insert in his app, Transportr, the routes and connections of the buses of Florianópolis-SC, the capital of Florianópolis and one of the main cities in the south of Brazil. He requested basic information to try to publish open data about the city's bus network. All he received were images of lines drawn manually in a map. Because the administration was unable to respond to a simple request for the location of the bus stops, he had to go to each one of them himself, eventually mapping the entire network.

What this example illustrates is how much something as simple as information could increase the use of public transport, if it were disclosed. Information, however, does not seem to be a priority. Grote presented this case in the same Open Street Map conference, and, just like Pedro Guedes, he also believes that adopting free public transport is one of the most important steps toward changing the way things are. More people using and valuing the public transport system means more people caring for it and therefore actively participating in decisions that are now considered merely technical. Opening data—all the data collected and hoarded by public transport agencies—and making public transport free are directly connected, he believes.

Conclusion

Movimento Passe Livre became a reference point and it still is fundamental to spreading ideas about social justice and transport. The movement is not, and will not be, a force that will take over and change the political and economic system as a whole, at least not in the way it is now constituted. Nevertheless, in a context of emerging conservative forces, *Movimento Passe Livre* may be essential to avoid setbacks in public transport policies.

The bottom line is: starting to face reality and addressing real and concrete social issues such as the transport crisis may be the first step toward reconstructing hope for social justice and for Brazilian democracy itself. Free public transport can be a direct connection to a different, fairer, and more equal country.

[14]

Right to the City: Mexico

Lorena Zárate

Overview

The struggles for spatial justice, human rights and democracy have a long history in Mexico. Since the late 1960s, urban social movements have played a key role in influencing the political agenda and the definition of public policies based on community-led projects and initiatives.

Against this backdrop, the adoption of the Mexico City Charter for the Right to the City in 2010 was both a result—and an important game changer—not just locally but internationally. Drafted inside a collective process that included local grassroots organisations, NGOs, academics and professionals, as well as international civil society networks and the local government, several of its contents were taken as a basis for the recently approved Mexico City's Constitution (2017), the first for this city as well as one of the few in the world to explicitly incorporate the Right to the City.

For many people around the world, the right to the city is a political tool that can galvanise a broad range of social actors, claims and proposals to advance the understanding of the city as a common good. Within its framework, protecting and guaranteeing existing rights as well as promoting new rights is equally possible and relevant.

This is the case in Mexico City. Access to adequate public

transportation and the need to develop an integrated mobility strategy and plan linked to a new vision of the city are priority issues on the city's metropolitan agenda. Social pressure and political will seem to be aligning in recent years. Has the moment arrived to make bold steps to advance the right to mobility? Will other cities follow Mexico City's lead and adopt their own constitutions, integrating the Right to the City and the Right to Mobility?

The march for democratic change in Mexico City

Struggles for spatial justice, human rights and democracy are certainly interconnected and have a long history in Mexico's capital city. The massive internal migration that took place, for the most part between the 1950s and 1970s, confirmed for *campesinos* and the working class the rampant disconnections between the promises of modern urban life and the cruel reality of having to struggle for a place to survive, usually in the periphery.

As for many other Latin American countries, the economic opportunities offered by an accelerated but limited process of industrialisation strongly promoted by the national government aligned neither with adequate nor sufficient housing policies. Squatting and self-building practically became the norm of Mexico City sprawl, under the form of the *colonias populares*.[1]

Mutual aid and community organising processes ignited social movements that claim access to land, housing and public services, including water, sanitation, electricity and transportation. Grassroots and non-profit organisations, with the support of academics and professionals, as well as progressive branches of the Catholic Church, engaged in small-scale collective projects in marginalised and impoverished neighbourhoods and in city-wide mobilisations to make their voice heard, and pressure local and federal authorities to pay attention to their demands and proposals.

Given decades of authoritarian governments "elected" under fraud and corruption, the demands for rights and democracy were inevitable and visible, especially in the Capital District (*Distrito Federal*). The student repression and killings of 1968, the spontaneous and rich social organising that took place after the deadly 1985 earthquake (showing extraordinary solidarity and claiming the right to stay in the central

---

1. 40% of Mexico City is comprised of so-called "informal" (self built) housing. Designated sometimes as "shanty towns," most are now consolidated with adequate building materials and municipal services. Not all have regularized tenure or property rights but this does not mean that people feel insecure—particularly true for those families with a long-standing presence and strong social ties in the neighbourhood.

neighbourhoods), and the opposition victory in the 1988 elections, were all clear signs of the political transformation the country was undergoing.

Institutional change introduced in the late 1990s allowed for the first democratically elected government in the city. The progressive Party of the Democratic Revolution (*Partido de la Revolución Democrática*, or PRD) has been in power in Mexico City since 1997, introducing relevant transformations in social policy and citizens' participation in the political and cultural life of the city. Over the past two decades, progressive initiatives from social movements and civil society organisations were translated into normative and policy changes regarding a broad range of issues, from housing and neighbourhood upgrading programs,[2] relevant improvements in urban mobility, child care and economic support for single mothers, students and the elderly, to sexual and reproductive rights, Indigenous peoples' and LGBTQ rights, to mention just a few.

The Mexico City Charter for the Right to the City and the Right to Mobility

Pressure from below: the elaboration and negotiation process

Against this backdrop, the Mexico City Charter for the Right to the City, signed in 2010,[3] could be seen as both a result and a game changer. Drafted inside a collective process that included local grassroots organisations, NGOs, activists, academics and professionals, as well as international civil society networks and the local government, some of its content was taken as a basis for the recently approved Mexico City Constitution (February 2017),[4] the first for the capital city, as well as the first one in the world to explicitly incorporate the Right to the City.

Born as an initiative of the Urban Popular Movement (*Movimiento Urbano Popular*, MUP), with the support of the Habitat International Coalition – Latin American Office (HIC-AL), its most direct antecedents are in two international events promoted by these organisations in Mexico City's historic centre: the World Assembly of Urban Inhabitants (October 2000)[5] and the Mexican Chapter of the World Social Forum

2. From 1999, the Housing Improvement Program (*Programa de Mejoramiento de Vivienda*) has provided more than 300,000 interest-free loans to improve housing conditions for lower-income households in the city: more recently, it has been complemented by the Barrio Improvement Program (*Programa de Mejoramiento Barrial*).
3. By no coincidence, at the 200th anniversary of the Mexican Independence and 100th anniversary of the Mexican Revolution. Habitat International Coalition, "Mexico City Charter for the Right to the City," http://www.hic-gs.org/document.php?pid=5407.
4. Mexico City Government, "Mexico City Constitution" [in Spanish], http://cdmx.gob.mx/constitucion.

(January 2008).[6] During the first, hundreds of social movements' representatives, from 35 countries, were engaged in dialogues and exchanges about "the city we want." At the second, thousands of Mexican activists and citizens took part in a three-day-long public debate about the right to the city, where the idea of developing a local Charter on this topic was first presented and discussed.

Because of the latter, a Promotion Committee was established to facilitate the debate and negotiation process of the Mexico City Charter for the Right to the City, integrating the MUP, HIC-AL and the Federal District Human Rights Commission (CDHDF); later joined by the Coordination Space of Civil Organisations on Economic, Social and Cultural Rights (Espacio DESC) and the Federal District Social Attorney's Office.

From April 2008 to June 2010 this Committee was responsible for organising public events, academic seminars and cultural activities with children and youth to collect relevant inputs and proposals for the Charter. During that period, more than fifty coordination and drafting meetings were held, and several communication materials and a graphic campaign in public transport were produced for awareness raising purposes. Concurrently, members of the Committee participated in conferences, courses, workshops, and radio programs to disseminate information on the Right to the City and ask for contributions to the Charter.

In March 2010, during the Fifth World Urban Forum organised by UN-Habitat and the Ministry of Cities of Brazil under the motto "Right to the City: Bridging the Urban Divide,"[7] the Draft Mexico City Charter for the Right to the City was presented and discussed for the first time with an international audience. Back in Mexico, the official signature of the Charter took place at the famous Metropolitan Theatre, with more than 2,000 people as witness, representing hundreds of social, academic, professional and governmental institutions, who also symbolically signed the final text.

Since its signature, the Charter has been appropriated and used by different organisations and communities to claim their rights and denounce abuses from private and public actors, including the Mexico City government. Middle-income neighbours affected by the construction of the *Supervía Poniente* (Western Superhighway) and

5. Habitat International Coalition-Latin America office, "World Assembly of Urban Inhabitants," http://www.hic-al.org/anterior/index.html.
6. América Latina en Movimiento, "Posicionamiento de la Mesa sobre Derecho a la ciudad y al hábitat" [Position of the Bureau on the right to the city and the habitat], https://www.alainet.org/es/active/21681.
7. UN-Habitat, "World Urban Forum 5," http://mirror.unhabitat.org/categories.asp?catid=584.

concerned by the environmental destruction it provoked, raised public awareness and presented a legal complaint quoting the Charter and highlighting the contractions of the government's policies and projects, while pedestrians and bicyclists used it as a reference for their right to mobility.[8] At the same time, on the opposite side of the city, a very active low-income community was engaged in the development of their own sub-district Charter (*Carta Iztacalquense por el Derecho a la Ciudad*), directly exercising a democratic decision-making process, as well as implementing urban agriculture, and several other social and cultural projects.[9]

The Mexico City Charter has also had international influence, and its principles and proposals can be found in documents such as the Global-Charter Agenda for Human Rights in the City (2011)[10] and the New Urban Agenda (2016),[11] both of which explicitly recognised the right to the city.

The main contents

As specified in its Preamble, the Charter calls for the achievement of an inclusive, liveable, just, democratic, sustainable and enjoyable city. It aims to stimulate processes of social organisation; strengthen the social fabric; and foster active and responsible citizenship. Furthermore, it promotes the construction of an equitable, inclusive and social/solidarity-based urban economy that guarantees the productive inclusion and economic strengthening of traditionally marginalised and excluded sectors.

Its promoters agree that this instrument aims to confront the most profound causes and manifestations of exclusion: economic, social, territorial, cultural, political and psychological. It is explicitly posed as a social response, an opposition to "city-as-merchandise," and an expression of the collective interest. As an initiative advanced by the urban social movement "from below" and adopted by a city-level government, the charter explicitly seeks to go beyond realizing human

8. For media repercussions about this case, see: Mariana Suárez Esquivel, "La *supervía* viola sistemáticamente derechos humanos de la comunidad" [The *supervía* systematically violates the human rights of the community], *La Jornada*, July 29, 2012, http://www.jornada.unam.mx/2012/07/29/capital/032n1cap; Judith Amador Tello, "La Supervía: Violación al derecho a la ciudad" [The Supervía: Violation of the right to the city], *Proceso Magazine*, September 12, 2012, http://www.proceso.com.mx/319633/319633-la-supervia-violacion-al-derecho-a-la-ciudad.
9. See: Colectivo de Organisaciones Civiles por la Democracia Participativa en Iztacalco, "La Carta Iztacalquense por el Derecho a la Ciudad" [Iztacalquense Charter for the Right to the City], *DFensor*, monthly magazine of the Federal District Human Rights Commission, no. 10, October 2014, http://cdhdf.org.mx/wp-content/uploads/2015/05/DFensor_10_2014.pdf.
10. United Cities and Local Governments, "Global Charter-Agenda for Human Rights in the City," https://www.uclg-cisdp.org/en/right-to-the-city/world-charter-agenda.
11. United Nations Conference on Housing and Sustainable Urban Development, Habitat III, "The New Urban Agenda," http://habitat3.org/the-new-urban-agenda.

rights *in* the city, to also include a focus on realizing the collective right *to* the city and the rights *of* the city.[12] This represents a complex approach that demands the linking of the human rights theme in its integral conception (civil, political, economic, social, cultural and environmental rights) to that of democracy in its diverse dimensions (representative, distributive and participative).

The Mexico City charter builds on the collective experience of similar initiatives, including Brazil's City Statute (2001), the Montreal Charter of Rights and Responsibilities (2006) and the World Charter on the Right to the City (2005),[13] from which it directly took its definition of the right to the city:

> The right to the city is the equitable use (usufructo equitativo) of cities according to principles of sustainability, democracy, equity and social justice. It is a collective right of urban inhabitants that confers upon them the legitimate right to action and organization, based on respect of their differences, cultural expressions and practices, with the objective of exercising their right to self-determination and attaining an adequate standard of living. The right to the city is interdependent with other internationally-recognised human rights, including civil, political, economic, social, cultural and environmental rights, as defined in international human rights treaties.

For many, the right to the city is a political tool that can galvanise a broad range of social actors, claims and proposals to advance the understanding of the city as a common good. Within its framework, protecting and guaranteeing existing rights as well as promoting new rights is equally possible and relevant.

The charter identifies six fundamental principles that incorporate an amalgam of individual and collective human rights, understood as being interdependent and indivisible to promoting the right to the city. Notably, these components include legal rights, social and political claims and material conditions (see figure 4).

12. The rights *of* the city refer to the need for strengthening local autonomy by legislating and conferring upon cities a full legal status with powers, resources and tools that can be enjoyed both by local governments and citizens. The concept may refer to the administrative, political and economic rights of the local governments in relation to national/federal authorities, as well as to the presence and role of local authorities vis-à-vis the international and multilateral institutions (United Nations, World Bank, International Monetary Fund, etc.). For more on this topic see: *Role of local government in the promotion and protection of human rights*, Final report of the Human Rights Council Advisory Committee to the thirtieth session of the UN Human Rights Council (A/HRC/30/49), http://www.ohchr.org/EN/HRBodies/HRC/AdvisoryCommittee/Pages/LocalGovernmentAndHR.aspx.
13. See Art. I, on the Right to the City in, Habitat International Coalition, Housing and Land Rights Network, "World Charter on the Right to the City," http://www.hlrn.org/img/documents/World Charter Right to City May 05.pdf.

Strategic Foundations	Vision
Full exercise of human rights in the city (new understanding of citizenship)	A city in which all persons (regardless of gender, age, economic and legal status, ethnic group, religious or political affiliation, sexual orientation, place in the city, or any other such factor) enjoy and realize all economic, social, cultural, civic and political human rights and fundamental freedoms, through the construction of conditions of individual and collective wellbeing with dignity, equity and social justice.
The social function of the city, of land and of property (combatting speculation and gentrification)	A city that assures that the distribution of territory and the rules governing its use can thereby guarantee the equitable use of goods, services and opportunities that the city offers. In other words, a city in which collectively defined public interest is prioritized, guaranteeing a socially just and environmentally balanced use of the territory.
Democratic management of the city	A city in which its inhabitants participate in all decision-making spaces of public policy formulation and implementation, as well as in public budget formulation, planning and control of urban processes. It refers to the strengthening of institutionalized decision-making (not only citizen consultancy) spaces, from which it is possible to do design, follow-up, screening, evaluation and reorientation of public policies.
Democratic production of the city and in the city	A city in which the productive capacity of its inhabitants is recovered and reinforced, in particular that of the low-income, traditionally excluded and marginalized sectors, fomenting and supporting the social production of habitat and the development of social and solidarity economic activities. It concerns the right to produce the city, but also the right to a habitat that generates income for the families and communities and strengthen the people's economy, not just the increasingly monopolistic profits of the few.
Sustainable and responsible management of the commons (natural and energy resources, as well as cultural patrimony and historic heritage) of the city and its surrounding areas.	A city whose inhabitants and authorities guarantee a respectful and responsible living relationship with nature, in a way that makes possible a dignified life for all individuals, families and communities, in equality of conditions but without affecting natural areas and ecological reserves, cultural and historic patrimony, other cities or the future generations.
Democratic and equitable enjoyment of the city	A city that reinforces social coexistence, through the recovery, expansion and improvement of public spaces for all, that allow community gathering, leisure, and creativity, as well as the critical expression of political ideas and positions.

Figure 4. Six fundamental principles/strategic foundations of the Right to the City.

The charter also incorporates at least two important principles addressing the right to the city as first articulated by French philosopher Henri Lefebvre in the 1960s: first, the right to participate in decisions affecting urban inhabitants and the production of urban space; and second, the right to appropriate urban space in favour of its use value over exchange value.[14]

While public transport is not explicitly mentioned at this high-level analysis in the Mexico Charter, urban mobility and transportation are clearly deeply related to each of the six principles in the Right to the City charter (and, as we will see below, it gets specific and detailed treatment elsewhere in the document). Here we focus on four of the main themes.

The second principle, treating the social function of land and property, a key component of the right to the city agenda, calls for an integrated approach to land use that privileges social justice, inclusion and re-distribution of limited resources. Access to the opportunities, goods and services that the city offers is strictly related to mobility options and is key to overcoming spatial segregation. By giving priority to low-income populations, in most cases living in the periphery, public transport systems can be fundamental in reducing inequality. At the same time, planning and fiscal measures can control speculation and gentrification processes that usually displace low and middle-income populations to the city outskirts, raising car-dependency and increasing service costs for public transport.

The third principle addresses public participation in decision-making. As with any other area of public policy, and given its particular character in urban and metropolitan areas, urban mobility and transportation policies and programs should be determined in a participatory way, and be publicly monitored and evaluated. Citizens and communities should be part of the decision-making process, to prioritise infrastructure and services and funding allocation, both at neighbourhood and city/region levels.

The fifth principle addresses the sustainable city. Being responsible for a large proportion of the gasoline consumption, land use and pollution in cities, transportation and mobility systems are central to achieving sustainability goals. By giving priority (in planning and budgetary measures) to public transport and non-motorised options, human settlements can significantly reduce their ecological footprint. Transportation is strictly linked with efficient waste collection, management and recycling systems, and is also fundamental for guaranteeing access to water in many peripheral neighbourhoods.

14. This latter point underpins the tactical urbanism gestures occurring in many cities today.

Last but not least, enjoyment of public spaces is inextricably linked with urban mobility and transportation. Streets and avenues, public transport stations, markets, bike paths, parks, libraries and even university campuses, hospitals and other public buildings and their grounds, are public – or quasi-public – spaces by definition and constitute a significant percentage of the urban area. At the same time, accessing parks, green areas, recreational, cultural and community centres, and other collective facilities and infrastructures requires public transportation for the vast majority of city residents.

This intimate connection between mobility and access to public space is so strong that a growing number of voices concur that any discussion of public spaces must also include a definition of the right to mobility as one of it main components, and vice-versa.

So, it is not surprising that both the Mexico City and the World Charter for the Right to the City have recognised the right to public transportation and urban mobility. The Mexico City Charter explicitly mentions the right to public transportation and to urban mobility as part of the "inclusive city" proposals (section 3.2.1)[15] and calls for actions to move forward a more sustainable, productive and safe city, such as: to **expand** those public transport networks which are most high-capacity, efficient, non-polluting, safe, comfortable, accessible, and affordable, and advance toward multi- and inter-modality transportation (section 3.3.5); to **locate** employment-generating productive and service activities in otherwise exclusively residential areas to decrease transportation demands, risks, costs, and negative impacts on the economy and social coexistence (3.4.6), to **strengthen** security programs for women in public transportation (section 3.7.6).

As we will explore in this chapter, in recent years these principles and proposals have been explicitly quoted and analysed by several groups promoting the right to mobility. Among them, it is worth highlighting the impressive special report on this topic that the Federal District Human Rights Commission published in 2013.

Mobility in Mexico City

As a valley originally formed by five different lakes, canoes and boats were for centuries the principal means of transportation in *Mexico Tenochtitlan*. The Spanish colonizers brought horses and other animals that were also used for moving people and goods. Until the 1950s, all

15. This echoes language in the World Charter on the Right to the City, as part of the section dedicated to Rights to Economic, Social, Cultural, and Environmental Development of the City (Part III).

these could be seen running side by side with trams in Mexico City streets and canals.

(As grandparents, environmental activists and experts know, the famous "City of the Palaces" was–at that time–covered by hundreds of rivers and canals, the majority of which are now underground or dried up. By looking at the name of some streets and avenues in a current city map, it is possible to know where some of those canals and rivers were located: *Canal de la Viga, Rio Churubusco*, and others.)

With the massive internal migration, and the so-called urban explosion in the mid-twentieth century, the first public bus systems were created to try to cope with the new high demand for transportation. But the policies and services were not enough and, according to experts, the 1960s marked the moment when car mobility began to be prioritised and new fast avenues and urban highways were built.[16]

Mexico City's population rose from just over 3 million in 1950, to 7 million in 1970. Interestingly, the number of vehicles grew even more rapidly than population, increasing more than three times between 1950 and 1960 (from 74,000 to almost 250,000); and had multiplied ten times by 1970 (up to 720,000). Over the same period, the number of buses only doubled (from just over 4,000 in 1950 to 9,900 in 1970).

At the end of the 1960s Mexico City's first Metro line was built and by 1986 it was already serving 4.2 million trips per day (about the same number as today). Most of the lines were built during the 1980s,[17] at the same time that massive bus systems were completed, which are responsible for the majority of trips (6.4 million/day).

Only in 1994 did the city name it's first Secretary of Transportation, and the first official *Transport Integral Program* appeared in 2002. Despite good intentions, the norm continued to be overcrowding, delays, traffic jams and pollution. Although Mexico City's population has remained stable since the late 1980s (at around 9 million), population growth in the metropolitan area accounts for more than double that number (21 million in 2015).

The Mexico Valley Metropolitan Zone (*Zona Metropolitana del Valle de Mexico*, ZMVM) is composed of 16 *delegaciones* (boroughs or districts) of the former Federal District (now officially called *Ciudad de México*, according to the recently passed Constitution), 59 municipalities from the *Estado de México* and one from Hidalgo State. The ZMVM is a high, almost enclosed valley located at 2,330 meters above sea level. It has an area of 4,715.3 km2, with a density of 5,920 people per square

---

16. Statistics included in this section come from *Informe Especial sobre derecho a la movilidad en el Distrito Federal.*
17. A few more Metro lines were added in the 1990s, the most recent one was finished in 2012.

kilometre.[18] The United Nations ranks the ZMVM as the 6th largest urban agglomeration in the world and it is expected to reach almost 24 million by 2030, with most of this growth in the peripheral areas.[19]

According to available data, there is an estimated 11 million trips per day in Mexico City alone; if the metropolitan area is considered, this number doubles (of the 22 million trips, 80% are within Mexico City, the rest mostly in Mexico State, in particular in Ecatepec, Nezahualcóyotl and Naucalpan, where many of the *colonias populares* are located).[20]

The public transport network in Mexico is vast and complex. It includes different services provided by a combination of public and private actors, such as:

- Collective Transport System-Subway (*Sistema de Transporte Colectivo-Metro*)
- Bus Rapid Transit (*Sistema de Corredores de Transporte Publico de Pasajeros del Distrito Federal, Metrobus*)
- Electric Transportation System (*Sistema de Transportes Eléctricos, Tren Ligero y Trolebus*)
- Passenger Bus Transportation Network (*Red de Transporte de Pasajeros*, RTP)
- Licensed collective services by buses, mini-buses and vans
- Individual Bike Transportation System (*Sistema de Transporte Individual* ECOBICI).

Impressively, compared to other North American cities, more than two thirds of daily commutes are by public transportation. This is a very large constituency of voters who depend daily on the public system.

Modal split varies considerably depending on the purpose of the trip and the place. Those going to school: 42% walking; 38% public transportation. Those going to work: 18% walking; 25% driving; 47% public transportation. People in peripheral *delegaciones* (lower-income for the most part) walk to school 3-4 times more than those living in more central areas (richer neighbourhoods). The proportion is almost the opposite when considering trips in private cars.

---

18. Significantly lower than other megacities, like New York or Sao Paulo.
19. United Nations, Population Division, Department of Economic and Social Affairs "World Urbanization Prospects: The 2014 Revision. File 11a: The 30 Largest Urban Agglomerations Ranked by Population Size at Each Point in Time, 1950-2030," https://esa.un.org/unpd/wup/CD-ROM/Default.aspx.
20. The most recent—partial—census on transportation is from 2007: the update is delayed until the end of 2017. Some figures here are from the National Institute of Geography and Informatics (INEGI) in 2015 as reported by Paulina López, "La movilidad de la Ciudad de México en la Encuesta Intercensal 2015" [The mobility of Mexico City in the Intercensal Survey 2015], *La Brújula*, February 9, 2016, http://labrujula.nexos.com.mx/?p=680.

The growth of cars

Studies affirm that over the past two decades there has been an alarming increase in car use in Mexico, and public spending has focused heavily on car infrastructure. Indeed, in 2011 66% of resources earmarked for public works went to automobile infrastructure, while 22% were allocated to public space, public transport and cycling infrastructure.[21] However, if the funds dedicated to the construction of Line 12 of the subway is removed, the amount allocated to public space and cycling infrastructure falls to only 0.31% of the total. The federal government grants different budgetary resources to state and local governments for infrastructure, mobility and accessibility. However, this has typically been allocated increasingly towards infrastructure supporting private car use.

In parallel, since the early 2000s, housing policy and financial instruments, both public and private, under the influence of World Bank recommendations,[22] have resulted in considerable growth of housing at the urban edge of the Mexico City agglomeration, resulting in higher car dependency and longer commutes:

> Namely, these new, housing developments have been created outside city limits and not even within the existing urban sprawl, where all urban services are to be found, including transport. This has made the inhabitants (highly) reliant (on) cars. Duhau (2008) reported that three quarters of the heads of families in a housing complex in San Buenaventura, Ixtapaluca, Estado de México, commuted to work in their own cars, putting in two to four hours a day in transit time.[23]

Coverage and Fares

The Mexico City government defines the maximum fares for all public transport services based on an annual review (including those under licensed service providers). Trips are free for the elderly, people with reduced mobility, as well as for pregnant women and children under five; reductions of nearly 40% are offered to single mothers, students and other low-income populations.

Public transport is heavily subsidised in Mexico City; as per 2017, fares for public services range between $4-7 (US$0.22-0.39/€0.18-0.33).[24] But

21. Source: [IDTP] Institute for Transportation and Development, *Transforming Urban Mobility in Mexico. Towards Accessible Cities Less Reliant on Car* (Mexico: IDTP and British Embassy in Mexico, 2012).
22. World Bank, *Housing: enabling markets to work*. A World Bank policy paper (Washington DC: World Bank, 1993).
23. Emilio Duhau, "Los nuevos productores del espacio habitable" [The New Producers of Livable Space], Ciudades, no. 79 (2008): 21-27.
24. Specific rates: Passenger Bus Transportation Network $4 (US$0.22/€0.18), Metro and Tren

the cost of single tickets, on average, is double in the State of Mexico, from where at least a third of trips originate. The fares might seem very cheap for a North American or European reader, but it is important to keep in mind that the average monthly income for the Mexico City Metropolitan Area is around $3,500 (US$195/€163) and that transportation costs can consume up to half the family income.

Quality and Sustainability[25]

In general terms, the average trip on public transport is long and continues to grow. It rose from an average of 53 minutes in 2007 to 1 hour and 20 minutes in 2009; this means a total of roughly 16 hours per week per person, in trips to and from work and/or school.

There are still no comprehensive monitoring and evaluation systems in place but some reports show that most people using public transport are not pleased with the service: 65% complain about bad or very bad quality; 80% affirm it is insecure; 90% say it is not comfortable; and 70% believe it is slow.

Serious pollution has been a critical issue on the city's agenda for several decades. Despite several reduction efforts, 76% of the pollution in the metropolitan area still comes from transportation, causing 4,000 deaths/year.

Different mobility paradigms, now getting aligned?

In the face of this situation, during the past decade urban mobility and transportation has been one of the key topics on the political and normative agenda. A growing number of actors, with a substantive list of demands and proposals, have become more visible and more vocal.[26] From bicyclists and pedestrians, to NGOs and private foundations—in some case with the support of foreign governments (like France or Britain) —a clear call for a 'paradigm change' is being made to place mobility and accessibility (to goods, services and opportunities, not just transportation of people and things) as the cornerstone of public debates and policies.

Ligero $5 (US$0.28/€0.23), Metrobus $6 (US$0.33/€0.28), Micro-buses and vans $4-7 (US$0.22-0.39/€0.18-0.33, depending on travel distances).
25. All data for this subsection from Gabriel Tarriba, and Gabriela Alarcón, *Movilidad competitiva en la Zona Metropolitana de la Ciudad de México: diagnóstico y soluciones factibles.* Resumen ejecutivo [Competitive mobility in the Metropolitan Zone of Mexico City: diagnosis and feasible solutions. Executive Summary] (Mexico: Instituto Mexicano para la Competitividad (IMCO), 2012), http://imco.org.mx/wp-content/uploads/2012/1/costos_congestion_en_zmvm2_final_abril.pdf.
26. Some of those include: @Bicitekas, @mujeresenbici, @Peatonico, @Pedestre, @Liga-Peatonal, @banquetalibre, @IDTP, @IMCO, @EmbarqMexico, to mention just a few.

All of them demand a clear strategy prioritising improvement in quality of life, public health and the functioning of the city-region through the promotion and protection of non-motorised mobility, improvement of public spaces, expansion of integrated public transport systems (improving quality and accessibility), dis-incentivising private car use, reducing polluting emissions and promoting clean energy. Some explicitly propose a right to mobility[27] while others are more interested in reverting the economic losses that the current situation entails for the private sector, for families, and the city-region as a whole.[28]

As a result, claims and recommendations around inclusion, equity, social and spatial justice, human rights and the right to the city concur, and sometimes overlap, with those of integral urban and territorial planning, sustainability and climate change, productivity and competitivity (see figure 5).

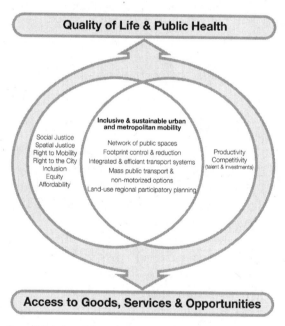

Figure 5. Relation of the Right to the City to other concepts.

In the context of the last national and local elections (2012), and amid the discussion of several so-called "structural reforms" (many of them highly controversial given their clear neoliberal inspiration/orientation),

27. See Federal District Human Rights Commission and ITDP, *Informe Especial*, 2013.
28. Tarriba and Alarcón, *Movilidad*, 2012.

an interesting process of Dialogues on Urban Reform took place during 2013, as part of the definition of the National Development Plan, and the new/revised contents for the General Law on Human Settlements, Territorial Planning and Urban Development (1976).

Organised by three private foundations (Centro Mario Molina, Instituto Mexicano para la Competitividad-IMCO and EMBARQ), and presented as an independent and non-partisan initiative, they gathered a wide range of actors with proposals to address what they defined as the 3D model of cities in Mexico ("D" for distant, disperse and disconnected). The result is a 70-page publication, "Urban Reform: 100 ideas for the Cities of Mexico,"[29] launched that same year.

The dialogues and proposals are organised around six main themes: territorial planning, metropolitan dimension, compact city, mobility, housing policies, neighbourhood revitalisation and innovation. The main objective for the mobility component is to improve mobility conditions in cities through the implementation of integrated public transport systems, the promotion of non-motorised options, and the elaboration of policies and programs for a more rational use of the private automobile. Of the 100 proposals, 22 are dedicated to recommendations around mobility and transportation, 10 to housing policies and 11 for neighbourhood revitalisation.

Against this backdrop, it would be difficult to read the contents of Mexico City's recently approved Mobility Law (2014) as a mere coincidence.[30] For the first time, the city has a law that is focused on transportation and that explicitly recognises the right to mobility (Art. 5) as the right of every person and the collectivity to have access to a mobility system for satisfying their needs and full development. "Mobility" is defined as journeys of people and goods through different means of transportation, with the goal that society can satisfy its needs and access opportunities that the city offers (for example, a job, education, health and recreation).

Also new is the hierarchy of mobility that the law establishes: pedestrians (in particular, people with limited mobility and special needs); bicyclists; passengers of public transport systems; providers of public transport systems; providers of private distribution of goods and merchandises; and last on the list of priorities, the users of private automobiles.

29. Organisers claim that more than 500 people participated in the seven Dialogues. A list of presenters and full documents are available at Embarq: "Reforma Urbana. La gran reforma que México necesita" [Urban Reform. The great reform that Mexico needs] http://www.movili-dadamable.org/reforma-urbana/50-100-ideas.
30. Asamblea Legislativa del Distrito Federal, "Ley de Movilidad del Distrito Federal" [Law of Mobility of the Federal District], 2014, http://aldf.gob.mx/archivo-ba20960fb6570ec7d4ee34c30ee2d733.pdf.

Most of the principles that should now be observed when designing and implementing policies, programs and public actions regarding mobility, recall some of those proposed by human rights activists and institutions: security/safety, accessibility, equity, efficiency, quality, sustainability, participation and co-responsibility. They also include resilience, multimodality and technological innovation.

The newly created Secretary on Mobility (SEMOVI), replacing the previous Secretary of Transportation and "*Vialidad*" (SETRAVI), will be responsible for formulating, stimulating, organising and regulating the development of mobility in the city, taking the right to mobility as its reference and ultimate goal in the elaboration of public policies and programs.

At the same time, SEMOVI will oversee the approval of the Integral Plan of Mobility and the Integral Plan of *Seguridad Vial*, aligned with the Mexico City General Programs on Development, Urban Development, Ecological Management and the ZMVM Planning. An advisory board on mobility and security was also created with the participation of different sectors and actors.

Finally, as part of the culmination of a decade-long process, the recently approved Mexico City Constitution includes the right to mobility (Art. 13, E) as the right of every person under conditions of security/safety, accessibility, comfort, efficiency, quality and equity. Priority will be given to pedestrians and passengers of non-motorised vehicles, and a culture of sustainable mobility will be promoted. The Constitution requires that the authorities take necessary measures to guarantee the exercise of this right, in particular the equal use of space and creation of an integrated public transport system, promoting low-emission options and respecting the rights of the most vulnerable users at all times.

Linkages with urban and territorial planning and sustainability are also clear through the commitments to prioritise the development and consolidation of collective public transport; stimulate the use of non-polluting vehicles or those with reduced emissions, and the creation of connected and safe infrastructure for pedestrians and bicyclists; guarantee accessibility; promote citizens' participation in the definition of public policies; and promote inter-institutional coordination at the metropolitan level.

Moving forward: open questions and challenges

As the previous official city slogan claimed, Mexico is a "city in movement". A long history of social mobilisation and political change is always present and is constantly being renewed in a small area that today concentrates about 21 million people. The challenges in such a megacity are immense, and the improvements are never enough.

During the past decade, the Right to the City and the Right to Mobility have appeared as explicit topics on the public agenda. A broad range of sectors and actors are committed to the tasks of raising awareness, experimenting with concrete alternatives and catalysing legal and institutional transformation to achieve a more just, democratic and sustainable city.

As one of the world's big metropolises, Mexico City is well aware of urban policies applied in other cities. Urban mobility is perhaps one of the topics where the direct inspiration from other cities is more evident and explicit. Former mayors from Bogotá and New York City—to mention just two well-known examples—are regular visitors to, and advisers of, the Mexico City government. At the same time, as shown in the preceding sections of this chapter, the circulation of ideas and practical tools have been a common practice both for the social and the private sector.

In recent years, new Bus Rapid Transit systems, bike paths, pedestrian infrastructure and pocket parks have been introduced at an accelerated pace, augmenting the mobility options for thousands of citizens and improving infrastructure in many neighbourhoods. At the same time, with regular programs like the *"paseos en bicicleta"* (which closes several main roads and avenues to cars every Sunday, in various districts of the city, combined with free recreational and cultural activities), it is clear that efforts are being made to foster a new culture on mobility, more inclusive and respectful of the different means of transportation, in particular non-motorised means.

However, it is also evident that these changes have been focussed primarily on already well-served central areas and have not had a significant impact on the low-income and traditionally marginalised communities. Conversely, some of those new services present affordability challenges and have in fact widened the social and spatial injustice (for example higher fares or non-integrated fares, which make those living in the periphery pay double, while people living in central areas can just bike or walk to work, through beautiful and well-maintained public spaces).

One can argue that different paradigms have entered into dialogue, and their confluences are now more explicit and visible. But several questions remain open. Will those confluences be enough to advance in the desired direction? Tensions and contradictions are always latent and keep appearing. How will they be managed?

We all know that the normative framework (Constitution, Laws) is not enough to guarantee the changes we need/we want. What conditions and mechanisms will be required for these changes to be implemented and monitored in a democratic and participatory way?

Even with political will, lack of coordination between institutions, policies and programs might jeopardize the possibility of advancing in a positive direction (urban and housing/mobility vs. transportation/ environmental regulations). How do we overcome fragmentation, duplication, overlapping, contradictions and gaps?

Some governments claim that it is only by privatising their public transport systems that they will be able to offer a more efficient service, meeting the needs of the population, creating in turn affordability and accessibility challenges. Who decides public budget priorities and to whom the funding directed (investments, loans, subsidies)?

Finally, there are also unexpected negative outcomes of well-intended policies, like those trying to promote densification and mixed-income housing in the central areas while controlling urban sprawl (known in Mexico City as "Bando 2" and "Norma 26"); or the improvement of public spaces and mobility options and services (like new Metro or Metrobus lines/stations, Individual Bike Transportation Systems, etc.) that can easily result in speculation, gentrification and displacement of low-income and marginalised groups, once again, to the periphery. Which instruments do we have to prevent and reverse these negative outcomes?

Open questions mean a necessarily open and collective learning process is required, including the critical review of our actions and omissions. And, as its inhabitants know, public debate and social mobilisation will continue at the core of any possibility of moving forward to make the Right to the City and the Right to Mobility a reality in Mexico City. We hope the lessons learned here spark efforts in other cities, as we move towards a more just and ecological city for all.

[15]

Value Capture: Linking Public Transport to Land Value

Jan Scheurer

Overview

This chapter summarises current practices in western developed cities to collect financial contributions for the operation of public transport services from sources other than public transport users' fares and general revenue of governments. In a number of European cities, salary-packaged annual passes issued by employers or educational institutions, or other periodical passes for unlimited journeys, make up a large majority of public transport tickets sold. The influence of this practice in shaping attitudes and travel behaviour is discussed, and it is argued how reliance on a large pool of periodical subscribers can, in the perception of public transport users, mark a hybrid experience between a fare-free system and a system that collects fares on a trip-by-trip basis.

From this insight, our focus will shift to the generation of (spatial) accessibility as the most critical benefit of a city's public transport service. In this context of enabling urban intensity and place-making, land users stand to gain as much as the travelling public from high-quality public transport. This nexus leads us to explore the question: what if it was land owners rather than passengers who, on a beneficiary-pays basis, provided the bulk of the funding for public transport operations? A discussion of the practicalities of such a shift, and the opportunities and constraints it would likely encounter in a contemporary policy environment, concludes this chapter.

Introduction

The question of who benefits from public transport is critical to any debate about how to best fund its operation. Traditionally, in most western developed cities a mix of 'user fee' or fare revenue and government subsidies have paid for public transport services. In this model, the implicit beneficiaries are considered to be a mix of the system's fare-paying users (passengers) and a form of generalised public interest, which can range from the provision of a welfare service for those without access to a private car, to the desire to reduce negative externalities of excessive car traffic such as road congestion, environmental damage or urban blight by making public transport more competitive in the travel market. More recent trends of public agencies outsourcing public transport operations to private-sector contractors or franchisees have not necessarily modified these funding arrangements in principle. They may have redistributed some entrepreneurial risk and may or may not have succeeded in shifting the ratio between user and public contributions to the operational task, but the basic assumptions about public transport's principal beneficiaries remain in place.

This chapter explores alternatives to this understanding and argues that one of the key benefits of public transport in urban areas is the generation of spatial accessibility. Put very succinctly: good transit to *land parcels* in a city increases the *value* of these parcels: in this view, good public transport also—and perhaps principally—benefits the *owners of land* in the city. Hence, it is suggested they should contribute financially to its provision and operation.

By providing a network of train stations and surface travel corridors, public transport effectively links a web of 'accessibility hotspots' across an urban area. This specific quality of access is automatically factored into the price of land, such that properties in the vicinity of public transport stations or stops tend to attract a price premium over those at a greater distance. Using new-generation data-driven tools to precisely measure this increased accessibility, this added value to sites becomes quantifiable and can inform the question whether property owners, in addition or alternatively to direct users or governments, might be regarded as the primary beneficiaries of public transport services and therefore a significant potential source of funding for such services.

Other beneficiaries that have recently been drawn into funding arrangements for public transport in a range of developed cities are employers, on the assumption that good public transport services generate increased access to labour markets and facilitate the economically desirable clustering of businesses into high-density, car-reduced urban environments; and motorists, on the assumption that the presence of popular public transport options also facilitates the management of an efficient road system where congestion is reduced.[1]

The next section will briefly introduce a selection of such models, followed by a more in-depth discussion of how the nexus between public transport provision and spatial accessibility can be harnessed into a comprehensive land tax regime that could potentially complement or even replace passenger fares and/or direct government subsidies to public transport operations.

So, who pays, when it isn't the person who rides the bus?

In their overview of alternative funding mechanisms for public transport, Ubbels et al differentiate between beneficiary-pays and polluter-pays approaches, though in practice there is some overlap between the two categories.[2]

Beneficiary-pays approaches include employment taxes, property taxes, developer levies and charges, and impact fees. One of the most well-known and long-standing examples of an employment tax, a striking example of an **'employer pays'** model, is the *versement de transport* introduced throughout France in stages since 1971. The *versement de transport* is a component of the payroll tax for employers above a certain business size (ten employees), and located within the commuter shed of a participating urban centre. Revenue is collected by the local authority and—importantly—must be spent on public transport capital investment or operation, or to subsidise fares. All French urban areas with a population of 100,000 or more make use of the tax, as do a majority of smaller conurbations (20,000-100,000 population). Over time, the share of funds collected from the *versement de transport* outgrew that collected directly from user fares.[3] For example, in the Paris metropolitan region in 2015, 39.9% of the regional transport agency's operational budget originated from the *versement de transport*, compared to 28.5% from user fares.[4]

1. Barry Ubbels, Marus Enoch, Stephen Potter, and Peter Nijkamp, eds., *Unfare Solutions. Local Earmarked Charges to Fund Public Transport* (London, UK: Spon Press, 2004).
2. Ubbels et al., *Unfare Solutions*, 2004.
3. Bruno Faivre D'Arcier, "La situation financière des transports publics urbains, est-elle durable?" [Is the financial situation of urban public transport sustainable], Les cahiers scientifiques du transport 58 (2010): 3-28

Ubbels et al acknowledge the boost to public transport funding and particularly the substantial investment in metro, tram and other fixed-route transit systems that revenue from the *versement de transport* has facilitated in French cities.[5] However, they also point to the vulnerability of this funding source during economic downturns, when employment rates decline just at a time when the provision of good public transport services is paramount for households experiencing economic hardship. As a consequence, over time the share of *versement de transport* revenue spent on operations grew at the expense of capital investment, leading to city authorities interested in further expanding their transit systems to look for additional sources of funding for this purpose.

Payroll tax supplements have also long been used to finance public transport investment and operations in Vienna (Austria), as well as in Portland and several other US cities. Another common feature of the fare policy of many European transit agencies is to collaborate with employers to offer discounted annual travel passes to employees as part of salary packaging arrangements; in Hamburg, for example, these are used by nearly 20% of all passengers.[6] In Vienna, annual travel passes are offered at a heavy discount (€365 (US$410) for 365 days, the equivalent price of 166 single tickets), with the result that it is now more common among the Viennese to own such a pass, allowing for unlimited travel on all public transport modes, than to own a private car In many jurisdictions within and outside Europe, tertiary institutions collaborate with transit agencies to include semester travel passes in their students' enrolment fees; all students (and sometimes staff) thus receive the benefit of free travel on public transport regardless of their rate of usage.[7] In Quebec, the *Université de Sherbrooke* and its student associations have implemented just such a scheme as part of a forward-thinking project to make the campus more ecological.

These long-term public transport passes made accessible through employment or enrolment arrangements, or through deliberately discounted prices on behalf of the transit agency's incentive policies, act like subscriptions to users: they reduce the marginal cost of each journey to zero for an entire year (or semester). Public transport thus becomes an automatic benefit packaged with one's job, educational training or, at an attractive and affordable cost, one's mere status as a citizen of a particular metropolis.

4. [OMNIL] Observatoire de la Mobilité en Île-de-France, "Financement des dépenses de fonctionnement pour les transports en commun" [Financing of operating expenses for public transport], 2017, http://www.omnil.fr/spip.php?article73.
5. Ubbels et al., *Unfare Solutions*, 2004.
6. [HVV] Hamburger Verkehrsverbund, "HVV-Verbundbericht 2013," 2013, http://www.hvv.de/.
7. Jeffrey Brown, Daniel Baldwin Hess, and Donald Shoup, "Fare-Free Public transport at Universities: An Evaluation," *Journal of Planning Education and Research* 23, no. 1 (2003): 69-82.

From the perspective of a transport user, this experience can be considered a halfway point between a fully user-paid and a fully fare-free public transport service. For the purpose of our inquiry, it represents a joint funding contribution to public transport by two groups of beneficiaries: users on the one side, with an interest in financial and practical convenience to access public transport, and employers, educational institutions and municipalities on the other side, each with an interest in maximising public transport usage.

Other potential contributors to public transport identified in Ubbels et al are **motorists**.[8] The authors discuss these contribution in the 'polluter pays' category, even though motorists can arguably also be considered beneficiaries of a well-functioning and well-used public transport system to the extent that it alleviates road congestion and takes pressure off the parking supply. Mechanisms to extract financial contributions towards the cost of public transport from motorists include earmarking a component of fuel levies or vehicle registration charges, or of congestion charges payable by individual motorists on a per-journey or per-day basis, applied either to a designated central area (like, for example, in London and Singapore) or to a particular piece of toll road infrastructure (like, for example, in Oslo and San Francisco).

The most widespread cross-funding arrangement from motorists to public transport appear to be levies on parking, collected either directly from motorists as a part of normal parking fees, or indirectly as an annual charge for the owners or operators of parking facilities. In some cities, developers are encouraged (or mandated) to pay cash-in-lieu fees to the local authorities rather than provide parking spaces in their developments, with the proceeds dedicated towards non-car transport and accessibility projects, including public transport.

Lastly, Ubbels et al discuss other developer contributions and property taxes as examples of beneficiary-pays forms of public transport funding.[9] Again, the view here is that **property owners** directly benefit in increased land value from the provision of public transport to their land. There is a range of models to share the cost of capital investment in infrastructure with land owners along new or improved public transport facilities. Medda categorises these into the three main groups: betterment taxes, accessibility increment contributions and joint development mechanisms.[10] Betterment taxes are defined as recurrent levies—for example, an annual tax—on land owners, property owners

8. Ubbels et al., *Unfare Solutions*, 2004.
9. Ubbels et al., *Unfare Solutions*, 2004.
10. Francesca Medda, "Land Value Finance for Transport Accessibility: A Review," *Journal of Transport Geography* 25 (2012): 154-161.

or businesses that benefit from a public investment, such as improved public transport accessibility. Accessibility increment contributions are custom-made fiscal instruments such as variable tax rates or one-off impact fees, designed to directly raise funds for measures that improve the amenity of a particular revitalisation area. Joint development mechanisms are public-private partnerships to conduct infrastructure and urban intensification projects in tandem.

What these models have in common is the notion that proximity to good public transport access, particularly to fixed-route modes such as heavy or light rail, is generally associated with a premium in property values. Mobilising this premium, which would otherwise solely accrue to land owners as a windfall profit, for the development or operation of public transport is known as **value capture**.[11] In the next two sections, we will examine this context in more detail by introducing the concept of quantifiable spatial accessibility on public transport.

Public transport proximity and performance as a land owner benefit

What is the benefit of accessibility—the proximity of land to public transport, and the performance of public transport found there—to land owners, and how can it be measured?

The following paragraphs are sometimes a bit technical, but what I am trying to describe here is an approach that can be adopted by cities to enable capturing this added value in quantitative terms.

The public transport-land use system generates spatial accessibility through the interplay of network configuration and performance, service standards and the distribution and clustering of land use activities throughout the urban fabric. Spatial accessibility is thus a proxy for, and an outcome of the degree of land use-transport integration achieved, within a settlement area both globally and locally.[12] Levels of accessibility differ across an urban area, depending on the centrality and connectivity of each public transport node, and the speed, frequency and capacity of the public transport modes that serve it. Using accessibility measures, we can identify the associated benefits to users as they vary according to geographical location. And we can also map them to a high degree of accuracy.

11. James Robert McIntosh, Peter Newman, Roman Trubka, and Jeff Kenworthy, "Framework for Land Value Capture from Investments in Transit in Car-Dependent Cities," *Journal of Transport and Land Use* 10, no. 1 (2017): 1-31; See also, Medda, "Land Value," 2012.
12. Karst T. Geurs, and Bert Van Wee, "Accessibility Evaluation of Land-Use and Transport Strategies: Review and Research Directions," *Journal of Transport Geography* 12, no. 2 (2004): 127-140; and Todd Litman, "Measuring Transportation: Traffic, Mobility and Accessibility," *ITE Journal* 73, no. 10 (2003): 28-32.

A range of tools have been developed to quantify accessibility benefits and to facilitate integrated transport and land use planning in practice.[18] The Spatial Network Analysis for Multimodal Urban Transport Systems (SNAMUTS) tool, co-designed by the author of this chapter, focusses specifically on the role of public transport to facilitate movement and accessibility in metropolitan areas and has to date been applied to 25 developed cities on four continents.[14]

SNAMUTS assesses spatial accessibility on public transport from a variety of angles by devising separate indicators for each and by visualising them both for metropolitan areas as a whole and for activity centres within each metropolitan area. These indicators include measures capturing a number of important factors in the public transport system, including: the ease of movement within a network (derived from travel times and service frequencies), the number of transfers that have to be done on public transport journeys, the spatial reach (travel time contour) of journeys within a pre-defined time window, the extent of coverage of the settlement area with services of a specified minimum standard of frequency and operational span within walking distance, the extent to which specific locations on the network act as conduits for movement, the capacity of specific network elements to absorb future increases in patronage and travel opportunities, and the extent to which the network facilitates user flexibility in navigating the system with minimal need to consult timetables or maps.

A composite measure takes in the results of each of these component indicators and translates them to a scale from 0 to 60, with higher values indicating greater overall public transport accessibility. These results are visualised in scale maps that allocate values and colour brackets to each activity centre catchments, as shown in Figure 6 below for Melbourne (Australia), which has almost 200 defined activity centres (spatial clusters of travel origins and destinations), and Figure 7, for Montreal (Canada) which is provided as a second example of the mapping. However, Montreal will not be discussed in this chapter.

Theoretically, it is therefore possible to allocate a quantitative public transport accessibility standard to each land parcel as a proxy for the benefit a land holder enjoys as a result of the provision of the public transport network.

It is important in this context that SNAMUTS and other accessibility measures do not merely capture a binary measure of transit endowment

---

13. M. te Brömmelstroet, C. Silva, and L. Bertolini, eds., *Assessing Usability of Accessibility Instruments* (Amsterdam, Netherlands: COST, 2014).
14. Carey Curtis, and Jan Scheurer, *Planning for Public Transport Accessibility: An International Sourcebook* (Oxon, UK: Routledge, 2016).

(such as, is a property located within 400 metres of a bus stop or not) but also a scalar, geographically differentiated measure of transit performance (what is the service level offered at that particular bus stop and how well does the bus service connect me to the rest of the city).

However, is it possible to translate this accessibility measure into a mechanism to raise funds for public transport operations that are complementary to or could even substitute for user fares?

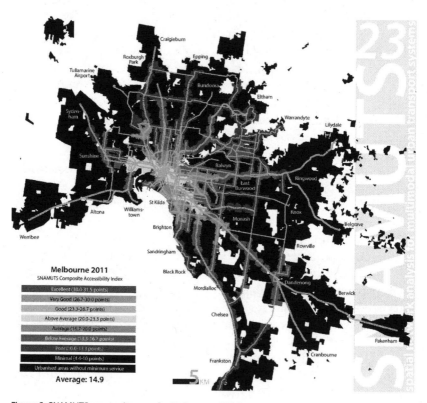

Figure 6: SNAMUTS composite map for Melbourne (2011)

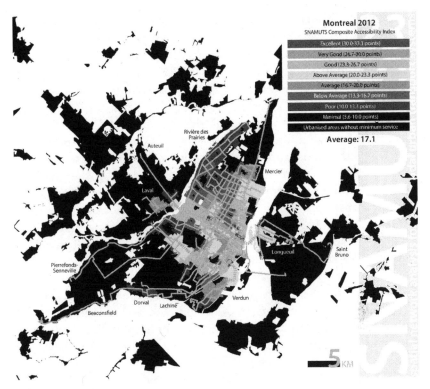

Figure 7: SNAMUTS for Montreal

The land tax discussion

A betterment tax, as defined above, is a hypothecated levy—an annual tax—applied on either the site value (classic land tax) or the capital-improved value of land (property tax). We will consider a specific example before reflecting more generally on the merits of land taxes compared to other forms of property-related taxes.

In the case of London's CrossRail (Elizabeth Line) project, added accessibility value has been captured by way of a Business Rate Supplement,[15] which is applied to all non-residential properties above a specified threshold valuation and is expected to raise approximately 28% of the construction costs of the railway. However, the Business Rate Supplement is charged at a uniform rate across the whole of Greater London; this practice is criticised as insufficiently equitable by Roukouni and Medda[16] since it does not take into account the varying extent of

15. Anastasia Roukouni, and Francesca Medda, "Evaluation of Value Capture Mechanisms as a Funding Source for Urban Transport: The Case of London's CrossRail," *Procedia – Social and Behavioural Sciences* 48 (2012): 2393-2404.
16. Roukouni and Medda, "Evaluation of Value Capture Mechanisms," 2012.

accessibility improvement achieved by the new rail line in different parts of the city. The decision-makers did not apply the results of an accessibility measure, like SNAMUTS, when implementing this tax.

Roukouni and Medda recommend a differentiated Business Rate Supplement based on accessibility benefit (or, since this effect has not been quantified at a great level of spatial detail in London, a differentiation based on a borough's distance from the new rail line) as a somewhat fairer way to pay for this new public transport line. They also recommend supplementing the tax by a Stamp Duty (a one-time transaction tax exacted at the time of purchase of the land) on residential land, also charged at rates that depend on distance from the new infrastructure. Implicit in their argument is that both businesses and residents are beneficiaries of the new public transport and should pay their fair share to build it. The burden should not only fall on public transport users and general tax revenue.

In a broader analysis in an Australian context, Wood et al evaluate the comparative merits of stamp duties, a transaction tax that is payable every time a property changes ownership and which is levied in all Australian jurisdictions, and the alternative of a broad-based land tax, applied to all urban land uses, including residential.[17] They cite widespread criticism of stamp duties as inefficient fiscal instruments: unlike, for example, taxes on transport fuels which are justified in order to raise funds for the public task of combating the externalised effects of air pollution and transport congestion, property transactions are generally not associated with a negative impact on community wellbeing.

Furthermore, stamp duties are considered regressive for having greater relative impact on lower-income groups, who tend to spend a larger share of their income on housing than higher-income groups. Stamp duty is also known to negatively affect housing affordability (as it adds to property prices) and, by inflating the cost of property transactions, slow the process of land use intensification in public transport-accessible neighbourhoods. As more and more cities devise place-making strategies around transport hubs in a bid to integrate land use and transport, and to prioritise pedestrians and reduce the impact of automobiles in activity centres,[18] taxation regimes that slow this process are considered counter-productive to urban policy goals.

---

17. Gavin Wood, Rachel Ong, Melek Cigdem, and Elizabeth Taylor, "The Spatial and Distributional Impacts of the Henry Review Recommendations on Stamp Duty and Land Tax," *Australian Housing and Urban Research Institute (AHURI)*, Final Report No 182 (Melbourne (VIC)/Perth (WA), Australia, 2012).
18. Carey Curtis John L. Renne, Luca Bertolini, eds., *Transit Oriented Development: Making it Happen* (Surrey, UK: Ashgate, 2009).

In contrast, a broad-based land tax applied to all urban land uses is likely to be capitalised into the value of land, provided the urban land market is sufficiently competitive. This is because the market value of land reflects the level of expected future revenue streams derived from the use of the land for development, on-sales or rental tenancies. To the extent that these revenue streams are subject to a land-based tax and thus reduced, downward pressure is exercised on land values, and affordability is improved for both residential and non-residential uses. Simultaneously, by being applied to the site value rather than the capital-improved value of a property, a broad-based land tax adds pressure on land owners to put vacant or underutilised urban sites to better use and, as long as agricultural land in the outskirts of the city is not subject to the tax (thus reducing the financial incentive to urbanise it), can act as a mechanism to encourage intensification within the existing urban footprint.[19]

These views are echoed by Kavanagh[20] and Putman[21], who argue in the tradition of 19th century tax reformer Henry George,[22] advocating the reduction (and eventually, abolition) of many existing taxes such as income and business taxes and their replacement by a broad-based land tax on account of macroeconomic efficiency (as a disincentive against the accumulation of economic rent through property speculation), equity and fairness: unlike labour or business, land is immobile and unambiguously traceable, and not in a position to exercise tax avoidance within its jurisdiction.

There are thus many theoretical advantages of a broad-based land tax, along the lines proposed by George, as a model for revenue collection towards the public good. Moreover, most developed cities have sophisticated and detailed land registries and usually already collect some form or other of property-based charges from land owners. The administrative infrastructure for raising a broad-based land tax, or a betterment tax earmarked specifically for public transport using an accessibility measure like SNAMUTS, is therefore generally already in place. But can it be harnessed for this purpose in practice?

---

19. Wood et al. (2012), "Spatial and Distributional Impacts," 2012.
20. Bryan Kavanagh, *Unlocking the Riches of Oz; A Case Study of the Social and Economic Costs of Real Estate Bubbles, 1972 to 2006* (Melbourne (VIC), Australia: The Land Values Research Group, 2007).
21. G.R. Putman, "The Georgist Case for a Vacancy Tax," http://www.grputland.com/2016/12/georgist-case-for-vacancy-tax.html.
22. I recommend any interested reader to explore Henry George's ideas further, as he proposed a unique and attractive solution to taxing property in the city. His Wikipedia page (https://en.wikipedia.org/wiki/Henry_George) is a good place to start.

Can land taxes fund public transport operations?

In this section, we will conduct a thought experiment, which will remain necessarily somewhat cursory, but can help outline the scope of a betterment tax raised to fund public transport operations in full in a medium-sized Western metropolis (Melbourne, Australia), allowing for the abolition of user fares as well as the redirection of current public subsidies for public transport operation towards other fiscal goals, including some compensation for hardship experienced by this shift, as discussed below.

This thought experiment, in other words, proposes not only the elimination of the user-fee contribution to public transport operations, that would make public transport "free" but also of the regional government's contribution.

Melbourne's metropolitan region had approximately four million inhabitants in 2011. In international terms, it is a low-density, space-consuming city, counting 28.3 residents and jobs per urbanised hectare of land. In the 2011-12 financial year, the State Government of Victoria spent A$2.95bn (US$2.22bn/€1.98bn) on operating expenses for Melbourne's metropolitan public transport system, which consists of a 15-line electric suburban rail network and a 250-km tram network and buses, all franchised to separate private operators. In that year, approximately 25% of these expenses were recovered from passenger fares.[23] Melbourne's public transport system attracted 126 passenger journeys per metropolitan resident per year in 2011, more than in any other Australasian city but significantly less than in typical Canadian, European or Asian cities of comparable size.[24]

Australia's 2011 census divides urban land into collection areas of uniform land uses (mesh blocks) classified into several categories, which allow for an approximate determination of the extent of private land that can be subject to the betterment tax.[25] The assumption is that such a tax will be levied on land in the categories of residential, commercial and industrial only; the land use categories of agricultural, parkland, hospital/medical, education, transport, water and other are exempt. Mesh block boundaries for all land uses encompass roads, streets and pedestrian pathways providing access to the properties; these usually make up between 20% and 30% of total urbanised land. To arrive at

23. [DTF] State of Victoria, Department of Treasury and Finance, *2013-14 Budget Papers*, 2013, http://www.dtf.vic.gov.au/Publications/State-Budget-publications/2013-14-State-Budget/2013-14-Budget-Papers.
24. Curtis and Scheurer, *Planning for Public Transport Accessibility*, 2016.
25. [ABS] Australian Bureau of Statistics, *Census 2011 – Mesh Block* Counts, 2012, http://www.abs.gov.au/websitedbs/censushome.nsf/home/meshblockcounts?opendocument&navpos=269.

an approximate net figure of taxable land, the land area used in our calculation has thus been reduced to 70% of that shown in the mesh block count.

With these caveats, the 2011 census identifies 148,675 hectares (367,383 acres) of potentially taxable land in the Melbourne metropolitan area. However, a large proportion of this land does not have public transport access at the SNAMUTS minimum standard within walking distance—figure 6 shows these areas shaded in black. It is reasonable that a betterment tax to fund public transport operations should only be levied on land that is actually serviced by public transport at this minimum standard, i.e. the areas shaded in traffic light colours in figure 6. Together, this core area makes up 37,121 hectares (91,728 acres) of taxable land.

To raise the A$2.95bn (US$2.22bn/€1.98bn) required annually to fund public transport operations across metropolitan Melbourne, a betterment tax would thus have to be charged at an average level of A$79,500 (€53,297) per hectare (US$24,200 per acre) per year, or A$7.95 (€5.33) per square metre (US$0.56 per square foot).

Public transport accessibility, however, is not distributed evenly across these areas. For this reason, we have converted the SNAMUTS composite accessibility score shown on in figure 6 into an exponential scale resulting in differentiated betterment tax rates according to accessibility level, ranging from a rate of A$42.85 (€28.73) per square metre (US$3.00 per square foot) in the immediate vicinity of the largest rail station in the central business district (Flinders Street) to a rate of A$1.26 (€0.84) per square metre (US$0.09 per square foot) near the outer terminus of a rail line at the urban fringe (Belgrave).

Or in other words, a medium-sized business occupying 5,000 square metres (53,820 square feet) in a central business district office tower (assuming a Floor Area Ratio of 20:1) would be liable to an annual betterment tax of A$9,165 (US$6,897/€5,810); a mid-rise apartment in an inner suburb with train and tram access (North Richmond; 100 dwellings per net hectare/40 dwellings per net acre) would be charged A$1,559 (US$1,173/€988), and a single-family house in an outer suburb with tram access (Bundoora; 20 dwellings per net hectare/8 dwellings per net acre) would be charged A$885 (US$666/€561).

A residence in a suburb without public transport access at the minimum standard—the black areas in figure 6—would not be subject to the tax. It is notable that the two latter figures—the estimated tax on a mid-rise apartment and a single-family house—are at roughly similar levels to the annual rates currently charged by the local councils (which, hence, would effectively double for the property owner with the application of the betterment tax); these are, however, calculated as a percentage of property valuation rather than based on land area. It is also notable that the spectrum between these two figures encompasses the cost of a full-price annual public transport pass for metropolitan Melbourne (A\$1,306.50 or US\$983/€744 in 2012), an expense a regular user – the person living at that address who uses public transport – would no longer have in a fare-free system. The marginal cost of using public transport would drop to zero.

The accessibility standards and the derived betterment tax rates shown are, of course, not static; they are subject to continuous change as the public transport network and infrastructure expands or contracts, service levels improve or deteriorate and land use intensifies or atrophies. Effectively fare-free public transport may lead to a surge in ridership and require higher service frequencies that add to operational costs in the short term, as well as greater capital investment towards new infrastructure and increased passenger capacity of existing infrastructure in the longer term. The construction of the betterment tax around spatial accessibility, however, includes an in-built incentive for governments to expand the minimum service standard (i.e. improve public transport service frequencies) to cover more currently underserviced areas in order to broaden the tax base, as well as to improve both network and service levels in order to increase the tax rate in line with improving accessibility standards. In addition, the inherent incentive of a land tax for private property owners to put urban land to the most lucrative use will help increase density around public transport.

Can a betterment tax therefore generate an ongoing synergistic outcome in both fiscal and planning terms—providing a stable and growing revenue base for transit as well as indirectly encouraging a more transit-oriented urban form?

Discussion and Conclusion

The betterment tax suggested in this paper differs from most similar instruments discussed in the literature and implemented in practice. First, value capture instruments are most commonly instigated to support specific packages of capital investment in public transport rather than to recover operational costs,[26] such as in the London example quoted above. As such, they tend to apply only for a specific time, related to the period during which the project in question is planned and implemented, and during which associated property price

26. P. Newman, E. Jones, J. Green, and S. Davies-Slate, *Entrepreneur Rail Model. Tapping Private Investment for New Urban Rail*, Discussion Paper, (Perth (WA), Australia: Curtin University, 2016).

gains are likely to materialise.[27] Second, it is usually the intention of value capture mechanisms to levy only the margin of added property value that can reasonably be attributed to the new or improved infrastructure: should other factors influencing property prices simultaneously reduce or neutralise this effect, revenue from the value capture instrument may fall accordingly.

Conversely, the proposal for a betterment tax made here concerns an instrument to raise revenue for the cost of public transport operations already in existence, levied in perpetuity while adapting to the changes in operational costs as network and service levels evolve, and charged at a level approximate to the quality of public transport accessibility provided, rather than a percentage of actual property prices or land values.

Importantly, it is borne out by ample evidence[28] that the level of public transport accessibility is already priced into land values with or without a betterment tax, though this relationship may not be quite as linear as suggested by the calculation of the tax level outlined above. People are willing to pay a premium for land near quality public transport hubs. Like every tax reform, the introduction of such an instrument, while enabling fare-free public transport and other compensatory measures, will produce winners and losers and thus create some controversy.

As discussed earlier, any type of land tax, including the betterment tax discussed here, is designed to exercise pressure on land owners to intensify the use of their property as they will need to secure a revenue base in order to pay the tax. This effect would likely range from the avoidance of vacancy and dereliction to the construction of buildings with greater density and/or higher value uses. All other influences being equal, the betterment tax would therefore instigate or accelerate an urban development trend towards a density pyramid directly proportional to the level of spatial accessibility on public transport.

While such an outcome appears desirable from the goal of optimising land use and transport integration, it may generate some unwanted side-effects. For example, it may either add to threats of redevelopment in heritage-protected neighbourhoods whose historic lower density is integral to their unique character, or failing that, add to their growing exclusivity and thus exacerbate gentrification pressures and contribute further to socio-economic inequalities in cities.[29]

27. McIntosh et al., "Framework for Land Value Capture," 2017.
28. See McIntosh et al., "Framework for Land Value Capture," 2017.
29. Richard Florida, *The New Urban Crisis. How our cities are increasing inequality, deepening segregation, and failing the middle class – and what we can do about it* (New York (NY), USA: Basic Books, 2017): and Ian Woodcock, Kim Dovey, Simon Wollan, and Ian Robertson, "Speculation and Resistance: Constraints on Compact City Policy Implementation in Melbourne," *Urban Policy and Research* 29, no. 4 (2011): 343-362.

Furthermore, a new land tax could be considered a form of financial hardship on residents who can be characterised as asset-rich, but cash-poor (such as retirees who own their residence outright, but live on a government pension), as well as on those who are not regular users of public transport.

From a transport sustainability point of view, there is arguably no case for protecting financial privileges of people who choose the private car over public transport—but the same is not true for people who predominantly walk and cycle: a land tax hypothecated towards public transport would incur a perverse incentive for travel behaviour change away from non-motorised modes. This could be partially mitigated by systematically adding free bike-sharing services to the public transport portfolio.

It is also imperative that a property's eligibility and valuation for the purpose of the betterment tax be determined at a more fine-grained level of geographical detail than the SNAMUTS tool can provide with its reliance on mesh blocks (or equivalent statistical units in cities outside Australia) and the undifferentiated inclusion of 400-metre or 800-metre catchments. In practice and to optimise the perceived fairness of the instrument, tax levels may have to decay gradually with growing distance from the public transport stop even within these walkable catchments, and allow land owners and building users a say when defining the boundaries. This procedure adds to the public effort required to set up the new land tax regime in ways that ensure both its functionality and its acceptability to the community.

Finally, for the user perception of the betterment tax it is highly relevant how exactly it is administered. Will a new accessibility-related public transport levy be raised from the end user of a property—the owner-occupier or renter—as a utility charge, akin to existing fees for water supply or rubbish collection, or will it be collected directly from land owners? In the former case, it is likely that there will be a greater and continuous public sensitivity concerning the administration of the charge, including the presence of lobby groups that seek to minimise it even at the cost of deteriorating public transport accessibility. In the latter case, the effects on residents and businesses are more indirect: it can be expected that land owners will attempt to pass the new cost on to renters, but as argued above, the presence of the betterment tax based on transit accessibility may partially neutralise this by exercising downward pressure on land values in general and thus improving housing affordability in both the ownership and rental sector. The same effect also works as a counter-incentive to developers who may be tempted to avoid the betterment tax by taking their projects away from public transport access, where the tax is not applied. It is, however, outside the scope of this paper to more accurately quantify such effects, or the way in which their various embodied incentives may interact.

This paper has argued for a broad-based betterment tax determined by the level of public transport accessibility throughout a metropolitan area, as an alternative method to passenger fares and direct government subsidies to fund the operation of public transport systems. Compared to existing alternative funding sources for public transport such as employer taxes, charges to motorists or even value capture mechanisms dependent on actual land or property values, a land tax based on transit accessibility—a data-driven calculation that carefully measures residents' and businesses' actual geographical access to the public transport system and the quality of that access from their home address—can provide an extraordinarily stable revenue stream, free from the ups and downs of employment or property markets, or the future fortunes (or not) of the car-based, petrol-powered transport system.

On the other hand, a broad-based, hypothecated tax or levy of this type is virtually unprecedented in any of the world's metropoles, and it will take some courageous pioneers to successfully steer its implementation through the inevitable political controversy and fallout that will likely accompany it.

Concluding Remarks

Free public transportation, on its own, cannot solve the problems faced by societies and cities as we enter the second quarter of the 21st century. What they can do is signal a city's clear intention to prioritize collective means of transportation as an unequivocal response to both growing urban poverty, social inequality and climate change.

This signal must also be coupled with efforts to prioritize public transportation in the urban space (enabling busses to surpass private cars in rapidity of transport). But cities can do more than giving a signal. They can take concrete steps to tackle big problems. About 100 cities with free public transport are showing this.

Many of them also signal and support a clear desire to replace the urban model that has been privileged for the past 100 years—first in North America and later exported to cities around the world—to break and remake our cities in another mold.

So any city that puts free public transport at the heart of a transport system that also encourages bicycle and walking would present an encouraging model which people and politicians around the world to follow, in the global north, the global south, in developed and developing countries and regions with emerging industry. For those whose cities have not yet been disfigured by highways and bridges and tunnels, it would be a better model to follow than those designed around the wrong transportation system.

Some argue we need to dismantle our automobile manufacturing giants and repurpose them to solve mobility problems, finding collective and carbon neutral solutions, as suggested by Noam Chomsky in a lecture at Concordia University in Montreal.[1] The ongoing unrepentant and reckless behaviour of automotive giants around the diesel scandal in Germany betray their fundamentally anti-social nature. Given our current ecological crisis, and such unethical and illegal behaviour from the car companies, dismantling the automobile giants starts to sound reasonable. It starts to sound like an imperative.

Let us briefly consider how we got into this dilemma in the first place and why—despite what we now know—we continue to reproduce this auto-insanity:

Since the invention of the automobile, cities have been rebuilt and reimagined following a sprawling urban form. Early in the 20th century, automobile-makers and their political servants wowed citizens of the world with an offer of freedom and unlimited cheap mobility in miraculous and magical 'cities of the future', most notably the Futurama exhibit by General Motors at the New York World Exhibition in 1939, in front of which tens of millions of citizens, city-builders, and policy makers paraded to learn about the 'city of tomorrow'.

Such marketing events were followed by brutal and ingenious city-breakers like Robert Moses, who not only imposed massive changes onto New York City at great social and economic cost, but also trained cadres of politicians and ambitious civil servants from cities across the country on how to get the job done, as brilliantly exposed in Robert Caro's epic and highly readable biography *The Power Broker*. See, for example, his description of the construction of the Cross-Bronx Expressway, in *One Mile*.

Another key to getting the city car-makers wanted was to destroy the competition. The big three US auto manufacturers systematically acquired—and dismantled—the only competition to their invention: extensive and functioning electric networks of tramways that had been built in almost every city, and used by tens of millions daily. Exactly how they did this is detailed in scintillating prose by Snell in his account submitted to Congress in 1974. The transcript of his report is especially compelling reading. We opened this book with a citation from his opening remarks to the United States Congress in 1973.

But much of the city highway infrastructure was built in the decades following the Second World War—tens of thousands of bridges and tunnels—and cities not only in North America but right around the globe are now saddled with an enormous retrofit headache. Also, what is to be done with the millions of square kilometres of low density sprawling city, totally dependent on the private car? And why do cities continue to build like this?

1. Alejandra Mellan-Morse, "Noam Chomsky Breaks Down Neo-Liberalism for Concordia," *The Link*, October 29, 2013.

According to many accounts, we are on the verge of a transport revolution in driverless vehicles. If driverless vehicles are privately owned, reproducing the patterns we currently see in many cities, we risk another great ecological and congestion nightmare, potentially doubling the vehicular kilometres travelled, while the driverless car returns to a parking lot at home.

If we adopt driverless vehicles, they must be publicly managed and integrated into our public transport system. Public authorities must play a significant role in implementing this transport "revolution" that doesn't help to create sensible, decent and ecologically sustainable work.

We already know Uber's low-wage precarious employment model, where the driver assumes capital costs and risks, while this ruthless corporation uses unscrupulous accounting practices to skirt its tax-paying responsibilities in the relentless pursuit of profit and share-value, hundreds of thousands of jobs in the taxi industry are at risk. With the arrival of driverless Ubers, the drivers themselves will evaporate.

Robots are rapidly replacing many jobs around the world. Earlier this year, Apple announced plans to replace a million workers in China last year with robots. They are in retail stores and caring for seniors. Artificial intelligence and big data are bringing sweeping changes to the service sector, in finance, law and even medicine. And don't forget the problem of monitoring and controlling the citizens that is connected with such a development.

Driverless vehicles, because they never need to park, might provide a solution to the parking problem, but they also need space—the streets which could be better used: for walking, cycling, expansion of green spaces or a range of other socially or ecologically beneficial uses.

Here is the paradox: land at transport hubs is best used for housing, so residents can walk or bike to their connection. But for these hubs to serve a regional function, this land must also be used for parking. If we remove the parking, via collectively-owned driverless vehicles, the problem may be significantly reduced. Of course, measures to protect residents from escalating land values around transport hubs to halt rapid gentrification would have to be implemented.

In the North American context, but also in emerging mega-cities in the global south, the person living in the urban periphery makes a choice to live there. Perhaps it was cheaper to buy a place large enough for a growing family. Perhaps you were priced out of the city-centre by gentrification. Perhaps fresh(er) air and more living space are important factors. Perhaps it is what you grew up with and always knew. But undoubtedly, for those living at the periphery, the daily commute ranks near the top of inconveniences for choosing this location. This person is locked into a life pattern that involves not only a daily commute, but thousands of kilometres a year in the car to get groceries, buy shoes, take the kids to the doctor. Nearly everything must be done by automobile.

If you are in the business of selling gasoline and automobiles, like General Motors, you couldn't have chosen a better 'city of tomorrow'. "If we can just convince people that this is way to live, we will guarantee our revenues forever," you can almost hear them smirking, in the whispered comic voice of Jim Gaffigan. In the United States and Canada, an army of post-war real estate developers building the American Dream in every city, laying the groundwork for a guaranteed revenue model with every house sold, while also automatically creating land values for commercial developments only accessible by automobile, and crucial for daily provisions of suburban housing: the shopping mall with butterfly-wing parking lots.

With rising costs of housing in cities around the world, increased levels of household debt, skyrocketing costs in education and medical care, all spiralling out of control, it seems unlikely the public purse could afford any new major expense—and never free public transport.

Let us have a closer look into the costs, the true costs, of owning a car:

- **direct financial costs:** the automobile itself; the fuel, which costs nearly as much as the purchase price of the vehicle over its lifetime; insurance; maintenance and debt financing; parking charges; parking fines;
- **indirect financial costs:** municipal road construction and maintenance (the lion's share of many municipal budgets); highways, bridges and tunnels (some of the most expensive charges in any country);
- **social costs:** commute times (and lost opportunity costs); road rage; shoveling it out of snowbanks (a problem in northern climates);
- **health costs:** accidents; from car-related pollution: cardio-vascular disease, cancers, premature infants for those living near highways; obesity; extreme climate events due to climate change;
- **environmental costs:** air quality; landscape fragmentation; climate change; habitat destruction; impacts on water quality; climate change; and these lists could all go on.

Experts, activists and politicians at the municipal level need to package and communicate these true costs of owning an automobile, both to their constituents and to other levels of government, in a compelling and visible way. Then, they need to spell out an effective, realistic and affordable alternative, that will compete directly with the private automobile on speed and reliability of service. They need to speak directly to the people—and so to the people in the urban periphery—in a language that resonates clearly with their everyday lived reality. Many of these people are not happy with the status quo.

They would support a political call to reconsider the pricing structure of transport in their city. The first step would be to provide an exceptional public transport service: clean, on time, state of the art. Major reinvestments to improve the quality and connectivity of the service, and making it the clear priority for moving people in the city with reserve bus lanes—as a start. At this point, the city could eliminate the price barrier: announce free public transport measures. These are the carrots: great service, fast, clearly the priority mode of transport, and free to use.

This bold city would now be in a position to introduce some sticks. In the short term: remove lanes on highways; increase gas taxes and add tolls to bridges; reduce speed limits; increase parking rates; tax kilometres travelled. But eventually: dismantling highways, densifying the cities, reducing space for cars, and (re)making our cities for people, again.

Considering different finance models for public transport, and then for free public transport, is both worthwhile and helpful. International experience is interesting. But only in a few cases will it be possible to import a concrete model. A solution that may work in France, given its legal and societal morays, may not be useful in Germany or Mexico. But the question about finance for public transport becomes even more complicated once you try to decide what is socially just. If authorities put taxes on gas, roads and bridges, what about those low-income workers who depend on the use of a car with no real alternative, should they be penalized?

Considering the broad principles in support of social justice and equity in funding public transport and any free public transport program, we propose the discussion focus on principles such as:

- The rich should contribute to support others less well-off;
- Citizens should pay according to their income and the very poor should not pay at all;
- The profiteers who own the automobile system should pay;
- Following bonus-malus, anything that pollutes or causes harm to others should pay more, while low and zero emissions vehicles would pay less;
- Employers should pay according to their economic strength;
- Following polluter-pays, established in some jurisdictions, consumers of fossil fuels should pay more;

- Anyone who could take public transport, but doesn't do so, should pay for using the car and for parking.

But finally, who can help bring about free public transport financed according to these principles? In cities around the world, there is already a range of actors and agents actively campaigning for free public transport, some of which we have explored in this book.

Our research distinguishes several different approaches. First, there are groups like Planka.nu, in Sweden. Planka.nu is horizontally managed and has no formal leadership, with links to the student movement, trade unions and the Swedish Left Party. While their focus is on fair transport and mobility rights, they also work with refugee and migrant rights groups in the broader struggle for a more just society. They have a radical critique of society, but take direct action to reflect the world they want to live in, based on values of solidarity and good health. Of course, they reject the 'car society' completely. And they have lots of fun.

The second group of actors work in coalitions on the left, such as those found in Toronto. The group pushing change is overtly socialist, and their ultimate goal is a revolutionary change in society, breaking old structures of production and consumption, to completely remake society. Free public transport is a tangible goal for working people, around which they can conduct that broader discussion.

The third group consists of residents working for a city in which people of all nations can live together peacefully and in solidarity, examples of which are found in the countries of former Yugoslavia. Their working style is a kind of ongoing social forum that has a working group on the issue of free public transport. This first edition of our book does not include examples from this group, but their work promotes greater resident participation in decision-making, for clean air and a safe environment, and against privatization and social-marginalisation, particularly of migrants and refugees.

The fourth group consists of traditional vehicles in the political arena—political parties—such as the Scottish Socialist Party, which has campaigned for free public transport for many years. This political party has chosen the protection, democratisation and expansion of the commons as its primary political goal, inviting voters to signal their support in the traditional ballot box.

Finally, some free public transport movements are driven by public administrations who are deliberately working to expand democratic participation of civil society and citizens. These experimental administrations have been responsible for trying out different forms and different approaches to free public transport and have learned by doing. Sometimes free public transport is offered only at certain times in the day, at rush hour or during the middle of the day when the transport network is less crowded. Or for certain groups of people, such as children or seniors. Or it is free only in designated areas of the city, the downtown area perhaps, as in some US cities like Portland. And of course, some have provided free public transport to all of their citizens, in the city-centre and in the suburbs, with Tallinn in Estonia as Europe's greatest example.

The efforts of these five groups, each working in their own ways and using their own particular strategies, need to be supported and strengthened and connected with others also working hard to make our cities and societies more socially and ecologically just, and more people-centred, in the march forward to achieving the right to mobility—the right to the city—in all cities of the world.

We hope our book is a small contribution towards strengthening these efforts.

Activists for Free Public Transport of all cities and regions around the world unite!

Author's bios

Paula Aftimus is a journalist and a bicycle enthusiast. However, her favorite means of transportation is walking, not only because it's free but because it's the best way to discover a city that is constantly changing. Although she doesn't hate cars, she openly wishes half of them could be exchanged for a free, better and wider public transport. Unimpeded to come and go, broadly and collectively, people might remember that they never needed a car in the first place and that those "menacing" strangers who share the city with them, well, they are just people. Usually nice ones.

Allan Alaküla has been representing Tallinn in Brussels since 2007 during which his main job was to sell the most innovative /smart /green /eco /sustainable /inclusive /cohesive city worldwide, not always easy when every other city is trying to sing the same song in the EU. Representing the world capital of free public transport from 2013 made a big difference, because the topic sells itself. Living permanently in Tallinn, Allan considers himself a (free) public transport addict – using daily a (free) commuter train and a (free) tram. On the weekends, he can't avoid driving his private car but that may change soon, as Estonia aspires to become the first free public transport nation in the autumn of 2018.

Prof. Michael Brie is senior fellow at the Institute for Critical Social Analysis of the Rosa Luxemburg Foundation in Berlin in the field of history and theory of socialism and communism. He is chief-editor of the series Contribution to Critical Transformation Research (the fourth volume was published in 2016) and researcher in the field of projects of free public transport in Europe. He served as a long-time member of the program committee of the party The Left. Michael recently published a book entitled *Karl Polanyi: A Socialist Thinker For Our Time* (Montreal, Canada: Black Rose Books, 2017). The crisis of the car industry in 2008 and the decision of the German government to subsidise car production by the so-called wreckage bonus inspired him to engage for alternative solutions in the field of mobility.

Dr. Georgios Daremas holds a B.A in Sociology, an M.A in Sociology/ Anthropology and a PhD in Political Philosophy (Sussex University, UK). He has taught for many years Cultural and Media theory in tertiary education. He has co-authored a textbook on Sociology of Work (in Greek, 2000) and written numerous academic articles and chapter contributions on Hegel, Marx, Critical theory, theories of democracy and mass media analysis. He has conducted many empirical researches in political communication, media audiences' reception and contemporary social and political beliefs. He is currently working on editing a book on forms of direct democracy.

Judith Dellheim studied political economy in Leningrad, earning her PhD in 1983, after which she worked in the foreign trade office for the GDR government. Since 1990, she has been working on economies of solidarity, on political parties and movements, and on economic policies. She has been a member of the Federal Board of Germany's Party of Democratic Socialism (PDS), a free-lance scientific consultant, and since 2011, a senior researcher at the Rosa Luxemburg Foundation. Obviously, she has experienced project failures–something she also hopes will happen to our "car society"–but, unfortunately, despite great efforts, the first attempt to launch a powerful movement in Berlin for free public transport also failed. But Judith keeps a sense of humour.

Michelle DeRobertis, M.S., P.E., is currently enrolled in the doctorate program at the University of Brescia, Italy under Professor Maurizio Tira. Her area of research is the effectiveness of traffic limited zones, known in Italy as "Zone a Traffico Limitato". A graduate of University of California, Berkeley, she is a registered civil and traffic engineer in California. Prior to enrolling in the PhD program, she had 30 years of transportation engineering and planning experience in both the public and private sector. Her areas of expertise are bicycle and pedestrian transportation, traffic safety and sustainable communities. She has published numerous articles on sustainable transportation policies and the need to consider public transit, biking and walking as seriously as the automobile.

Max Jäggi was a member of a Swiss collective of journalists that went to Bologna in August 1974, to cover the story of a neo-fascist bomb attack. The three members ended up spending ten months there instead of the planned two days, and ended up writing a book about the remarkable city, published in English in 1977, called *Red Bologna*.

Wojciech Kębłowski is a critical urban geographer, and a PhD candidate at *Université libre de Bruxelles* (IGEAT) and *Vrije Universiteit Brussel* (Cosmopolis). He is currently working on a doctoral thesis that explores the geography and politics of fare-free public transport, bringing insights from Aubagne (France), Chengdu (China), Tallinn (Estonia) and Żory (Poland). His research focuses on developing critical perspectives on transport, inspired by urban theory as well as political economy. Wojciech further studies diverse urban "alternatives," looking at their capacity to empower their inhabitants, to challenge urban power relations, to construct an urban utopia.

Anna Nygård was born in Helsinki, Finland and grew up in a suburb west of Stockholm, Sweden. As a teenager, she dreamt of changing the world and joining the local anarcho-syndicalist youth federation seemed like the right way to start. At 16 she couldn't possible imagine that the recently started fare free public transport campaign would take her places like Mexico, where she participated as keynote speaker at the Towards Carfree Cities Conference in 2011. Less surprising is that she's now being recognised by guards in the Stockholm subway, thanks to Planka.nu's many fare dodging tutorials on youtube.

Jason Prince, an urban planner, has two decades of experience in local economic development, pedestrian-oriented planning, and non-profit housing development. Between 2008 and 2013, Jason headed up a research-action project out of McGill University's School of Urban Planning, working at local and regional levels to change how Montrealers move in their city, pushing for quieter, safer neighbourhoods and actively fighting provincial government plans for a larger inner-city highway intersection, the Turcot Interchange. Prince co-edited a bilingual book on the struggle, published just 3 days before public hearings began on this controversial project: *Montréal at the Crossroads* (Montreal, Canada: Black Rose Books, 2009). Prince currently teaches the social economy and public policy, part-time, at Concordia University's School of Community and Public Affairs, while also coaching non-profit businesses at PMEMTL CentreVille. Jason has two children, aged 10 and 11.

Herman Rosenfeld is a retired staff-person with the Canadian Auto Workers Union, (now UNIFOR). He previously worked in an auto assembly plant. He has taught politics and labour studies at McMaster and York Universities. Currently, he is an activist with Free Transit Toronto, TTCriders and the Fair Fare Coalition. He is a member of Socialist Project and has written numerous articles on politics and unions for left publications and does educational work on union and socialist political issues. He is the author of "American Social Democracy: Exceptional but Otherwise Familiar," in *Social Democracy After the Cold War*, edited by Bryan Evans ad Ingo Schmidt, Athabasca University Press, 2012.

Daniel Santini is a journalist and works as project coordinator at the Brazilian office of the Rosa Luxemburg Foundation. He is allergic to traffic jams and believes that free public transport is the best solution for cities, both ecologically and socially. From June 2010 to April 2013, he maintained the blog Other Ways (*Outras Vias*, in Portuguese), about Car Free Cities, Critical Mass and public transportation. In 2012, he crossed the Amazon forest by bicycle with two friends, on an expedition called Cicloamazonia. He never met a bike that he didn't wanna ride.

Dr. Jan Scheurer is a Senior Research Fellow at Curtin University, Perth (Australia) and a Senior Lecturer/Honorary Associate at RMIT University, Melbourne (Australia) and Barcelona (Spain). In collaboration with Prof Carey Curtis (Curtin University) and colleagues, he developed the award-winning Spatial Network Analysis for Multimodal Urban Transport Systems (SNAMUTS) accessibility tool, summarised in their 2016 publication *Planning for Public Transport Accessibility: An International Sourcebook* (Routledge) and their website at www.snamuts.com. Jan teaches and researches into urban design and planning, transport and land use integration, social and cultural dimensions of mobility, and the policy impact of disruptive transport technologies.

Maurizio Tira is Full Professor of Town and Regional Planning and Rector at the University of Brescia (Italy). He has headed up several EU-funded research programs on town planning and mobility. He chaired the COST Action TU0602 "Land Management for Urban Dynamics" research project and was invited as an expert to the OECD in working groups on pedestrian and cyclist safety, and as invited expert at the European Transport Safety Council. He is President of the National

Centre for Urban Studies, past president of the local Agenda 21 Association and member of the Board of the Italian Society of Urban Planners. Author of about 250 books and papers, he has been invited as a speaker to many conferences in Italy and abroad.

Lorena Zárate is the President of Habitat International Coalition. She has been involved in the elaboration and dissemination of the World Charter (2001-2005) and the Mexico City Charter for the Right to the City (2008-2010). She has co-edited and published books and articles and has widely participated as a speaker, in particular within the World Urban Forum and the World Social Forum. Since 2014, she is co-coordinator of an international project to promote a Global Platform for the Right to the City, that actively participated at the Habitat III process and the discussion of the New Urban Agenda.